Classic Guards

CLASSIC SPORTS

JONATHAN KNIGHT, Series Editor

Classic Bucs: The 50 Greatest Games in Pittsburgh Pirates History
DAVID FINOLI

Classic Steelers: The 50 Greatest Games in Pittsburgh Steelers History
DAVID FINOLI

Classic Browns: The 50 Greatest Games in Cleveland Browns History
Second Edition, Revised and Updated
JONATHAN KNIGHT

Classic Cavs: The 50 Greatest Games in Cleveland Cavaliers History
Second Edition, Revised and Updated
JONATHAN KNIGHT

Classic Pens: The 50 Greatest Games in Pittsburgh Penguins History
Second Edition, Revised and Updated
DAVID FINOLI

Classic Bengals: The 50 Greatest Games in Cincinnati Bengals History
STEVE WATKINS AND DICK MALONEY

Classic 'Burgh: The 50 Greatest Collegiate Games in Pittsburgh Sports History
DAVID FINOLI

Classic Reds: The 50 Greatest Games in Cincinnati Reds History
JOE HEFFRON AND JACK HEFFRON

Classic Guards: The 50 Greatest Games in Cleveland Baseball History
JONATHAN KNIGHT

Classic Guards

THE 50 GREATEST GAMES IN CLEVELAND BASEBALL HISTORY

Jonathan Knight

The Kent State University Press • Kent, Ohio

ISBN 978-1-60635-514-5 (Paper)
ISBN 978-1-63101-589-2 (ePub)

The manufacturer's authorized representative in the EU for product safety is Mare Nostrum Group B.V., Mauritskade 21D, 1091 GC Amsterdam, The Netherlands, email gpsr@mare-nostrum.co.uk.

Cataloging information for this title is available at the Library of Congress.

FOR JACOB

—maybe someday you'll have a field named after you.

Contents

“What’s in a name? That which we call a rose by any other name would smell as sweet.”
—William Shakespeare, *Romeo & Juliet*

Preface

Put simply, a lot of people thought the name shouldn't have been changed.

When Cleveland's baseball team decided the time had come to retire its well-established nickname, the announcement was met with a cauldron of mixed emotions. People had grown attached to the name of their beloved ballclub and were reluctant to let it go just like that.

In fact, some didn't. One defiant Cleveland media outlet went so far as to keep referring to the team by its old name for a couple of years after the official switch.

Be that as it may, the decision had been made that it was the right thing to do. And despite the criticism swarming around the decision, the team did take it seriously and considered a handful of options before settling on the one it chose, "anxious to get a nickname that couldn't be turned into a joke," as one reporter explained.

Joke or not, when the new name was finally announced, nobody really loved it. It felt as if—in perhaps an appropriate analogy—it had come out of left field. The *Plain Dealer* tried to spin it by explaining that "the name will recall fine traditions . . . looking backward to a time when Cleveland had one of the most popular teams. . . . "

A columnist begrudgingly accepted the new name but grumbled, "wait until they start to lose." One influencer opined that the name would just be temporary and might be changed again if a better option came along. Ideally, he added, "the team would go out and make a name for itself," so those who didn't like the new selection could use that instead.

Alas, none of that happened. The name, for better or worse, stuck. And gradually, after a few years of the old name still being bandied about, whether by habit or outright obstinance, people adopted the team's new identity.

Thus, they became the Cleveland Indians.

Considering the brouhaha that change prompted in 1915, it should have come as little surprise a century later that the process, response, and notable resistance played out in a very similar way when the time for a name change came round once again. After careful consideration, a new name was announced. Some hated it, few truly liked it, all needed time to adjust. The reasons prompting the name change may have been different, but every other aspect was essentially the same. While perhaps not repeating itself, history had certainly rhymed.

And for as much as the early twentieth-century Cleveland baseball team differs from its early twenty-first-century descendants, the tales of the two name changes serve as historical pillars, demonstrating the concrete connection between the past and the present. Not unlike the huge sandstone Guardians of Traffic statues ensconced on the Hope Memorial Bridge just outside the ballpark that the now Cleveland Guardians call home.

Changing the name of the team in 2022 was neither a detachment from nor a whitewashing of its history. It was, after all, technically the fifth official nickname the franchise has been known by, which isn't even counting the handful of other names the city's initial professional baseball entries carried.

And for those who argued that "Guardians" didn't represent or reflect anything about Cleveland, in a way, that very detail also helped carry on the city's baseball tradition. Whether you see a reflection of the city in "Guardians" or not, certainly we can all agree that it's at least as emblematic as "Blues." Or "Bronchos." Or "Infants." Or "Naps." Or "Spiders."

Or, for that matter, "Indians."

Even at the time of that choice in 1915, there was a bit of revisionist history going on behind the scenes. A few days after the announcement, some industrious reporters dug back and retconned justification by tying the name to Louis Sockalexis, a talented Native American ballplayer who'd played for the National League's Cleveland Spiders in the late 1890s. While certainly garnering attention from an audience largely made up of fans who'd never laid eyes on a Native American, Sockalexis didn't leave any real legacy on the field or the city. True, he was baseball's first Native American player, but this was never cited nor celebrated by the team at the time of the announcement. Particularly since he'd played in less than a hundred games over three seasons for a franchise that would soon cease operations and be all but forgotten. And, not for nothing, he also drank himself to death at the age of forty-two, passing away just over a year before the "Indians" nickname was selected.

So if "Guardians" doesn't represent the city, then it's a perfect fit for a franchise that has never quite done that with its team names anyway.

If nothing else, all of this underscores that the one name that truly defines this franchise isn't "Guardians" or "Indians" or "Naps" or "Bronchos" or "Blues." It's "Cleveland." The nickname of the team can change, has changed, and someday may change again. But regardless of what letters are stitched across the jerseys or what logo appears on the caps, it's all connected, deriving from the same bloodline, extending the same narrative. Framing it in a modern vernacular, it all lives within the same cinematic universe.

Accordingly, the fifty vignettes making up the list of greatest games you hold in your hands cover every nook and cranny of that universe. From the franchise's initial baby steps as the Blues in the early 1900s to its decade-long run as the Naps through its century as the Indians and now its new dawn as the Guardians, it's all represented here. From Napoleon Lajoie to Bob Feller to Rocky Colavito to Omar Vizquel to José Ramírez. From Indians to Guardians and back again.

This list of the fifty greatest games in Cleveland baseball history has evolved over the years and will naturally continue to. New games replace old ones like diners coming into and out of a busy restaurant. As always, the present marches on and history is created—constantly enlivening and refreshing that which we knew before. But this list, certainly open to (and inviting) discussion and debate, is intended to both celebrate the history of the franchise and, in its own way, protect and preserve it.

Which, perhaps appropriately, is exactly what a guardian sets out to do.

#50

INDIANS 5, CHICAGO WHITE SOX 4
SEPTEMBER 24, 2013

From the Depths of Despair to the Height of Delirium

On a cool September night at Progressive Field, it had taken just a matter of minutes to epitomize the full roller-coaster experience of the Indians' 2013 season.

After five years of abject irrelevance—bottoming out with a ninety-four-loss disaster in 2012—there had been marked improvement in Terry Francona's first season as Cleveland manager. Recovering from a rocky April and then an eight-game losing streak in June, the Indians had endured, surging over the .500 mark and remaining in contention for a playoff spot throughout the summer. Still, as September began, they were a long shot to reach the postseason, with a pack of more experienced clubs already in the race.

Rather than folding under the pressure, the Indians found a groove and began playing their best baseball of the season, gradually leapfrogging their way up the standings. Still, after a loss in Kansas City on September 18, they were on the outside looking in, trailing the Tampa Bay Rays and Texas Rangers for the final wild card spot, with the Baltimore Orioles right on their heels. With ten games remaining, it would take a remarkable finish for Cleveland to snag its first postseason appearance in six years.

Yet over the next week, a remarkable finish appeared to be in the works. The Indians swept a four-game weekend series with Houston to surge ahead of the Rangers in the race. But they'd need to keep the streak going during a two-game set with the last-place Chicago White Sox before heading to Minnesota for the final series of the season.

In a pitcher's duel between Chicago starter Hector Santiago and Cleveland's Ubaldo Jimenez, the White Sox clawed to a 2–1 lead in the seventh, but Indians outfielder Michael Brantley tied the score on the first pitch of the bottom of the frame with a home run. Second baseman Jason Kipnis soon followed with a two-out RBI single to push Cleveland ahead 3–2.

The lead endured to the ninth, when talented but erratic closer Chris Perez was called upon to close things out. Perez had racked up 123 saves over the previous four seasons, including twenty-five in 2013, but was rarely dominant, occasionally outspoken while being critical of Cleveland fans, and at times prone to ninth-inning meltdowns that cost Cleveland ballgames.

Which is exactly what appeared to happen. On his third pitch of the night, Perez surrendered a game-tying home run to Chicago's Dayan Viciedo. Then, after striking out the next two batters, Perez gave up another homer—this one to Alejandro De Aza—that put the White Sox ahead 4–3. With a chorus of boos cascading out of the stands, Perez gave up another single and Francona removed him, replacing him with reliever Bryan Shaw, who got the final out of the inning.

Rocked on their heels, the Indians would have one final chance to try to prevent a demoralizing defeat that could potentially derail their playoff drive. Brantley laced a one-out single, but third baseman Mike Aviles struck out, and the Indians were down to their last out. Francona decided to roll the dice and called on forty-two-year-old Jason Giambi to pinch hit.

In his nineteenth season, Giambi had enjoyed a long and successful career, establishing himself as one of the league's best power hitters with Oakland and the New York Yankees in the late 1990s and early 2000s. After admitting during the league's widespread investigation into steroid use that he'd taken performance enhancing drugs at times during this era, Giambi had endured, playing another ten years. After he left the Yankees, he moved back to Oakland and then Colorado, serving as a reliable substitute and pinch hitter, but more importantly, as a beloved elder statesman and clubhouse leader that younger players could lean on. Such was the goal when the Indians signed him as a free agent the previous winter, and it had worked. Despite appearing in less than half of Cleveland's games and collecting barely thirty hits, Giambi had made a positive impact on a young team that was battling for a playoff spot.

And now, the chances of grasping that spot largely rested on his shoulders.

With the season hanging in the balance, Kipnis stood beside Francona on the top step of the dugout, hoping for a miracle. In the back of their minds was the home run Giambi had hit against Chicago back in July to break a ninth-inning tie and, as it happened, make him the oldest player to ever hit a walk-off home run. "We were both like, 'One more time. One more time. Just lightning in a bottle. Come on. Get it one more time,'" Kipnis recalled.

After Brantley stole second, with the Chicago infield shifted right to close up gaps for the left-handed-hitting Giambi, the veteran initially considered trying to tap a grounder between second and third in the hopes of reaching base on an infield single, advancing Brantley, and keeping the inning going. Instead, he opted for more.

On a 1–1 slider from White Sox closer Addison Reed, Giambi blasted a drive high into the September night. It sailed over the right-field fence and landed deep in the seats as the crowd erupted and Giambi tossed his bat aside, thrusting his arms in the air. The elder statesman of the Cleveland clubhouse had snatched victory from the jaws of defeat and provided the Indians with an incredible 5–4 victory that kept their playoff hopes alive.

"I don't think I even touched the ground," Giambi said of his trip around the bases. "They might have been able to appeal because I don't know if I even touched any of the bases."

As Giambi completed his journey around the base paths, he side-stepped into home plate and then was mobbed by his teammates in celebration. Most of the fans remained standing and applauding as the team left the field, refusing to leave the ballpark and instead insisting on basking in the glow of the dramatic victory a little longer.

Everyone, it seemed, understood the magnitude of what had just happened. "From the depths of despair to the height of delirium all in the span of ten minutes," broadcaster Matt Underwood described to his television audience.

It was a fitting metaphor for the Indians' yo-yo journey of a season. It was their eleventh walk-off victory of 2013, but undoubtedly the most important and most meaningful. "I almost started crying when he hit that ball," first baseman Nick Swisher said. "If you lose that game, man, you never know what's going to happen. We're in that position right now where we've got to win out. We've got to *win*."

And win is what the Indians continued to do, as Giambi's heroics served as a pair of defibrillator paddles that restarted the Indians' playoff drive. They proceeded to romp over Chicago the following night for a sixth straight win. Then they traveled to Minnesota and completed a four-game sweep over the Twins to close out the season with ten straight victories—something no major-league team had done in more than forty years—and clinch a playoff spot on the final day.

While the winning streak and successful playoff run were made up of countless ingredients and performances, it was Giambi's dramatic home run that became the emblem of the achievement and the hallmark of the Indians' season. And the veteran, having spent more than two decades playing professional baseball, was the first to appreciate just how special it was.

"This is the stuff you dream about," he said that night. "Coming down the stretch, trying to get a playoff berth. It doesn't get any bigger. It really doesn't."

White Sox	0	0	0	1	0	0	1	0	2	=4
Guardians	0	1	0	0	0	0	2	0	2	=5

CHICAGO

	AB	R	H	RBI
De Aza cf-lf	5	1	2	2
Ramírez ss	5	0	1	0
Gillaspie 3b-1b	3	1	1	0
Konerko 1b	4	0	1	0
Semien 3b	1	0	0	0
Dunn dh	4	0	0	0
García rf	3	0	1	1
Viciedo lf	4	1	2	1
Anderson c	0	0	0	0
Beckham 2b	4	1	1	0
Phegley c	1	0	0	0
Danks ph-cf	1	0	0	0
TOTAL	35	4	9	4

	IP	H	R	ER	BB	SO
Santiago	6⅓	6	3	3	2	1
Jones	1⅔	1	0	0	0	2
Reed (L)	⅔	2	2	2	0	2

CLEVELAND

	AB	R	H	RBI
Bourn cf	3	0	1	0
Carson rf	0	0	0	0
Giambi ph	1	1	1	2
Swisher 1b	3	0	0	0
Kipnis 2b	4	0	1	1
Santana dh	3	0	1	0
Raburn rf	3	0	0	0
Stubbs cf	0	0	0	0
Cabrera ss	4	1	0	0
Gomes c	4	0	1	0
Brantley lf	4	2	3	2
Aviles 3b	4	1	1	0
TOTAL	33	5	9	5

	IP	H	R	ER	BB	SO
Jiménez	6⅓	5	2	2	3	7
Allen	⅔	1	0	0	0	1
Smith	1	0	0	0	0	2
Perez	⅔	3	2	2	0	2
Rzepczynski	0	0	0	0	0	0
Shaw (W)	⅓	0	0	0	0	0

Attendance: 21,083

#49

INDIANS 10, NEW YORK YANKEES 9
SEPTEMBER 23, 1997

What a Way to Win It

It had been a schizophrenic season for the Cleveland Indians. After back-to-back dynamic seasons that saw the team win nearly 200 games, the '97 Tribe managed to stay competitive but fell well short of expectations. As a campaign of ups and downs neared its conclusion, the Indians encapsulated the entire experience in one unforgettable night.

Returning home from a grueling fourteen-game road trip that netted an unsurprising 7–7 record, the Tribe's magic number for clinching its third straight American League Central Division title stood at two. With a win that night and a loss by the second-place Chicago White Sox, Cleveland could hoist the flag on this cool September evening at Jacobs Field. The only thing standing in its way was the franchise's ultimate nemesis.

Earlier that summer, the New York Yankees' longtime dominance over the Indians became a national story when the Yanks became the first major-league team to defeat another 1,000 times. Now, while the Indians were lethargically meandering toward the finish line, the defending-champion Yankees were in an all-out sprint trying to catch Baltimore atop the AL East. Adding insult to injury, for inexplicable reasons the Yanks had dominated the Indians at Jacobs Field since its opening three years before, winning fourteen of eighteen games there. And though New York had already secured a playoff berth, it actually had more to play for than the Indians—and in the early going, the game unfolded accordingly.

Constantly harassing Cleveland pitcher Charles Nagy, the Yankees surged to a 3–0 lead in the second aided by a walk, a Cleveland error, and an infield single. The Tribe answered when catcher Sandy Alomar popped a two-run homer in the bottom of the inning, but New York first baseman Tino Martinez did likewise in the third to make it 5–2. The New York lead stretched apparently out of reach with two-run innings in the fifth and sixth to put the advantage at 9–2. With Yankee hurler Kenny Rogers cruising and manager Joe Torre replacing several regulars, it appeared the Indians' celebration would have to wait for another night.

But the tide began to turn in the bottom of the sixth. After Manny Ramirez singled to start the inning, third baseman Matt Williams doubled to score Ramirez and later scored himself on a ground out by Alomar. With two down, Kevin Seitzer beat out an infield single and second baseman Tony Fernandez launched a home run to left to pull the Indians within three.

After a scoreless seventh, Cleveland struck again in the eighth on a David Justice homer and an RBI single by Fernandez. In the ninth, Torre brought in steady reliever Jeff Nelson, who walked leadoff batter Bip Roberts. After Omar Vizquel sacrificed him to second, Nelson whiffed Ramirez to put the Yankees one out away from victory. Matt Williams walked, then Justice fell behind 0-and-2, and the Tribe was down to its final strike. But Justice ripped the next pitch to center, scoring Roberts to tie the contest and sending Williams to third. With what was left of the capacity crowd roaring and clapping to the drumbeat of bleacher icon John Adams, up stepped Alomar, who had already enjoyed a magical season. The fairy tale continued as he mirrored Justice's single right up the middle, scoring Williams to give the Indians an improbable 10–9 win.

Players spilled out of the dugout and mobbed both Williams and Alomar. The Yankees walked off the field stunned—both at their sudden collapse and at the Indians' excitement. After racking up a combined forty-six victories in their last at-bat in 1995 and 1996, it marked the first time in sixty-three chances the '97 Tribe won a game it was trailing after eight innings. But this wasn't just any comeback. "The Indians made the kind of rally that Hollywood would call too contrived for belief," Bill Livingston wrote in the *Plain Dealer.*

Once the dust had settled, the Indians' attention turned to Chicago to see if the night could become even more memorable. The final inning of the White Sox-Minnesota game was broadcast on the Jacobs Field scoreboard and thousands of fans remained in their seats. With the Twins leading 5–3, former Indian Albert Belle led off the Chicago ninth with a strikeout, delighting the crowd back in Cleveland. Two outs later, the White Sox had lost and the Indians were once again champions of the Central Division. The players returned to the field wearing commemorative T-shirts and caps to celebrate with their fans, high-fiving them and spraying champagne into the stands. "It is unbelievable what we did to come back," Nagy said amidst the jubilation. "To come back against a team like the Yankees . . . well, it makes me want to hug everyone here in this clubhouse."

"This was a season in which we couldn't worry about how many players we lost to trades, free agency, or injuries," Alomar said. "We had to find ways to win, and we did."

"What a great game," Justice added. "It was a playoff-type atmosphere out there."

An atmosphere which would be recreated over the course of the next four unforgettable autumn weeks.

Yankees	0	3	2	0	2	2	0	0	0	=9
Indians	0	2	0	0	0	4	0	2	2	=10

NEW YORK

	AB	R	H	RBI
Curtis lf-cf	5	0	0	0
Sanchez ss	5	1	1	1
O'Neill rf	4	1	1	0
Williams cf	3	2	2	1
Pose pr-lf	1	0	0	0
Martinez 1b	5	2	2	2
Fielder dh	5	1	3	2
Girardi c	3	1	2	1
Posada c	1	0	0	0
Fox 3b	3	0	0	0
Bush 2b	4	1	2	2
TOTAL	39	9	13	9

	IP	H	R	ER	BB	SO
Rogers	6	7	6	6	1	1
Irabu	1⅓	2	2	2	0	3
Stanton	⅔	1	0	0	0	0
Nelson (L)	⅔	2	2	2	2	1

CLEVELAND

	AB	R	H	RBI
Roberts lf	4	1	0	0
Vizquel ss	4	0	0	0
Ramirez rf	5	1	1	0
Williams 3b	4	2	1	1
Justice dh	5	2	3	2
Alomar c	5	2	3	4
Seitzer 1b	3	1	2	0
Thome ph-1b	1	0	0	0
Fernandez 2b	4	1	2	3
Grissom cf	3	0	0	0
TOTAL	38	10	12	10

	IP	H	R	ER	BB	SO
Nagy	5	9	7	6	2	6
Weathers	1	3	2	2	1	0
Shuey	1⅓	1	0	0	1	0
Morman	1	0	0	0	0	1
Mesa (W)	⅔	0	0	0	0	0

Attendance: 43,039

#48

INDIANS 5, BALTIMORE ORIOLES 4
OCTOBER 9, 1997

Like a Thief in the Night

No one doubted that the Baltimore Orioles were the better team. Soaring into the 1997 American League Championship Series on a wave of momentum after a stunning upset of New York in the Division Series, the Indians had emotion on their side and not much else. Baltimore, winners of ninety-eight games during the regular season, had better pitching, a more balanced lineup, and had knocked the Tribe out of the playoffs the previous year. What's more, the Orioles had been itching to face New York and avenge their five-game defeat in the previous year's ALCS, so the incoming matchup with the Indians was seen as a letdown. Having to play Cleveland, wrote the *Baltimore Sun,* "is like hearing that Congress declared war on Sweden." The view was the same from coast to coast, since fans knew the Tribe probably didn't belong in the postseason at all, let alone in the championship series. The plucky Indians had their fun against the Yankees, but few doubted the ride would soon come to a screeching halt.

Game One at Baltimore's Camden Yards bore this out. The Indians only managed four hits and gave up a pair of home runs as the Orioles coasted to a shutout victory. The second game followed a similar script on a balmy Thursday evening as Baltimore looked to take a choke hold on the series. After Cleveland right fielder Manny Ramirez gave the visitors early hope with a two-run homer in the first, legendary Cal Ripken Jr. blasted his own two-run shot off Charles Nagy to tie the contest in the second.

Each team spoiled scoring opportunities in the fourth with inning-ending double plays before Baltimore broke through again in the sixth. Shortstop Mike Bordick delivered a two-out, two-run single to put the home team up 4–2. Cleveland went down in order in the seventh against Scott Kamieniecki—who'd relieved starter Jimmy Key in the fifth—and in the eighth the Indians would now have to face reliever Armando Benitez, coming off a dominating regular season in which he'd racked up 106 strikeouts in just over seventy-three innings. Throughout 1997, Benitez established himself as the finest setup man in the American League, maintaining the lead in forty-three of forty-four chances. True to form, Benitez whiffed Jeff Branson to open the inning, then fanned Tony Fernandez after a walk to Sandy Alomar. The Dominican flamethrower was one out away from handing the ball to dominating closer Randy Myers in the ninth to secure a two-game lead in the series.

Benitez then worked the count full to Tribe pinch-hitter Jim Thome, and Thome checked his swing on a ball-four slider for a walk to extend the inning. With two on and two out, up stepped Tribe center fielder Marquis Grissom, who had been hooked up to an IV before game time to combat dehydration from a case of the flu. Though he didn't take batting practice, Grissom was in the lineup that night and had gone two-for-three while returning to the locker room to throw up between innings. Since he'd arrived in Cleveland in a trade from Atlanta that spring, Grissom had a difficult time both transitioning to American League pitching and replacing fan favorite Kenny Lofton in center field. Now he'd face a pitcher who'd struck him out the only two times they'd faced one another with a playoff series' momentum hanging in the balance. Tightening the vice, the Indians had blown multiple scoring opportunities all night, going zero-for-eight with runners in scoring position. With Myers warming in the bullpen, if Grissom couldn't come through here, the Indians would return to Cleveland with their backs to the wall.

With the count 1-and-1, Benitez tried to slip a slider past Grissom. The quiet veteran turned on it with what little strength he had left and smashed the pitch deep into left-center field. It floated over the fence, stunning and silencing Baltimore fans already talking about the World Series. The team Baltimore hadn't been at all excited to play and was certain to beat had somehow snuck to a 5–4 lead. And after Paul Assenmacher and Mike Jackson cruised through the eighth and Jose Mesa closed out the ninth in businesslike fashion, the Tribe had completed a remarkable come-from-behind victory that defied explanation. "How can you explain something that came in the night like a thief and stole a game that the Indians seemed certain to lose?" Bill Livingston asked in the next morning's *Plain Dealer.*

Suddenly, the ridiculous magic, which had charmed the team throughout the New York series, had returned—and anything seemed possible. "This has become the kind of season that always happens to other teams," Livingston explained, "teams called the Amazin' Mets and the Miracle Braves.

"Amazin' miracle. It was that, all right."

The aftershocks of the three-hour, fifty-three minute contest—the longest nine-inning game in LCS history—followed the teams back to Cleveland, kicking off perhaps the wildest and most memorable weekend in Indians history.

Indians	2	0	0	0	0	0	0	3	0	=5
Orioles	0	2	0	0	0	2	0	0	0	=4

CLEVELAND

	AB	R	H	RBI
Roberts lf	5	0	0	0
Giles lf	0	0	0	0
Vizquel ss	3	1	0	0
Ramirez rf	4	1	1	2
Williams 3b	5	0	1	0
Justice dh	2	0	1	0
Branson ph-dh	2	0	0	0
S.Alomar c	3	1	0	0
Fernandez 2b	2	0	0	0
Seitzer 1b	2	0	0	0
Thome ph-1b	0	1	0	0
Grissom cf	4	1	3	3
TOTAL	32	5	6	5

	IP	H	R	ER	BB	SO
Nagy	5⅔	8	4	4	2	1
Morman	⅔	0	0	0	0	0
Juden	⅓	0	0	0	0	0
Assenmacher (W)	⅔	0	0	0	1	2
Jackson	⅔	0	0	0	0	1
Mesa (Sv)	1	0	0	0	1	1

BALTIMORE

	AB	R	H	RBI
Anderson cf	4	0	0	0
R.Alomar 2b	5	0	0	0
Davis rf	5	0	1	0
Palmeiro 1b	4	1	2	0
Surhoff lf	3	1	1	0
Ripken 3b	4	2	2	2
Baines dh	3	0	1	0
Berroa ph-dh	1	0	0	0
Hoiles c	3	0	0	0
Bordick ss	3	0	1	2
Hammonds ph	0	0	0	0
TOTAL	35	4	8	4

	IP	H	R	ER	BB	SO
Key	4	5	2	2	2	4
Kamieniecki	3	0	0	0	1	1
Benitez (L)	1	1	3	3	2	3
Mills	1	0	0	0	1	2

Attendance: 49,131

#47

INDIANS 2, NEW YORK YANKEES 1 (11 INNINGS)
OCTOBER 5, 2007

Lord of the Flies

They lived deep within the dark waters of Lake Erie, morphing from larvae and emerging from the water into the inviting summer air to seek each other out in a short but frantic mating period. Though the lifespan of these tiny flying insects called midges only lasts a few days, on one muggy October evening, they would permanently etch their legacy into baseball history.

In their first playoff appearance in six years, the Indians mopped the floor with the veteran New York Yankees in Game One of their Division Series in a 12–3 rout. There was plenty at stake as the teams paired up for Game Two on an unseasonably warm Friday evening at Jacobs Field—the Indians didn't want to have to win a game at Yankee Stadium to stay alive, and the Yankees didn't want to fall behind by two games in a best-of-five series. With momentum up for grabs, both teams put their best foot forward.

Making his first postseason start on the mound for Cleveland was Fausto Carmona—the name by which the pitcher was known at the time. Five years later, it was revealed that his real name was Roberto Hernández and he'd falsified his identity to get a visa to the United States. (Here he is referred to as "Carmona," as he was known at the time.) Carmona was sharp early, mowing down the vaunted New York lineup. Seasoned Yankee hurler Andy Pettitte was nearly as effective, and the Indians blew an opportunity to draw first blood in the second when shortstop Jhonny Peralta was thrown out at home when he took too wide a turn around third base trying to score on a Kenny Lofton single. Instead, it was New York that surged to the early lead in the third when Melky Cabrera lofted a 2–2 pitch from Carmona into the right-field stands to make it 1–0. And there the score remained as the game became an old-fashioned pitching duel.

With thousands of tiny midges swirling through Jacobs Field on a warm October night, Cleveland pitcher Fausto Carmona (later known as Roberto Hernández) stays focused, propelling the Indians to a thrilling 2–1 extra-inning victory over the New York Yankees in Game Two of the 2007 American League Division Series. *Akron Beacon Journal.*

Time and again Cleveland squandered scoring chances. Two ground outs and a strikeout wasted a leadoff double by Jason Michaels in the third. Two at-bats with a runner at second in the fourth proved fruitless. Lofton was caught stealing third for the final out in the fifth. Center fielder Grady Sizemore led off the sixth with a triple but was stranded there, just as Peralta was left at second after a one-out double in the seventh.

Yet while the Indians scuffled at the plate, Carmona shone on the mound. After Cabrera's homer, Carmona permitted just two hits over the next six innings and not once did a New York runner reach third base. Even after he set down the Yankees in order in the eighth, it appeared Carmona's efforts would be wasted. Pettitte had been replaced with New York star rookie reliever Joba Chamberlain, who had allowed just one earned run in nineteen appearances on the season. But as Chamberlain and the Yankees took the field for the bottom of the eighth, they weren't alone. Attracted to the bright lights shining above the field and drawn to the perspiration of the players on it, a black army of midges swarmed into Jacobs Field and began to cover the Yankees as if reenacting a biblical plague. "They were like small pterodactyls," Tribe third baseman Casey Blake said.

Midges becoming a factor at Indians games were nothing new, dating back to the team's days at old Cleveland Municipal Stadium on the lakefront, but it had always been limited to three bursts of activity in the summertime. Yet with surprisingly warm temperatures in Cleveland that first week of October, the insects' life cycle had been altered and they'd arisen from the lake for one final swarm.

New York trainers were called onto the field to hose the players down with bug repellent, to no effect. Clearly distracted, Chamberlain walked leadoff hitter Sizemore on four pitches, then uncorked a wild pitch that sent Sizemore scrambling into second. Indians rookie Asdrubal Cabrera sacrificed Sizemore to third, bringing up designated hitter Travis Hafner. Hafner lined a shot toward right, but New York first baseman Doug Mientkiewicz was there to snag it and preserve the New York lead. Once again, it appeared Cleveland was about to spoil another golden scoring opportunity.

But the midges wouldn't allow it. Chamberlain lost control with another wild pitch, thrown so hard it sailed past catcher Jorge Posada and caromed off the backstop almost back to home plate. Sizemore sprinted toward home, realizing this was likely Cleveland's last shot to tie the game. "I saw it bounce back hard," Sizemore said, "but I was already committed. I knew it was going to be close so I didn't try anything fancy. I just went straight in." Posada recovered the ball and fired it back to Chamberlain just as Sizemore slid into home beneath him, toppling the beefy reliever then bouncing to his feet and thrusting his fist in the air. The capacity crowd went bonkers as the Indians had tied the score.

Chamberlain's flying nemeses continued to harass him as he hit Victor Martinez with a pitch, then walked Ryan Garko, putting the Indians into a position to take the lead. But Peralta struck out to end the eighth and the game toiled on.

The Yankees had a shot to go back ahead in the ninth when Melky Cabrera came up with a two-out single and stole second with the AL's home-run and RBI king Alex Rodriguez at the plate. In an epic nine-pitch at-bat, Carmona struck out the mighty Rodriguez to complete a masterful nine-inning, three-hit performance. "Fausto was unbelievable," Hafner would say later. "To give up one run in nine innings against that lineup is an amazing job." And while the midges had gotten into Chamberlain's head as much as on his skin, Carmona was unfazed. "The coolest part about that is Fausto didn't flinch," Garko said. "You saw what happened to their guy." But after going down in order in their half of the ninth, the Indians would need more.

Reliever Rafael Perez came on to shut down the Yanks in the tenth, then the Indians appeared poised to win. Sizemore led off with a strikeout but scrambled to first when Posada couldn't hang onto the third strike. He advanced to third on a Cabrera bunt and a Hafner ground out, then Martinez was intentionally walked and Garko was hit by a pitch to load the bases for Peralta. But just as he'd done in the eighth, he struck out to end the inning. Perez cruised through the top half of the eleventh and the Indians once again had victory in their grasp in their at-bat.

Lofton started the inning with a four-pitch walk, followed by a single to left by pinch-hitter Franklin Gutierrez. Casey Blake then dropped down Cleveland's fourth sacrifice bunt of the game, advancing both runners, and Sizemore was intentionally walked. After Asdrubal Cabrera popped out to first, the Indians fell to a woeful one-for-seventeen on the night with runners in scoring position. With two down, Travis Hafner was all that stood between the Indians and yet another missed opportunity.

Remembering his failures to bring home runners in the sixth, eighth, and tenth, Hafner worked the count full against Luis Vizcaino. The entire game hinged on the next pitch. "Bases loaded, 3–2, two outs," Hafner would say. "That's what you dream about as a kid."

The dream became reality when Hafner lined a changeup into right-center field to bring Lofton home and give the Indians an unforgettable 2–1 victory. And long-suffering fans who had seemed eternally snake-bitten saw broader, almost biblical symbolism in the way the victory arrived riding tiny wings. "By now," *Plain Dealer* columnist Bud Shaw wrote, "the town is so hungry even a mouthful of bugs in October tastes good."

But not nearly as good as a playoff victory over the New York Yankees.

Yankees	0 0 1	0 0 0	0 0 0	0 0	=1
Indians	0 0 0	0 0 0	0 1 0	0 1	=2

NEW YORK

	AB	R	H	RBI
Damon lf	5	0	0	0
Sardinha lf	0	0	0	0
Jeter ss	4	0	1	0
Abreu rf	4	0	1	0
Rodriguez 3b	4	0	0	0
Matsui dh	3	0	0	0
Posada c	3	0	0	0
Cano 2b	4	0	0	0
M. Cabrera cf	4	1	1	1
Mientkiewicz 1b	3	0	0	0
Duncan ph-1b	1	0	0	0
TOTAL	35	1	3	1

	IP	H	R	ER	BB	SO
Pettitte	6⅓	7	0	0	2	5
Chamberlain	1⅔	0	1	1	2	2
Rivera	2	0	0	0	1	3
Vizcaino (L)	⅔	2	1	1	2	0

CLEVELAND

	AB	R	H	RBI
Sizemore cf	4	1	2	0
A. Cabrera 2b	4	0	0	0
Hafner dh	6	0	2	1
Martinez c	3	0	0	0
Garko 1b	3	0	0	0
Peralta ss	4	0	1	0
Lofton lf	3	1	2	0
Michaels rf	1	0	1	0
Gutierrez rf	3	0	1	0
Blake 3b	4	0	0	0
TOTAL	35	2	9	1

	IP	H	R	ER	BB	SO
Carmona	9	3	1	1	2	5
Perez (W)	2	0	0	0	0	1

Attendance: 44,732

#46

INDIANS 7, CALIFORNIA ANGELS 5
JULY 18, 1995

Belle of the Ball

For a city starved for postseason baseball, it was a delectable hors d'oeuvre prior to the main course.

While the red-hot Indians were running away with the American League Central Division in what had already become a magical season, the California Angels had parked themselves in first place in the AL West and boasted the American League's second-best record behind Cleveland. Seemingly destined to square off in October, the teams met for a brief two-game series at Jacobs Field in mid-July in what was hyped as a preview of bigger matchups to come. The Angels dominated the first game and took an 8–3 decision, and the Tribe knew it needed to bounce back in the second game to avoid giving California any psychological advantage come playoff time.

Another sellout crowd packed into Jacobs Field, where Cleveland held a stunning 29–11 record. As the summer progressed, each Indians home game became a party, a reason for fans to celebrate before, during, and after the game. For the first time in four decades, the Tribe was the best team in baseball, and Cleveland couldn't get enough. Now, with a certified big game on tap, the home fans were even more wired than usual.

It mattered little when the Angels surged to a 3–0 lead in the fifth inning. The Indians were a comeback team with an offense that could erupt at any moment. And true enough, in the bottom of the frame, two-out RBI singles by Carlos Baerga, Albert Belle, and Manny Ramirez knotted the contest. But Cleveland dug another hole in the sixth when starting pitcher Mark Clark surrendered a two-run homer to Garret Anderson to make it 5–3. The Indians went down in order in the sixth and seventh, then couldn't take advantage of a pair of walks in the eighth. They went into the bottom of the ninth still trailing by two and now would have to face Major League Baseball's all-time saves leader—California closer Lee Smith. Despite the long odds facing their team, the Jacobs Field fans were roaring with confidence, knowing the Indians had already won fourteen games in their last at-bat in 1995, including ten at Jacobs Field. "These guys don't know when to fold their tent," Cleveland manager Mike Hargrove said. "Late innings around here can be a lot of fun."

Pinch-hitter Wayne Kirby opened the inning with a line drive to first base which bounced off the bag and first baseman J. T. Snow before carrying into foul territory as Kirby reached safely. Smith rebounded by striking out Jim Thome, though Kirby stole second. Shortstop Omar Vizquel followed with a rising line drive which tipped off the glove of shortstop Gary DiSarcina and fell for a hit. With the tide of momentum now officially turned, Baerga walked on four pitches. As he turned to trot down to first, he clapped his hands and pumped his fists at Belle, marching up to the plate.

It was baseball drama at its purest: bottom of the ninth, bases loaded, one team's closer against the other's cleanup hitter. Smith set the tone with two quick fastballs, getting ahead of Belle 0-and-2. After just missing outside, Smith tried to sneak a slider past Belle. It didn't work.

Belle pounded the ball toward straightaway center field. As it sailed through the summer night, the roar of the crowd grew louder, fans realizing what they were witnessing. Belle's blast cleared the center-field wall and landed in the picnic plaza 425 feet from home plate, the fourth grand slam of his career. Belle pumped his fist in the air as he rounded first, flooded by a tidal wave of cheers.

The Indians' 7–5 triumph was perhaps the most significant of the 100 they would earn in '95. Not only was it dramatic, but symbolic, marking Cleveland's twenty-fifth come-from-behind win on the year. It also encapsulated Belle's torrid finish to the campaign. Though he had just fifteen home runs over the first three months of the season, his grand slam off Smith would be the first in an amazing string of thirty-five homers over the final two months to close a season that would forever burn brightly in Tribe history.

"This team never gives up," Baerga said. "We have a positive attitude. If you have a positive attitude, things like this can happen."

Angels	0 0 1	0 2 2	0 0 0	=5
Indians	0 0 0	0 3 0	0 0 4	=7

CALIFORNIA

	AB	R	H	RBI
Phillips 3b	4	1	1	1
Edmonds cf	4	1	1	2
Salmon rf	4	0	0	0
Davis dh	4	0	0	0
Snow 1b	4	1	1	0
Anderson lf	4	1	2	2
Easley 2b	4	0	2	0
Fabregas c	4	1	1	0
DiSarcina ss	3	0	0	0
TOTAL	35	5	8	5

	IP	H	R	ER	BB	SO
Langston	7	9	3	3	2	3
Habyan	⅔	0	0	0	0	0
Patterson	0	0	0	0	1	0
Percival	⅓	0	0	0	0	0
Smith (L)	⅓	3	4	4	1	1

CLEVELAND

	AB	R	H	RBI
Amaro cf	4	1	1	0
Thome ph	1	0	0	0
Vizquel ss	5	1	3	0
Baerga 2b	4	2	1	1
Belle lf	4	1	2	5
Ramirez rf	3	0	2	1
Perry 1b	4	0	1	0
Winfield dh	3	0	0	0
Sorrento ph-dh	0	0	0	0
Alomar c	4	0	0	0
Espinoza 3b	3	1	1	0
Kirby ph	1	1	1	0
TOTAL	36	7	12	7

	IP	H	R	ER	BB	SO
Clark	6	8	5	5	0	4
Plunk	2	0	0	0	0	1
Assenmacher (W)	1	0	0	0	0	0

Attendance: 41,763

#45

INDIANS 2, BOSTON RED SOX 1
OCTOBER 3, 1998

The Team That Beat Tom Gordon

Boston relief pitcher Tom Gordon had become so noteworthy in baseball that he was about to earn distinction as a cultural phenomenon.

After toiling as a solid but far-from-spectacular starter for nearly a decade in Kansas City, Gordon was signed by the Red Sox as a free agent and moved to the bullpen. And in 1998, Gordon enjoyed the best season of his career. As Boston surged to ninety-two wins—a fourteen-game improvement from the year before—and a playoff berth, Gordon was the constant. Stepping into the vacant closer role, he became the game's most efficient reliever, racking up a league-best forty-six saves which included a record forty-three consecutive without a blown save. Much like Cleveland's Jose Mesa had done three years before, Gordon had redefined his career and become an overnight superstar. His fame would transcend the diamond, as the following spring, best-selling horror author and lifelong Red Sox fan Stephen King would publish *The Girl Who Loved Tom Gordon*, a chilling tale about a young girl who gets hopelessly lost in an immense forest and must survive with nothing but a small radio on which she could listen to her beloved Red Sox games and her favorite player, Tom Gordon. The stars had aligned for Gordon and the Red Sox, and, accordingly, it was not a good time for an opposing team to go toe-to-toe with destiny.

Yet that's exactly where the Indians found themselves. After clutch back-to-back victories, the Tribe took a two-games-to-one lead into Game Four of their best-of-five Division Series with the Red Sox on a drizzly, cool Saturday afternoon at Fenway Park. Though technically Boston was the team with its back to the wall, the Indians were also staring elimination in the face. If they couldn't put away the Red Sox on Saturday, they'd have to return to Cleveland for Game Five on Sunday and face untouchable Boston pitcher Pedro Martinez, who had mowed down the Tribe in the first game of the series. For all intents and purposes, both teams knew whoever won Game Four would win the series.

Boston manager Jimy Williams resisted public pressure to start Martinez on three days' rest for Game Four, instead tapping journeyman Pete Schourek, who had won just one game for Boston since the team purchased him from Houston in August. Yet for six innings, Williams looked like a genius. A day after Cleveland blasted four home runs, it managed just two hits over the first five innings as the Red Sox took a 1–0 lead on a fourth-inning homer by shortstop Nomar Garciaparra. Schourek was relieved after giving up a one-out double to David Justice in the sixth, but Derek Lowe retired Manny Ramirez and Travis Fryman to preserve the lead.

The Indians then dodged a huge bullet in the bottom of the inning when Red Sox third baseman John Valentin led off with a double and tried to score on a single to left by Mike Stanley. Justice, who had only played twenty games in left during the season, fired a perfect throw to the plate to cut down Valentin, and after a clutch three-pitch strikeout of Troy O'Leary by reliever Jim Poole with runners on first and third, the Tribe went to the seventh, down just one.

Looking to clinch victory, Williams went against the instinct that impelled him to start Schourek. Though Gordon hadn't started the eighth inning all year, with the season hanging in the balance, Williams called on him to open the inning. "He's done it for us all year," Garciaparra said. "He's the guy we want in there when the game's on the line." With Stephen King watching from the stands, Gordon retired Joey Cora on a fly ball, but then gave up a broken-bat single to center by leadoff hitter Kenny Lofton. Then Omar Vizquel, who was hitless in fourteen at-bats for the series, ripped a single to right. With the tying run now in scoring position, up stepped Justice, who had already enjoyed a sterling game but knew the entire Cleveland season might now rest on his shoulders. "When I walked to the box, I said this might be my last at-bat for the evening," he said later. "I wanted to put the ball in play with a chance to drive in a run."

After Gordon fired a strike past him and Lofton stole third, Justice ripped the next pitch—a fastball—into the damp autumn air. It rocketed over center fielder Darren Lewis's head and landed in the no-man's-land triangle of the quirky Fenway outfield, some 420 feet from home plate, and rattled around the nooks and crannies of the wall. Lofton scored easily to tie the game, and Cleveland fans watched breathlessly to see if Vizquel could make it around all the way from first. He did, and the Indians suddenly were ahead 2–1. Justice, who had hit .313 for the series, pumped his fist at second base in triumph. "David Justice did everything that we could have asked him to do," Indians manager Mike Hargrove said. "He showed you why David Justice is David Justice."

But, like King's protagonist, Cleveland wasn't out of the woods yet. Mo Vaughn ripped a one-out double in the bottom of the eighth, bringing Indian-killer Garciaparra up with a chance to turn the game around again. But this time, Garciaparra, who had rolled up a record eleven RBI in the series, grounded to third off Paul Shuey, who then got O'Leary to fly out to end the inning. Tribe closer Mike Jackson—who had been just as effective as Gordon in 1998 without the publicity—pitched a one-two-three ninth to send the Indians to the American League Championship Series for the third time in four years.

Though Gordon's heroics during the summer had gotten Boston to the postseason, long-suffering Red Sox fans—already enraged at Williams for not starting Martinez—now questioned his decision to bring Gordon on early. "That was the difference in the game," Vizquel said. "I don't think he was mentally ready to pitch the eighth. I don't think his mind was set to do it."

The following spring, Gordon's magical year was immortalized on bookshelves around the world. Meanwhile, the pitcher extended his string of consecutive regular-season saves to fifty-four before an elbow injury ended his season and forced him to sit out all of 2000. Released by the Red Sox, he found a new home in Chicago with the Cubs but never again found the dominance that carried him through the 1998 season.

And the Indians found their own little claim to fame, with their eighth-inning heroics in Game Four, earning a mention in King's postscript to his book. "There's a saying," King wrote, "one that most closers like Tom Gordon would probably agree with: some days you eat the bear . . . and some days the bear eats you."

After five months of pitching perfection, the Cleveland Indians became that second bear and, in so doing, were the team that finally beat Tom Gordon.

Indians	0 0 0	0 0 0	0 2 0	=2
Red Sox	0 0 0	1 0 0	0 0 0	=1

CLEVELAND

	AB	R	H	RBI
Lofton cf	4	1	1	0
Vizquel ss	4	1	1	0
Justice lf	4	0	2	2
Ramirez rf	4	0	0	0
Fryman 3b	2	0	1	0
Thome dh	3	0	0	0
Sexson 1b	2	0	0	0
Alomar c	3	0	0	0
Wilson 2b	2	0	0	0
Cora ph-2b	2	0	0	0
TOTAL	30	2	5	2

	IP	H	R	ER	BB	SO
Colon	5⅔	5	1	1	3	3
Poole	1	0	0	0	1	2
Reed (W)	⅔	0	0	0	0	1
Assenmacher	0	1	0	0	0	0
Shuey	⅔	0	0	0	1	0
Jackson (Sv)	1	0	0	0	0	1

BOSTON

	AB	R	H	RBI
Lewis cf	4	0	1	0
Valentin 3b	3	0	2	0
Vaughn 1b	4	0	1	0
Sadler pr-2b	0	0	0	0
Garciaparra ss	3	1	1	1
Stanley dh	3	0	1	0
Buford pr-dh	0	0	0	0
O'Leary lf	4	0	0	0
Hatteberg c	2	0	0	0
Benjamin 2b-1b	2	0	0	0
Cummings ph	1	0	0	0
Bragg rf	4	0	0	0
TOTAL	30	1	6	1

	IP	H	R	ER	BB	SO
Schourek	5⅓	2	0	0	4	1
Lowe	1⅔	0	0	0	0	2
Gordon (L)	2	3	2	2	2	0

Attendance: 33,537

#44

INDIANS 7, TORONTO BLUE JAYS 6
JUNE 28, 1992

Coming Attractions

From the pitch darkness of perhaps the bleakest period in the long history of the Cleveland Indians came a small, distant beam of hope. After losing a team-record 105 games in 1991, the Tribe proved little better to start '92, sinking to last place almost instantly and by late June stood fifteen games out and on pace to again lose 100 games.

Yet on an otherwise pedestrian Thursday afternoon at the corner of Carnegie and Ontario avenues in downtown Cleveland, the present yielded to the future. On June 25, 1992, team and city officials conducted the ceremonial groundbreaking for the Gateway project which, in two years, would culminate in the opening of a new ballpark for the forlorn Indians and their long-suffering fans. Former Tribe legend Mel Harder and current star Charles Nagy both threw symbolic first pitches over the spot where home plate would eventually rest, and for a few hours, the sorry current state of the franchise—currently mired in a five-game losing streak—yielded to the bright promise of tomorrow. But with the first-place Toronto Blue Jays storming into town for a weekend series, the respite would be brief.

Boasting the best record in the American League en route to their first world title, the Blue Jays coasted to a 6–1 win on Friday night, extending Cleveland's losing streak to six. On Saturday night, the Indians showed unusual perseverance, rallying for two runs in the eighth inning for a 6–4 win to avoid the sweep. With longtime Indian killer Jack Morris—who held a stunning 30–11 career record against Cleveland—pitching on Sunday, the home team's chances of taking the rubber match looked slim.

Those hopes dropped almost entirely to nothing in the first inning as Toronto scored three runs—the first on a home run by former Indian slugger Joe

Carter. Though the game was barely twenty minutes old, it appeared Morris (who would be an Indian himself within two years) had all the support he would need to shut down the staggering Tribe, which had scored just nine runs over its previous sixty innings.

But in between innings, something happened. In the short duration of a commercial break, the Indians transformed from a hapless last-place team into the energetic, inspirational juggernaut they would become upon the opening of the ballpark that was now nothing more than turned dirt.

Leadoff hitter Kenny Lofton had already made an impact in his first full major-league season, gradually taking over the center-field and leadoff spot from incumbent Alex Cole. While Cole had brought blazing speed and little else to the lineup, Lofton provided a complete package Tribe fans hadn't seen in decades. It was displayed in his first at-bat of this Sunday matinee, as he laid down a perfect bunt that rolled down the third-base line as Lofton reached first base. Veteran shortstop Felix Fermin followed with a single, then up-and-coming second baseman Carlos Baerga sliced a hit through the right side to score Lofton. The Tribe added another run when emerging power hitter Albert Belle grounded into a double play, scoring Fermin. But with the bases cleared and the rally apparently over, Cleveland heated up again. A single and two walks loaded the bases for another little-known youngster fresh up from double-A Canton-Akron who had yet to play fifty major-league games. Tall, skinny third baseman Jim Thome came through with a two-out single up the middle to score two runs and put the Indians on top. Though the game wasn't even an inning old, the crowd of 23,560—one of the largest of the season—recognized there was something different about the home team.

The resurgent Indians struck again in the second. Once again, Lofton led off the inning with a bunt single down the third-base line. He stole second and scored on another Baerga single to make it 5–3. By now, Morris was agitated. When Lofton came up again in the fourth, Morris fired a pitch toward Lofton's knees, sending him scrambling out of the batter's box. "That's the most bush thing I've ever seen," Indians manager Mike Hargrove said later. Lofton took a step toward the mound before being restrained and the fans rose to their feet. The game had now taken on added seasoning, particularly after Lofton returned to the box and laid down another bunt. This time Morris threw him out, but the message was clear. Lofton's daring symbolized the guts of a new team. "That's my game," he said. "After he threw at me, I had to bunt. I've got to stand up for myself."

With the afternoon now taking on a postseason atmosphere—not that any Cleveland fans knew precisely what that meant—the Indians took their 5–3 lead into the seventh. But once again they were haunted, first by their own incompetence when left fielder Glenallen Hill committed back-to-back errors, then by a specter from their past when Carter delivered a single to score Devon White and future Indian Roberto Alomar to tie the contest. Then in the eighth, Jeff Kent, another future Indian, blasted a home run to left center to put Toronto ahead for the first time since the first inning. For all their spunk, it appeared the Indians would lose for the forty-sixth time in seventy-five games.

But once again, a newfound resilience propelled the Tribe. Cole opened the Cleveland eighth with a walk, then moved to second on a sacrifice bunt. In the Indian dugout, normally by-the-book Hargrove decided to play a hunch. He pulled back Hill for pinch-hitter Paul Sorrento. On the surface, the move seemed illogical since Sorrento had struck out all three times he'd faced Blue Jays reliever Duane Ward in his career. Yet Hargrove, perhaps fueled by the unexpected energy of this promising afternoon, rolled the dice. And it paid off.

"He'd always gotten me with those sliders," Sorrento said of Ward. "This time, he got the slider up a bit, and I drove it." Sorrento blasted an 0–1 pitch over the fence in right center to put the Indians up, 7–6. The roar of the crowd made it sound twice as big. Hargrove again went against convention in the ninth, tapping recently acquired reliever Eric Plunk, who hadn't earned a save in three years, to slam the door. And slam it he did, putting down the Jays in order, including soon-to-be-Tribesmen Dave Winfield and Candy Maldonado, to sew up a satisfying 7–6 win. Perhaps more telling, the league's worst team had taken two of three from the best with stunning back-to-back comeback victories. "But Saturday night was only a game," Paul Hoynes wrote in Monday's *Plain Dealer.* "Yesterday was drama. A nine-act play with villains, goats, and heroes."

Starting with those two victories, Cleveland's 1992 season made a 180-degree turn. The Indians would post a 48–41 record over the remaining three months of the campaign—a small step for a baseball team, but a giant leap for a woebegone franchise. The team's unforgettable 1990s renaissance, which would culminate in a pair of pennants and six playoff appearances, had begun on a sunshiny June weekend with a last-place team teaching itself how to win.

More than a surprising victory, that Sunday afternoon on the shores of Lake Erie became a preview of coming attractions.

Blue Jays	3	0	0	0	0	0	2	1	0	=6
Indians	4	1	0	0	0	0	0	2	x	=7

TORONTO

	AB	R	H	RBI
White cf	3	1	0	0
R. Alomar 2b	5	1	1	0
Carter rf	4	1	3	3
Winfield dh	3	1	0	0
Olerud 1b	5	1	2	2
Maldonado lf	5	0	0	0
Borders c	4	0	0	0
Kent 3b	3	1	1	1
Lee ss	4	0	1	0
TOTAL	36	6	8	6

	IP	H	R	ER	BB	SO
Morris	7	10	5	4	2	3
Ward (L)	1	2	2	2	2	0

CLEVELAND

	AB	R	H	RBI
Lofton cf	4	2	2	0
Fermin ss	4	1	2	0
Baerga 2b	4	0	3	2
Belle dh	4	0	0	0
Martinez 1b	3	1	1	0
Cole ph	0	1	0	0
Howard lf	0	0	0	0
Whiten rf	2	1	1	0
Hill lf	2	0	0	0
Sorrento ph-1b	1	1	1	2
Thome 3b	4	0	2	2
Jacoby 3b	0	0	0	0
S. Alomar c	4	0	0	0
TOTAL	32	7	12	6

	IP	H	R	ER	BB	SO
Cook	5	4	3	1	3	2
Power	1⅓	2	2	2	1	2
Lilliquist	⅓	0	0	0	0	0
Olin (W)	1⅓	2	1	1	1	1
Plunk (Sv)	1	0	0	0	0	0

Attendance: 23,560

#43

GUARDIANS 9, TEXAS RANGERS 8 (10 INNINGS)
SEPTEMBER 28, 2025

The Guardiac Kids

Even before the first pitch, it already felt like the most bizarre regular-season finale in franchise history. And considering what had happened to get to this point, that only seemed appropriate.

At the midpoint of the summer, a Guardians season that had begun with so much promise was circling the drain. A ten-game losing streak—culminated with a three-game sweep at the hands of the first-place Detroit Tigers in Cleveland over the Fourth of July weekend—had dropped the Guardians to a whopping 15½ games behind the Tigers as they'd sunk into fourth place in the American League Central Division.

Their usually efficient offense was floundering. At one point in late June, Cleveland was shut out three times in four games and held scoreless five times in an eleven-day period. Even worse, their stalwart pitching staff was suddenly riddled with scandal. Just before getting swept by Detroit, starting pitcher Luis Ortiz was placed on non-disciplinary leave due to a league investigation that ultimately revealed he'd been taking bribes from gamblers to rig pitches during games. The news got even worse three weeks later when the investigation expanded to include star closer Emmanuel Clase, who'd already gathered twenty-four saves in 2025 after notching forty-seven the year before. It was a stunning body blow to the already woozy Guardians, who would now have to finish the season without arguably their most dominant player.

Standing at 40–48 with more than half the season gone, their top pitcher likely about to be kicked out of the sport, and no hope in sight, the Guardians had seen their season turn into an absolute disaster.

Then something strange began to happen.

It started gradually, and few took notice at first. They snapped out of the losing streak by winning eleven of their next thirteen games to claw back over the .500 mark and into second place in the division. But still eight games behind the Tigers and with a handful of other teams in the American League playoff race, the odds of salvaging the season still seemed long, particularly after a six-game losing streak in late August dropped them back under the break-even mark, and they now stood a distant 12½ games behind Detroit with thirty-two games to play.

Then the fuse truly caught.

In an inexplicable whirlwind, the Guardians would win fifteen of their next sixteen games, including ten straight, to trim Detroit's lead to a single game. It was one of the most remarkable turnarounds in the history of baseball, made all the more incredible when the Guardians beat the Tigers twice to start the final week of the season and surged into sole possession of first place. *Plain Dealer* columnist Terry Pluto started referring to the Guards as "the Little Team that Could." Others coined a different, perhaps more appropriate nickname—"Guardiac Kids," an homage to the swashbuckling Cleveland Browns teams of the late 1970s and early 1980s that regularly overcame long odds to win close games at the wire.

And things would only get goofier.

In the season's penultimate game on Saturday night, the Guardians pulled off a bizarre 3–2 walk-off victory over visiting Texas when Cleveland pinch-hitter C. J. Kayfus was hit by a pitch with two out and the bases loaded to drive in the winning run. The triumph allowed Cleveland to remain tied for first with the Tigers and clinch at least a wild-card playoff berth. Part of their mission had been accomplished, and it was something to behold, since the possibility of qualifying for the postseason seemed like a fantasy just a month earlier. But to truly cement their place in history, they needed to capture the division crown.

On a sun-splashed September Sunday at Progressive Field, the Guardians trailed late before a Jhonkensy Noel home run in the seventh and a sacrifice fly by second baseman Brayan Rocchio knotted the score at five in the eighth. Better still, just before Rocchio's heroics, word trickled into Progressive Field that the Tigers had lost in Boston, ensuring that even with a loss, thanks to an advantage in tie-breakers, Cleveland had indeed clinched the division championship. As the news flashed on the stadium scoreboard, the energetic fans rose to their feet and began celebrating. Which was both strange and a bit confusing to the players in the dugout. "I was wondering why the fans were so excited about a t-shirt toss," catcher Austin Hedges joked later.

For as fulfilling (and unusual) as the moment was, players and fans alike wanted to see the title won the right way, with a Cleveland victory. And yet, that appeared to slip from reach as the game tumbled into extra innings and Texas pinch-hitter Rowdy Tellez blasted a three-run homer in the tenth to put the Rangers up 8–5. It appeared that the Little Team That Could had finally run out of gas, and the Guardians would have to settle for winning the division on a tiebreaker.

Still, they had one more chance. In the bottom of the inning, catcher Bo Naylor ripped a double to score "ghost runner" George Valera, who began the tenth on second base, which cut the deficit to two. Then pinch-hitter Petey Halpin fouled off six pitches in a grueling nine-pitch at-bat to draw a walk, bringing Rocchio to the plate. On the fifth pitch from Texas reliever Jose Corniell, a 1–2 fastball clocked at 96 miles per hour, Rocchio blasted a high, arching shot straight down the right-field line. Sailing through the lengthening shadows of the gathering dusk, the baseball struck high off the foul pole, giving Rocchio just his fifth home run of the season and one of the most memorable moments in team history.

His teammates poured out of the dugout and gathered around home plate as Rocchio sailed around the bases, catapulting his batting helmet into the air as he rounded third. As he reached home plate, the crowd roared in triumph, now able to celebrate the team's thirteenth Central Division title in thirty years how they wanted—and with a dramatic flourish.

"It was incredible," Rocchio said afterward, "not only because of the honor and the walk-off, but knowing that we wanted to win the division the right way."

The moment served as an exclamation point on the greatest comeback in the history of baseball. No team had ever overcome a deficit that large to win a division or pennant, as Cleveland surpassed the 1914 Boston Braves—who'd rallied from a fifteen-game hole to win the National League flag. Perhaps more incredibly was how quickly the Guards had caught up when it mattered most, making up eleven games in the last twenty-four days of the season, the largest deficit ever overcome in the month of September.

All perfectly symbolized by a fittingly crazy finish in the finale.

"Just like the Guardians saving the best for the last part of the season," Pluto wrote in the *Plain Dealer*, "they did so in this game."

Rangers	0	2	2	0	0	1	0	0	0	3 =8
Guardians	2	0	1	0	0	0	1	1	0	4 =9

TEXAS

	AB	R	H	RBI
Helman cf	4	0	0	1
Freeman 2b	4	1	1	0
Pederson ph	1	0	0	0
Solano 2b	0	0	0	0
Jung 3b	4	2	1	0
García dh	4	1	1	0
Burger 1b	3	0	1	2
Tellez ph-1b	1	1	1	3
Duran ss	5	0	1	0
Heim c	5	1	0	0
Moore rf	1	1	0	0
McKinney ph-rf	3	1	0	0
Osuna lf	4	0	1	2
TOTAL	39	8	7	8

	IP	H	R	ER	BB	SO
Corbin	4	4	3	3	2	5
Coulombe	1	0	0	0	0	0
Milner	1⅓	2	1	1	1	2
Curvelo	1	2	1	1	0	1
Corniell (L)	1⅔	3	4	3	1	1

CLEVELAND

	AB	R	H	RBI
Kwan lf	4	1	1	0
Martínez cf-2b	3	2	1	0
Ramírez dh	5	0	2	0
Rodríguez rf	2	0	1	2
Valera ph-rf	2	1	0	0
Naylor c	4	2	2	2
Arias ss	3	0	0	0
Manzardo ph	1	0	1	0
Halpin pr-cf	0	1	0	0
Rocchio 2b-ss	4	1	1	4
Schneemann 3b	4	0	0	0
Noel 1b	3	1	2	1
Kayfus ph-1b	1	0	0	0
TOTAL	36	9	11	9

	IP	H	R	ER	BB	SO
Allen	4⅓	5	4	4	2	4
Festa	1⅔	0	1	0	0	2
Allard	2	0	0	0	0	2
Kent (W)	2	2	3	2	0	0

Attendance: 31,054

#42

INDIANS 22, NEW YORK YANKEES 0
AUGUST 31, 2004

The Yankee Massacre

After two years of sub-.500 baseball, there were low expectations for a young Cleveland team in 2004. True to form, the Tribe limped out of the starting gate, and following a seven-game losing streak in late May, its record was a meager 18–26. Yet gradually, the team started to improve and hovered around the .500 mark for much of the summer before catching fire in early August. The unassuming Indians won ten of eleven games to trim an eight-game deficit to Minnesota in the American League Central Division to one. Suddenly Cleveland fans were allowing themselves to think postseason.

But for as quickly as their team had become a contender, it dropped to pretender once again, losing nine straight games to again fall to eight behind, and the sudden promise was gone. In that momentum-killing skid, the Indians had managed to score a total of just twenty-three runs—an average of just over two per ballgame. The seeds of a playoff contender had been planted but hadn't taken root yet.

Meanwhile, as always, the New York Yankees were postseason-bound, boasting the best record in the AL going into a midweek series with the Indians in the Bronx. The Yankees would wind up the season winning more than 100 games and come within a victory of reaching their sixth World Series in seven years. And with the Boston Red Sox still nipping at their heels, the Yanks would enter September with plenty of motivation. Which is what makes what occurred on that Tuesday night so remarkable.

Things started well for the Indians with a one-out single by Omar Vizquel, who would then score the first of three first-inning runs on a bases-loaded triple by designated hitter Travis Hafner. The rout was on in the second when Vizquel came through again, this time with an RBI single, sparking another three-run inning. The triple threat continued in the third with three more runs—including two on a two-out double by Vizquel—to make it 9–0. New York finally held Cleveland scoreless in the fourth before things got downright ridiculous in the fifth.

Back-to-back doubles by first baseman Ben Broussard and second baseman Ron Belliard preceded a two-run homer by Coco Crisp. After Cleveland loaded the bases, third baseman Casey Blake walked to bring home the fourth run of the inning, then Broussard delivered his second hit of the frame, scoring two more runs. It was 15–0 after five—and the Indians weren't done yet.

They added another in the sixth on a Vizquel RBI double before New York pitchers finally settled and held the Tribe in check for the seventh and eighth. But Cleveland's offensive tilt-a-whirl began again in the ninth. After singles by Josh Phelps and Belliard, Jody Gerut blasted a three-run homer. After another walk to Crisp, Vizquel came to bat for the seventh time on the evening, and the usually partisan New York fans rose to their feet. Vizquel had collected six hits in his previous six at-bats, tying an American League record for a nine-inning game, and now would try to make history. But this time, he flied out to former teammate Kenny Lofton in center. Moments later, catcher Victor Martinez put the cap on with a three-run home run, completing Cleveland's second six-run inning of the night. The Yankees went down in order in the ninth, finishing the game with just five hits.

The final was 22–0—the worst loss in Yankee history and the largest shutout victory in Major League Baseball in 104 years. Cleveland rolled up twenty-two hits, including six extra-base hits and three home runs to go along with nine walks. And things could have been much worse had the Indians not left ten runners on base, including seven in scoring position. By contrast, in a three-game series with New York at Jacobs Field the previous week, the Indians had combined to score only twelve runs.

Personifying this dominance was Vizquel, who became the first Indian in twenty-four years to collect six hits in a nine-inning game. He scored three times and knocked in four runs, in one night raising his season batting average eight points. Somewhat lost in the run parade was a sterling pitching performance by Cleveland starter Jake Westbrook, who pitched seven shutout innings for the win. While the Indians were rolling to nine runs in the first three innings, Westbrook retired the first eleven New York batters and only once allowed a Yankee to reach third base on the night.

Both the Indians and their fans knew the blowout victory couldn't have come against a better opponent. New York owner and perennial loudmouth George Steinbrenner refused to talk to reporters after the game. "I think everybody has to look at this game and ask some questions," said veteran New York catcher Jorge Posada. "How good are we?"

The Indians had delivered the Yankees and their blustery fans a huge slice of humble pie. "New York and California are the same," Gerut said. "It's like no one can do it better than they can."

Just like no one can do it better than the Indians did that night.

Indians	3	3	3	0	6	1	0	0	6	=22
Yankees	0	0	0	0	0	0	0	0	0	=0

CLEVELAND

	AB	R	H	RBI
Crisp cf	6	4	2	3
Vizquel ss	7	3	6	4
Lawton lf	5	1	1	1
Ludwick rf	2	1	1	0
Martinez c	4	3	2	4
Hafner dh	6	1	2	3
Blake 3b	2	1	0	1
McDonald 3b	2	0	0	0
Broussard 1b	3	2	2	2
Phelps 1b	2	1	2	0
Belliard 2b	6	3	3	1
Gerut rf/lf	4	2	1	3
TOTAL	49	22	22	22

	IP	H	R	ER	BB	SO
Westbrook (W)	7	5	0	0	0	5
Guthrie	2	0	0	0	1	1

NEW YORK

	AB	R	H	RBI
Williams cf	4	0	0	0
Jeter ss	2	0	0	0
Wilson ss	2	0	0	0
Sheffield dh	3	0	1	0
Clark dh	1	0	0	0
Rodriguez 3b	4	0	1	0
Matsui lf	2	0	1	0
Crosby lf	2	0	0	0
Posada c	2	0	0	0
Flaherty c	2	0	0	0
Olerud 1b	3	0	1	0
Cairo 2b	3	0	1	0
Lofton rf	2	0	0	0
TOTAL	32	0	5	0

	IP	H	R	ER	BB	SO
Vazquez (L)	1⅓	5	6	6	2	1
Sturtze	3	6	7	7	2	1
Nitkowski	1⅔	3	3	3	3	1
Loaiza	3	8	6	6	2	3

Attendance: 51,777

#41

INDIANS 4, OAKLAND ATHLETICS 0
JULY 19, 1974

Good Luck, Bozzie

Put simply, it was an absolutely miserable time to live in America.

By the middle of the hot, depressing summer of 1974, Richard Nixon's presidency was limping toward its inevitable conclusion, with the chief executive finally agreeing to release edited transcripts of the recorded phone calls that would leave a permanent stain on history. The economy was stagnant, unemployment was rising, and there was little for Americans to be proud of.

Cleveland suffered its own black eye that June when the gold-mine promotional idea of Ten-Cent Beer Night turned into a fiasco that forced the Indians to forfeit a game with Texas. Despite the national embarrassment, the team saw no harm in holding the second scheduled Ten-Cent Beer Night on July 18, albeit with the beer rationed through a coupon system and 200 police officers on hand to quell any shenanigans. And, to the relief of the front office, there were no incidents, despite a crowd nearly twice the size of the one for the first Beer Night. It was the only piece of good news surrounding the Tribe, which had seen a 1½-game lead in the American League East Division following the first weekend of July vanish during a string of nine losses in ten games, including six straight.

The sour stretch continued with a loss to the red-hot Oakland Athletics, who opened a four-game weekend series at Cleveland Stadium with a 3–2 win on Thursday night. The A's, winners of the previous two World Series, held the best record in the AL and a comfortable lead in the West Division. With Gene Tenace, Sal Bando, Joe Rudi, and Reggie Jackson in the lineup, the Athletics boasted one of the best collections of power hitters in baseball. Already coasting toward a third straight title, it appeared no one could stop the Athletics. But on Friday night, someone did.

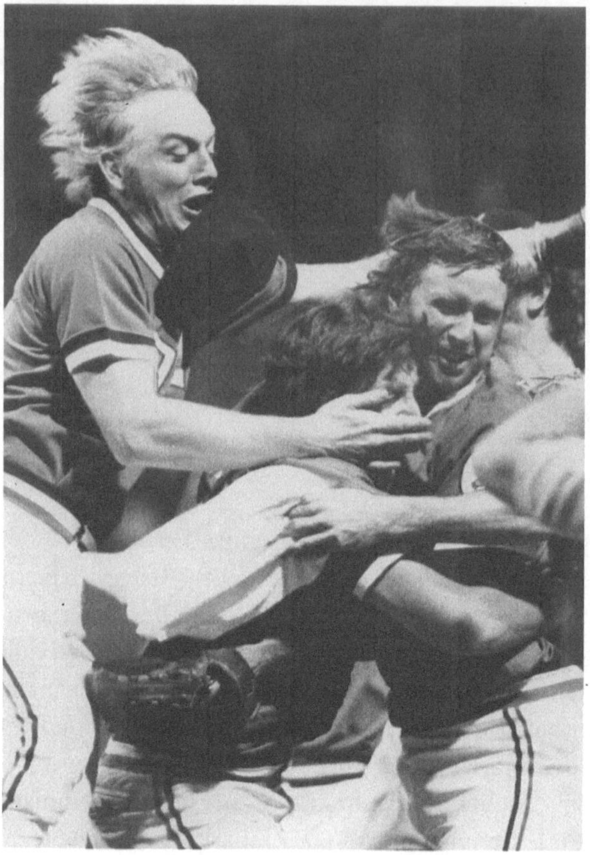

Cleveland pitcher Dick Bosman is mobbed by his teammates after completing perhaps the unlikeliest no-hitter in franchise history on July 19, 1974. Cleveland State University Library's *Cleveland Press* Collection.

It had already been a long year for Cleveland pitcher Dick Bosman. He'd come to the Indians from Texas the year before in a controversial trade for hurler Steve Dunning but went just 1–8 in twenty-two games with the Tribe. Then just after the '74 season began, the Indians made a deal with the Yankees that brought four new pitchers to the team—further burying Bosman on the roster. By mid-July, the thirty-year-old Bosman had won just one game on the year and his career appeared to be circling the drain.

The evening started innocently enough, with Bosman cruising through the first three innings and retiring the Oakland lineup in order. Meanwhile, the Tribe broke through for a pair of runs in the third on a rare homer by Joe Lis. It would be all the offense Bosman would need. His string of consecutive outs reached eleven in the fourth before he threw wild to first after fielding a Bando tapper along the third-base line and it got away from Cleveland first baseman Tommy McGraw for an error. But Bosman struck out Jackson to end the scoring threat and the inning, and from then on it was smooth sailing.

The embattled pitcher was magnificent, mowing down the world champs with surprising ease. Only three times did Oakland hitters even approach reaching base safely. In the fifth, Rudi smacked a grounder to the hole at shortstop, but the Tribe's Frank Duffy made a nifty backhand stop and threw Rudi out. Then in the seventh, Bando hit a sharp grounder up the middle which Bosman snared between his legs, then threw to first. And finally, in the eighth, A's first baseman Pat Borque hit a long fly to right field, but Charlie Spikes made a running catch on the warning track to end the inning. The Indians added two more runs in the fourth to make it 4–0, but the crowd of 24,302 was only interested in one thing: could Bosman get the no-hitter?

As the eighth inning came to a close, Reggie Jackson crossed paths with Bosman on his way out to the mound. "Good luck, Bozzie," Jackson said. Bosman just smiled. With the fans on their feet, Dick Green stepped into the batter's box. Green, who had broken up a no-hit bid by Baltimore's Wayne Garland in the ninth inning earlier that week, swung at Bosman's first pitch and hit a three-hopper to Buddy Bell at third. Bell threw him out. Pinch hitter Jesus Alou then hit a soft grounder to Jack Brohamer at second for out No. 2. History would ride on the shoulders of Oakland center fielder Bill North. With the crowd roaring like tempest waves against an ocean shore, North fouled off the first two pitches, then swung and missed at a perfect sinker for the final out. Dick Bosman had done it. His teammates rushed the field to mob Cleveland's newest hero.

The man whom the team hadn't even wanted three months before had just etched his name in the record books, pitching the thirteenth no-hitter in Indians history. Aside from his own throwing error in the fourth, not one Athletic batter reached base on Bosman, who threw a mere seventy-nine pitches—sixty of them for strikes. "It was a masterpiece," commented teammate Gaylord Perry, who would go on to win the American League Cy Young Award that year. Adding a sprinkle of irony on top of the magic, Bosman's catcher was the Indians' regular first baseman, John Ellis, playing backstop for the first time in two months with everyday catcher Dave Duncan getting the night off.

It may have been the low point of a magical season for Oakland, but eloquent Reggie Jackson pointed out the silver lining. "I'm glad he pitched a no-hitter," he said. "If we're going to get beat, we might as well get beat by a no-hitter."

After escaping his adoring teammates, who scurried to the locker room to spread out a trail of towels for the pitcher to walk on, Bosman addressed the crowd through a field microphone. "This is the culmination of everything I've worked for and dreamed about," said Bosman, who had never before thrown a no-hitter at any level. "I almost feel like I'm dreaming—and if I am, I don't want to wake up for a week or so."

But he did wake up bright-eyed and bushy-tailed on Saturday. Cleveland general manager Phil Seghi found Bosman in the locker room after the game and said, "Come up and see me first thing in the morning." He would tear up Bosman's old contract and give him a raise.

The Indians' losing streak was over and the everyday frustrations of the summer of '74 temporarily evaporated on that muggy Friday night on the lakefront. "It couldn't have come at a better time," said Tribe manager Ken Aspromonte, "and it couldn't happen to a more deserving guy."

Athletics	0 0 0	0 0 0	0 0 0 =0
Indians	0 0 2	2 0 0	0 0 x =4

OAKLAND

	AB	R	H	RBI
North cf	4	0	0	0
Campaneris ss	3	0	0	0
Bando 3b	3	0	0	0
Jackson rf	3	0	0	0
Rudi lf	3	0	0	0
Washington dh	3	0	0	0
Bourque 1b	3	0	0	0
Green 2b	3	0	0	0
Haney c	2	0	0	0
Alou ph	1	0	0	0
TOTAL	28	0	0	0

	IP	H	R	ER	BB	SO
Hamilton (L)	3⅓	5	4	4	0	4
Odom	3⅔	1	0	0	1	1
Knowles	1	1	0	0	0	0

CLEVELAND

	AB	R	H	RBI
Lowenstein lf	3	0	0	0
Torres lf	0	0	0	0
Duffy ss	4	0	0	0
Hendrick cf	3	0	1	0
Spikes rf	3	0	0	0
Ellis c	3	1	1	0
Bell 3b	3	1	2	1
McGraw 1b	3	1	1	1
Lis dh	2	1	1	2
Gamble dh	1	0	0	0
Brohamer 2b	2	0	1	0
TOTAL	27	4	7	4

	IP	H	R	ER	BB	SO
Bosman (W)	9	0	0	0	0	4

Attendance: 24,302

#40

GUARDIANS 1, TAMPA BAY RAYS 0 (15 INNINGS)
OCTOBER 8, 2022

SpongeBob Saves the Day

Shadows rarely cause problems.

The dark shapes created by an object obstructing a source of light are not really something most people ever truly think about or are concerned with. Unless, that is, it can affect your work—for example, as a photographer. Or maybe a gardener.

Or, in some cases, a baseball player.

On those occasions when the angle and location of the sun, the time of day, and time of year all line up just right in certain ballparks, shadows can wreak havoc on a batter's ability to read a pitch. For as the baseball passes into and out of the long shadows that stretch across the field as it travels from the pitcher's hand toward home plate, it becomes nearly impossible to visualize the spin and gauge the speed. Thus, batters tend to struggle until the shadows finally dissolve along with the waning daylight.

Ironically, those occasions tend to be more prevalent in October, when the sun sets a bit earlier. And the games matter most.

Problematic shadow conditions emerged on what began as a bright but crisp Saturday afternoon as the Guardians hosted the Tampa Bay Rays in the second game of their best-of-three Wild Card Series at Progressive Field. Cleveland had narrowly won the first contest the previous afternoon (under an overcast sky) in a 2–1 pitchers duel, and needed one more victory to close out the series and advance to the next round of the American League playoffs.

From the outset, both teams seemed determined to make Friday's low-scoring affair look like a shootout.

Cleveland starting pitcher Triston McKenzie and the Rays' Tyler Glasgow were equally brilliant early, with each team collecting only one hit apiece through the first four innings while racking up eleven total strikeouts. No runner reached second base until the sixth, when the Rays managed to put two on with two out before McKenzie enticed a fly out from Harold Ramírez to end the inning. The Guards then got their first chance to score in the bottom of the frame when two walks and a hit batter loaded the bases with nobody out. But third baseman José Ramírez struck out, then first baseman Josh Naylor grounded into a double play. The game remained scoreless and, though no one knew it yet, wasn't even half over.

With the stark shadows lengthening as the sun crept across the October sky, the teams toiled through scoreless inning after scoreless inning. Both teams' bullpens shuttled in new pitchers with the frequency of Uber rides in Public Square, and each new hurler proved just as successful at shutting down the opposing team's lineup as the one before.

When Naylor struck out with two down in the bottom of the ninth, the game tumbled into extra innings with no runs on the board and only five hits between the teams, all singles. The beat went on through the tenth and eleventh, with pitchers gathering eight more strikeouts, and the possibility of either team scoring felt as long as the shadows stretching across the infield. "It seemed swimming across Lake Erie to Canada with a tuba strapped to your back," Terry Pluto wrote in the *Plain Dealer,* "was easier than pushing a run across home plate."

Finally, in the twelfth, Tampa appeared to catch the break both teams had been waiting for. With runners on the corners and two out, Manuel Margot slapped a hard-hit ground ball down the third-base line and over the bag. It appeared the ball was headed for the left-field corner and a certain RBI double, but Cleveland's Ramírez, perfectly positioned near the bag, lunged into foul territory to spear the ball in his glove. He then made a lightning-quick pivot off his back foot and fired a long throw toward first in a desperate attempt to beat Margot. As Tampa Bay's Harold Ramírez came across home plate, the throw to first arrived just ahead of Margot, but low. Naylor stretched himself nearly entirely horizontal to catch the ball as it bounced off the dirt, barely keeping his back foot on the bag.

First-base umpire Quinn Wolcott called Margot out, and after a replay challenge by Tampa confirmed the call, the inning was over and the Guardians had escaped thanks to one of the greatest defensive plays in franchise playoff history. Had Ramírez not grabbed the ball and made a perfect throw, and had Naylor not managed to scoop up the baseball and keep his foot on first base, the Rays would have scored to take the lead.

"José kind of willed himself there to make that play," Cleveland manager Terry Francona would say later. "And Naylor . . . I don't know if it's a game-saving (play), it might have been a year-saving play."

The latter notion rung particularly true when Tampa Bay struck out the side in the bottom of the twelfth. The game marched on, still scoreless.

The Rays again threatened in the fifteenth. A pair of singles—marking the first time all day either team collected more than one hit in a inning—put runners on first and third with one out. But Cleveland reliever Sam Hentges, in his third inning of relief in what would be his longest outing of the season, struck out the next two batters to escape the jam.

With clocks ticking past 5 P.M. and the contest now approaching the five-hour mark, the game had long since passed the point of feeling surreal. That feeling intensified further when former Cleveland star pitcher Corey Kluber, now with the Rays, entered the game in his first relief appearance in nine years to face his old team, then subsequently proceeded to retire five straight batters.

Perhaps the only thing that could have made the atmosphere feel even more bizarre is what happened next—as the bottom of the fifteenth inning began, over the Progressive Field speakers crackled the theme song to the popular children's television show SpongeBob SquarePants.

Strange as it may have seemed, it served a purpose. This was the walk-up song selected by Cleveland rookie right fielder Oscar Gonzalez. While many players choose intense, bombastic songs intended to intensify and motivate them as they stepped up to bat, Gonzalez had the opposite mindset. He'd selected that song as he was coming up through the minor leagues, he said, to remind him that he's playing a game and should be having fun—just like the fun kids have when they hear that song and watch the show.

And on the second pitch of that at-bat—the 432nd pitch of the game—Gonzalez had the most fun of all.

He blasted a slider from Kluber high and deep to center field. "I knew it was a home run," Gonzalez would say later. "I knew it was a good connection and could tell by the angle of the ball."

Sure enough, the ball cleared the fence in center field 410 feet away, in one instant providing the Guardians with their first postseason series victory in six years.

For as suddenly and dramatically as it ended, it had been arguably the most grueling playoff game in team history.

The numbers told the tale. Fifteen innings, sixteen pitchers, thirty-nine strikeouts, 104 plate appearances. All resulting in just one run. Delivered by one swing, which, incredibly, marked just the eleventh total hit of the game and the first extra-base hit.

"I just kind of figured that it was going to take something like that," Francona said, "because it was a day when the pitching was having its way. Then when the shadows came, you could tell guys were having a tough time."

Beyond being remarkable, the game was also perfumed with history. The Guardians' longest postseason game ever, it marked just their second playoff walk-off homer and was the first time in the history of Major League Baseball that a postseason game had gone scoreless for at least fourteen innings.

Short as the series was, it would be memorialized for the incredible pitching on display. Altogether in the two games of the series, the Guardians scored only three runs but managed to triumph in both games only because their pitching staff had allowed just a single run in twenty-four innings of playoff baseball.

Yet ironically, that performance, certainly aided by shadows, would be overshadowed itself by an epic home run which would forever be associated with a cartoon character.

Rays	0 0 0	0 0 0	0 0 0	0 0 0	0 0 0 =0
Guardians	0 0 0	0 0 0	0 0 0	0 0 0	0 0 1 =1

TAMPA BAY

	AB	R	H	RBI
Díaz 3b-1b	6	0	0	0
Franco ss	5	0	1	0
Arozarena lf	5	0	1	0
Ramírez dh	6	0	0	0
Choi 1b	3	0	0	0
Bruján pr-2b	2	0	1	0
Paredes 2b	2	0	1	0
Walls ph-3b	3	0	1	0
Margot rf	5	0	1	0
Bethancourt c	2	0	0	0
Peralta ph	1	0	0	0
Mejia c	3	0	0	0
Siri cf	6	0	0	0
TOTAL	49	0	6	0

	IP	H	R	ER	BB	SO
Glasnow	5	2	0	0	0	5
Fairbanks	0	0	0	0	2	0
Adam	2	1	0	0	0	2
Rasmussen	1⅔	0	0	0	0	2
Cleavinger	1⅓	0	0	0	0	4
Armstrong	1⅓	1	0	0	0	3
Raley	1	0	0	0	1	2
Kluber (L)	1⅔	1	1	1	0	1

CLEVELAND

	AB	R	H	RBI
Kwan lf	5	0	0	0
Rosario ss	5	0	0	0
Ramírez 3b	6	0	0	0
Naylore 1b	6	0	1	0
González rf	5	1	2	1
Giménez 2b	5	0	0	0
Brennan dh	5	0	1	0
Hedges c	3	0	0	0
Miller ph	1	0	0	0
Maile c	0	0	0	0
Straw cf	4	0	1	0
TOTAL	45	1	5	1

	IP	H	R	ER	BB	SO
McKenzie	6	2	0	0	2	8
Karinchak	1	0	0	0	1	0
Stephan	1	0	0	0	0	2
Clase	1	0	0	0	0	1
Sandlin	⅔	0	0	0	1	1
Morgan	1⅓	0	0	0	0	2
De Los Santos	1	1	0	0	1	0
Hentges (W)	3	3	0	0	0	6

Attendance: 34,971

#39

INDIANS 3, BALTIMORE ORIOLES 2
SEPTEMBER 8, 1995

The Dance

In the time that lapsed between Indians postseason appearances, the team had played 6,430 games. Fourteen new Major League Baseball teams were born and nine different presidents resided in the White House. Along the way, Cleveland became the most humiliated team in the game, going better than thirty years without even contending for a pennant. While the decades of losing provided plenty of suffering, this dark generation was eclipsed by the unthinkable—the deaths of promising young pitcher Steve Olin and veteran reliever Tim Crews in a boating accident during spring training in 1993. A losing baseball team was inconsequential by comparison, and it would take nearly a full year for an already wobbly franchise to get back on its feet again.

But as summer gradually began to yield to fall in 1995, that multigenerational drought was about to come to an end. In what had become an almost ethereal season, the '95 Indians had simply overwhelmed the rest of the American League, sprinting to a twelve-game lead in the Central Division at the All-Star Break of a strike-shortened season, while throttling opponents all summer long. Heading into the first post–Labor Day weekend, the Tribe led second-place Chicago by 22½ games, and everyone knew it was just a matter of time before the official celebration of a division title could begin.

The Indians' first chance would come on a Friday night at Jacobs Field, which had become a mythical palace over the previous two years, where Clevelanders gathered every night to celebrate their first dominant baseball team in nearly a half century. And after a summer like the Tribe had enjoyed, *how* they clinched was just as important as *when*. "We definitely want to do it in front of our fans," said third baseman Jim Thome. "They deserve it as much as we do."

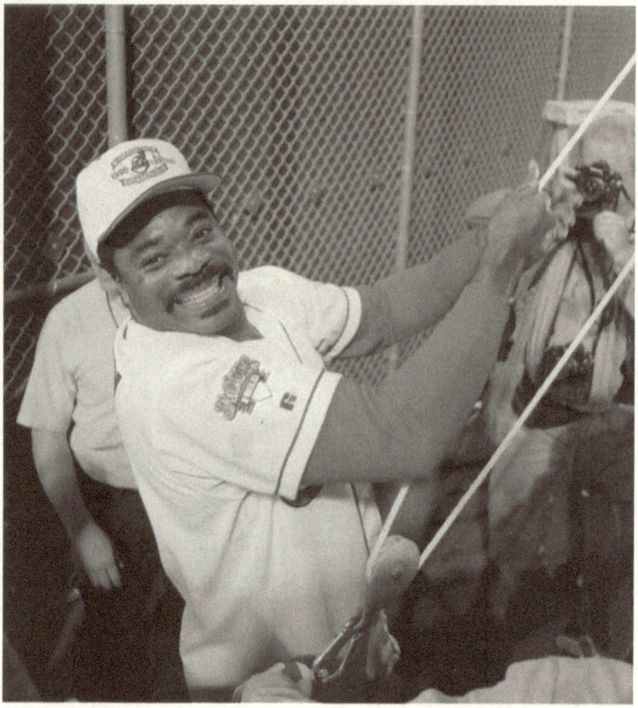

Veteran slugger Eddie Murray flashes an uncharacteristic smile as he hoists the banner, one most Indians fans thought they'd never see, proclaiming their first division championship of the Jacobs Field era following a 3–2 win over the Baltimore Orioles on September 8, 1995. *Akron Beacon Journal.*

The mediocre Baltimore Orioles were in town, led by iconic shortstop Cal Ripken Jr., who two days before had broken Lou Gehrig's previously thought unbreakable record of 2,130 consecutive games played. Appropriately, in his first game since making history, Ripken presented his team's lineup card at home plate to a rousing standing ovation from the Cleveland crowd. Meeting him there with the Indians lineup was veteran Eddie Murray, who had been a longtime teammate of Ripken's in Baltimore throughout the 1980s, and the diamond stalwarts greeted one another with a friendly embrace. Like Ripken, Murray symbolized a newfound maturity for a team that had for decades managed to avoid such a quality. But now, with the postseason one victory away, the Indians punched their time clock and took care of business much like the countless blue-collar workers who had followed the team over the previous forty years.

On a night oozing with appreciation for history, it seemed fitting that Murray should lead the way. After the Indians plated a run in the third, then loaded the bases, Murray ripped a two-run single to center to put the Tribe up 3–0 and provide all the necessary offense. Toeing the rubber for Cleveland that evening was Orel Hershiser, another seasoned vet whose career had been revitalized when he joined the Indians earlier that year. And though he was a newcomer,

Hershiser understood the magnitude of what was about to happen. "I wanted this game to be pressure-packed," he said. "I treated it like a Game Seven, a do-or-die game. I want to simulate what's going to happen later this year."

And as he had all year, Hershiser came through. He cruised through the first three innings, then coaxed a timely double play to thwart a scoring threat in the fourth. When Hershiser tired in the seventh, the reliable Cleveland bullpen took over, giving up just one hit over the final 2⅓ innings. When the Indians took a 3–2 lead into the ninth, the center-field bullpen door opened and out trotted closer Jose Mesa, who, perhaps more than any other Indian, reflected the team's sudden and unexpected rise to dominance. Molded into a reliever after a so-so four-year career as a starter, Mesa had become the best in the business, ripping off thirty-seven consecutive saves to set a new major-league record. Now, with a sellout crowd roaring and anticipating the end of a four-decade slump, it would be up to Mesa to deliver the goods.

He got Ripken to ground out to short, then forced Harold Baines to hit a weak fly to right center. After Chris Hoiles walked, Jeff Huson stepped up and popped the second pitch high into the September night. Thome followed the ball into foul territory and caught it just in front of third base—and Cleveland finally had a reason to celebrate. Players and coaches swarmed out of the dugout for a mass celebration on the infield as a waterfall of appreciation poured on them out of the Jacobs Fields stands. "After wandering in the baseball desert for four decades," Paul Hoynes wrote in the *Plain Dealer*, "Indians fans finally know why Chief Wahoo has been smiling all these seasons."

It was the second-earliest clinch date since the start of divisional play, yet with the start of the season backed up three weeks, it technically was the earliest clinch ever. "Clinching on September 8, with a lead of twenty-two-some games," Cleveland general manager John Hart said in the jubilant locker room, "this is Joe Hardy and *Damn Yankees*. I'll sign on for this every year."

With the players donning the commemorative T-shirts and caps fresh out of their boxes, they marched united into center field where they raised the flag proclaiming them division champions. As Murray guided the pennant by rope up to the top of the scoreboard, the Garth Brooks song "The Dance" played over the Jacobs Field speakers. And those who had been with the team two years before immediately recognized the significance—it had been Steve Olin's favorite song. Many players and coaches felt tears trickle down their faces as the flag caught the cool lake breeze in tune with the song, succumbing to the double dose of emotion. Primarily, they remembered their fallen teammate and knew he should be here with them.

But they also realized that after more than a generation of misery that carried off the field, the Cleveland Indians were finally invited to the dance that was postseason baseball.

Orioles	0	0	0	1	0	0	1	0	0	=2
Indians	0	0	3	0	0	0	0	0	x	=3

BALTIMORE

	AB	R	H	RBI
Anderson lf	4	0	0	0
Goodwin cf	3	1	1	0
Bass ph	1	0	1	0
J. Brown pr-cf	0	0	0	0
Palmeiro 1b	3	0	1	0
Bonilla rf	4	0	0	0
Ripken ss	4	0	0	0
Baines dh	4	1	1	0
Hoiles c	3	0	0	0
Hammonds pr	0	0	0	0
Huson 3b	3	0	1	1
Alexander 2b	1	0	0	0
Barberie 2b	1	0	0	0
TOTAL	31	2	5	1

	IP	H	R	ER	BB	SO
K. Brown (L)	6⅔	6	3	3	4	0
Lee	⅔	0	0	0	0	1
Benitez	⅔	0	0	0	0	0

CLEVELAND

	AB	R	H	RBI
Lofton cf	4	1	1	0
Vizquel ss	1	0	0	1
Baerga 2b	4	1	1	0
Belle lf	2	0	0	0
Murray dh	4	0	3	2
Thome 3b	4	0	0	0
Ramirez rf	4	0	0	0
Kirby rf	0	0	0	0
Sorrento 1b	4	0	0	0
Alomar c	2	1	1	0
TOTAL	29	3	6	3

	IP	H	R	ER	BB	SO
Hershiser (W)	6⅔	4	2	2	3	5
Assenmacher	1	1	0	0	0	0
Tavarez	⅓	0	0	0	0	1
Mesa (Sv)	1	0	0	0	1	0

Attendance: 41,656

#38

INDIANS 5, PHILADELPHIA ATHLETICS 2
SEPTEMBER 13, 1936

Teen Wonder

By the time the 1936 season reached its final month, there wasn't much excitement for the Indians—or anyone else in the American League, for that matter. The New York Yankees had already clinched the pennant and held a twenty-game lead over the fifth-place Tribe. With the last-place Philadelphia Athletics coming to League Park for a Sunday doubleheader, the Indians and their fans were already turning their attention to the future. And in the first game that afternoon, the future arrived.

Discovered by Tribe scout C.C. Slapnicka amidst the cornfields of Iowa at the age of sixteen the year before, young pitcher Robert William Andrew Feller had seen limited action with Cleveland since making his big-league debut in mid-July. But he had shown glimpses of his potential in his first four appearances, picking up a pair of victories. In his first career win on August 23, he struck out fifteen St. Louis Browns—a preview of things to come for the man who would soon be known as "Rapid Robert."

With his father William in attendance for the first time in his professional career that September Sunday, the younger Feller put forth "an electrifying performance that defies comprehension," Alex Zibin would write in the *Plain Dealer.* On a gloomy, drizzly afternoon, the teenager from Van Meter, Iowa, opened the game by walking center fielder Lou Finney, then rebounded to strike out the side in order. After the Indians plated a pair of runs in the bottom of the first, Feller again opened the second with a walk and then picked up two more strikeouts. Unveiling a blazing fastball, Feller continued to blow batters away, picking up two more strikeouts in the second, two in the fifth, and then striking out the side again in the sixth.

When Feller's control would start to waver, his infielders would stall, gathering at the mound to slow him down and buck up his confidence. "He had what he wanted when he needed it most," Zibin wrote, "and that was a tremendous fast ball, mixed in with a pretty good curve." Though he would yield nine walks, seven steals, hit a batter, and release a wild pitch, Feller would allow only two runs on two hits, with one of the runs scoring on a cunning double steal. Meanwhile, his teammates gave him all the support he'd need with two more runs in the third without a hit and another in the seventh.

Feller had fourteen strikeouts going into the eighth, with both his personal mark and the American League record within reach. He bested himself with a pair of whiffs then topped the twenty-eight-year-old league record with a strikeout of right fielder George Puccinelli in the ninth. It gave the young fireballer seventeen for the game—representing one for each year of his life. Now with five games under his belt, Feller had a whopping fifty-five strikeouts to his name.

Suddenly, the final two weeks of a fruitless season had meaning, and Feller picked up two more dominant victories, including a 9–1 triumph over Detroit in the season finale. Gaining confidence with each start, Feller would win nine games in 1937, seventeen in 1938 with 240 strikeouts, then become one of the finest pitchers in baseball in a dazzling 1939 season, winning twenty-four games and striking out 246 with a 2.85 ERA. It was the beginning of a stretch of dominance that would land him in the Hall of Fame with 266 career victories and more than 2,500 strikeouts.

And it all started with a skinny seventeen-year-old kid dominating a bunch of men on a dreary Sunday afternoon in what was supposed to be a meaningless game.

Athletics	0	0	2	0	0	0	0	0	0	=2
Indians	2	0	2	0	0	0	1	0	x	=5

PHILADELPHIA

	AB	R	H	RBI
Finney cf	1	1	0	0
Puccinelli rf	2	0	0	0
Moses rf-cf	2	1	1	0
Dean 1b	3	0	1	1
Johnson lf	4	0	0	0
Higgins 3b	2	0	0	0
Luby 2b	4	0	0	0
Peters ss	4	0	0	0
Hayes c	4	0	0	0
Gumpert p	3	0	0	0
Moss ph	0	0	0	0
TOTAL	29	2	2	1

	IP	H	R	ER	BB	SO
Gumpert (L)	8	7	5	3	5	2

CLEVELAND

	AB	R	H	RBI
Hughes 2b	3	2	1	0
Knickerbocker ss	2	2	1	0
Averill cf	2	1	1	2
Trosky 1b	4	0	2	0
Weatherly rf	4	0	0	1
Hale 3b	4	0	0	0
Heath lf	3	0	1	0
George c	4	0	1	0
Feller p	4	0	0	0
TOTAL	30	5	7	3

	IP	H	R	ER	BB	SO
Feller (W)	9	2	2	2	9	17

#37

GUARDIANS 7, NEW YORK YANKEES 5 (10 INNINGS)
OCTOBER 17, 2024

Christmas in October

It was getting easy to believe the Guardians didn't quite belong here.

After the first two games of the American League Championship Series in New York, heavy underdog Cleveland looked outmatched and overwhelmed, dropping both in ho-hum affairs controlled by the Yankees from start to finish. Now two defeats away from elimination in the best-of-seven series, the Guardians would return to Cleveland to try to find themselves and re-channel the never-say-die energy that had driven them to an American League-best forty-two come-from behind wins over the course of the season.

"We're one swing of the bat from being right back in it," manager Stephen Vogt opined after a 6–3 loss in Game Two. "That is who we are. We don't quit. We just need to keep being us."

Forty-eight hours later, those words would appear prophetic.

Before a packed house at Progressive Field on a Thursday night, the Yankees drew first blood in the second inning when catcher Jose Trevino singled home a run. But in what would prove to be a key moment, a pitch later, Cleveland pitcher Matthew Boyd picked Trevino off first base for the second out. Boyd then enticed second baseman Gleyber Torres to line out—which, without the pickoff, likely would have allowed New York's Alex Verdugo to tag up and score from third and put the Yankees up by two. It didn't appear to be that notable at the time, but it prevented Cleveland from digging itself into a hole for the third straight game and, more importantly, halted the Yankees' momentum that had gradually gathered steam all week long. And an inning later, the Guardians finally grabbed some momentum for themselves.

With one out in the bottom of the third, rookie designated hitter Kyle Manzardo blasted a two-run homer to give Cleveland its first lead in the

David Fry celebrates after hitting a game-winning home run that gave the Guardians a dramatic 7–5 victory over the New York Yankees in the tenth inning of Game Three of the 2024 American League Championship Series. © David Richard/USA TODAY NETWORK via Imagn Images.

series. Then in the sixth, second baseman Andrés Giménez singled home another run to make it 3–1. After Boyd tamed the New York bats through five innings, a potent Cleveland bullpen took over, keeping the Yankees off the scoreboard through the sixth and seventh. Then in the top of the eighth, after Hunter Gaddis allowed a two-out walk, the Guardians called on closer Emmanuel Clase to save the day just as he had done throughout 2024. Nearly unhittable all year, Clase had racked up a league-best forty-seven saves with a microscopic 0.61 ERA, cementing his reputation as one of baseball's most dominant pitchers.

It would be up to Clase to pick up up the final four outs to preserve the Cleveland triumph. But it wouldn't be easy—the next man up was as dominant a hitter as Clase was a pitcher.

New York slugger Aaron Judge, on the cusp of being named American League Most Valuable Player for the second time in three seasons, had gathered legendary statistics in 2024, posting a .322 batting average with fifty-eight home runs and 144 RBI. And he'd already wreaked havoc on the Guards in the ALCS, clubbing a game-clinching homer in Game Two and driving in four runs in just eight at-bats in the series.

It was a classic confrontation that represented what October baseball was all about. And perhaps fittingly, the outcome was dramatic.

After Clase got ahead in the count with two quick strikes, Judge blasted the fourth pitch—a 99-miles-per-hour fastball—just over the right-field wall to tie the game at three and silence the Cleveland crowd. Even more stunning, three pitches later, designated hitter Giancarlo Stanton did the same thing, depositing a 1–2 fastball into the center-field bleachers to give the Yankees the lead. Clase, who had only allowed two home runs in the entire regular season, had now given up two in consecutive at-bats when it mattered most. Consequently, in a matter of seconds, the Guardians had gone from the brink of victory to the cusp of defeat. It was, as Cleveland manager Stephen Vogt would describe later, like the team just got punched in the teeth.

The Yankees then scratched out another run in the ninth to make it 5–3. In the bottom of the frame, leadoff hitter José Ramírez reached first on an error, but Josh Naylor promptly grounded into a double play. Down to their last strike with two outs, center fielder Lane Thomas laced a double off the center-field wall to keep Cleveland alive, albeit just barely.

Stepping to the plate to pinch-hit was six-foot-three, 250-pound rookie Jhonkensy Noel, who, based on the alchemy of his overall girth and festive last name, had earned the affectionate nickname "Big Christmas." And while Noel had made an initial impact—homering in his first career at-bat after being called up from the minor leagues in June—he'd struggled as the season dragged on, hitting just .118 in the month of September and not hitting a home run in his last seventy-six plate appearances. Now the entire Guardians season would rest on the struggling Noel's shoulders.

After taking a first-pitch fastball for ball one, Noel unleashed on a low changeup from Yankee relief pitcher Luke Weaver. He crushed the baseball high into the autumn night, and it landed halfway up the left-field bleachers as the suddenly jubilant home crowd roared. Big Christmas had pulled off an October miracle—and in so doing, became the first rookie in the history of baseball to hit a game-tying homer in the ninth inning or later of a postseason game. Against all odds, the score was tied and the Guardians were still alive as the game shifted into extra innings.

Cleveland held the Yankees scoreless in the tenth, and with the ballpark still buzzing from Noel's heroics, Bo Naylor led off the bottom of the inning with a single, then advanced to third on a sacrifice bunt and a ground out. With two down, David Fry, who'd replaced Manzardo in the seventh and struck out with the tying run at second in the eighth, stepped to the plate. Fry had already had a memorable postseason, most notably by crushing a clutch home run in the fourth game of the American League Division Series against Detroit that enabled the Guardians to turn a late deficit into a narrow victory and force a deciding Game Five. But for as memorable as that homer was, Fry was about to top it.

After falling behind in the count to New York closer Clay Holmes, Fry blasted a fourth-pitch fastball deep to left field. Following a similar path to the ball Noel had hit one inning earlier, it landed several rows deep in the bleachers, giving the Guardians the tenth walk-off postseason victory in franchise history and rescuing a game they had appeared to have blown when Clase faltered in the eighth.

For all the dramatics, it perhaps symbolized what the Guardians had done all season long—one part of the team steps up when another falters. Even when it's the best closer in baseball.

"It was like, 'You know what, boys, he's picked us up all year,'" Fry said. "It's time we pick him up. There were just so many little moments in that game."

Little moments all adding up to a big occasion.

Kind of like Christmas. Only in October.

Yankees	0 1 0	0 0 0	0 3 1	0 =5
Guardians	0 0 2	0 0 1	0 0 2	2 =7

NEW YORK

	AB	R	H	RBI
Torres 2b	3	0	0	1
Soto rf	4	1	0	0
Judge cf	5	1	1	2
Stanton dh	3	1	1	1
Domínguez pr-dh	0	0	0	0
Chisholm 3b	4	0	1	0
Berti 1b	4	0	0	0
Rizzo 1b	0	0	0	0
Volpe ss	3	2	1	0
Verdugo lf	4	0	1	0
Trevino c	2	0	1	1
Wells ph-c	2	0	0	0
TOTAL	34	5	6	5

	IP	H	R	ER	BB	SO
Schmidt	4⅔	5	2	2	2	2
Hill	⅓	0	0	0	0	0
Hamilton	⅓	0	1	1	1	0
Mayza	⅔	1	0	0	2	0
Kahnle	1⅔	1	0	0	2	1
Weaver	1⅓	2	2	2	0	2
Holmes (L)	⅔	2	2	2	0	0

CLEVELAND

	AB	R	H	RBI
Kwan	4	0	0	0
Manzardo dh	3	1	2	2
Fry ph-dh	2	1	1	2
Ramírez 3b	4	0	1	0
Naylor 1b	5	0	0	0
Thomas cf	3	2	1	0
Schneemann rf	4	0	0	0
Noel ph-rf	1	1	1	2
Giménez 2b	5	0	1	1
Hedges c	2	0	1	0
Brennan ph	1	0	1	0
Naylor c	1	1	1	0
Rocchio ss	4	1	1	0
TOTAL	39	7	11	7

	IP	H	R	ER	BB	SO
Boyd	5	2	1	1	3	4
Smith	1	0	0	0	0	1
Herrin	1	1	0	0	1	0
Gaddis	⅔	0	1	1	1	1
Clase	⅓	3	2	2	0	0
Morgan	⅓	0	1	0	1	1
Walters	⅔	0	0	0	0	1
Avila (W)	1	0	0	0	2	2

Attendance: 32,531

#36

INDIANS 5, ATLANTA BRAVES 4
OCTOBER 26, 1995

Don't Wake Up a Dead Dog

After a dominant summer and a triumphant run through the American League playoffs, the Cleveland Indians' majestic 1995 season was about to fizzle out like a Fourth of July sparkler.

Their mighty bats had gone silent in the World Series against the Atlanta Braves, who won three of the first four contests behind stellar starting pitching. After dropping the first two games in Atlanta, the Tribe rallied for a clutch victory in Game Three at Jacobs Field but then dropped the critical fourth game in the late innings. Not only was Cleveland now just one loss away from extinction but, to keep the season alive, the Indians would have to beat the best pitcher in baseball.

Four-time Cy Young Award winner Greg Maddux had been nearly unstoppable that year, posting a 19–2 record in a shortened season with an amazing 1.63 ERA. He'd handcuffed the Tribe bats in the first game of the series, limiting Cleveland to two hits and no earned runs in nine innings. But the Indians were confident things would be better the next time Maddux took the mound. "Wait until we see him a second time," second baseman Carlos Baerga said. "It will be different then."

Another player hoping for a different result after Game One was Cleveland pitcher Orel Hershiser, who'd pitched well in the opener but took himself out of the game in the seventh inning when he felt he'd lost his release point. In retrospect, Hershiser felt he'd outthought himself, that he'd too easily tried to do what was best for the team rather than yielding to his fiery competitive spirit.

Win or lose, Game Five would be the Indians' final game at Jacobs Field in 1995, and like the seventy-nine that had come before it, a huge crowd packed into the steel jukebox at the corner of Carnegie and Ontario ready to rock. And it didn't take long.

In the bottom of the first inning, the ordinarily controlled Maddux walked Omar Vizquel on five pitches, then Vizquel moved into scoring position on a Baerga ground out. With two down, Cleveland cleanup hitter Albert Belle stepped to the plate looking to atone for what so far had been a sluggish series. Belle rifled the first pitch down the right-field line and into the Atlanta bullpen for a two-run home run that electrified the already wired home fans. Little did they know that with the celebratory pyrotechnics exploding above Jacobs Field, the real fireworks were about to begin.

Veteran Eddie Murray climbed into the batter's box and Maddux's next pitch sailed up and in toward Murray's head, causing the veteran to spin out of the way. Ordinarily a soft-spoken leader by example, Murray saw a message in Maddux's pitch and took a step toward the mound pointing at the Braves star. Atlanta catcher Charlie O'Brien interceded to keep Murray from getting any closer, and both benches cleared. In the mix of shouting players, Hershiser found Maddux.

"Were you throwing at him?" Hershiser asked.

No, Maddux explained, he was just trying to jam Murray.

Hershiser pondered the comment for a moment, then replied, "You can do better than that."

Order was restored and the game resumed, but Belle's home run combined with Murray's stand had sent a clear message: the Indians weren't going down without a fight. "Eddie's one of those guys, you know, he's quiet," Cleveland reserve outfielder Wayne Kirby said. "But don't wake a dead dog up . . . Maybe we needed it to regroup and get our cockiness back." Whether or not Maddux had intentionally thrown at Murray, the Indians tapped into a newfound energy while the Braves seemed rattled. "I think after that, [Maddux] lost it a little bit," Vizquel said later. "He was shaky."

Meanwhile, Hershiser was cruising, retiring nine of the first ten batters and twelve of the first fourteen. But when Marquis Grissom reached base on an infield single in the fifth to score Ryan Klesko, the game was tied at two and the Braves had taken back the momentum. Then, in the sixth, the Tribe put runners on the corners with two out when Jim Thome came through with a clutch single up the middle to put the Indians ahead, followed by another RBI hit from Manny Ramirez to make it 4–2. With the Jacobs Field crowd roaring once again, the Indians had taken control of the game.

Hershiser continued to roll into the eighth, when he gave up a leadoff single to Mike Mordecai. Up next was Tribe-killer Grissom, who would collect more hits than any other Atlanta player in the series. Grissom ripped a line drive right back up the middle, but with catlike reflexes, Hershiser reached across his body to snag the ball backhanded, then quickly spun and fired to first to double up Mordecai. With the fans on their feet, Hershiser circled the mound screaming, "Take that! Take that!" The competitive fire that had been lacking in Game One was back, surfacing again after he struck out Luis Polonia to end the inning. "Today I was all player," Hershiser said. "I stood taller and prouder."

In the bottom of the eighth, Thome added what appeared to be nothing more than icing on the cake when he launched a 436-foot bomb to center field for a 5–2 lead. The blast turned out to represent the game-winning run when Klesko knocked a two-out, two-run homer off Cleveland closer Jose Mesa in the bottom of the ninth to make it 5–4. Mesa rebounded to strike out Mark Lemke to close out a satisfying triumph, beating one of the best pitchers in the history of the game and narrowing the Atlanta lead to three games to two. Perhaps more importantly, with their backs to the wall, the Indians showed they weren't about to be intimidated by anyone.

"Everything they got, they earned," Maddux said.

Including the opportunity to fight another day.

Braves	0 0 0	1 1 0	0 0 2	=4
Indians	2 0 0	0 0 2	0 1 x	=5

ATLANTA

	AB	R	H	RBI
Grissom cf	4	0	1	1
Polonia lf	4	1	1	1
Jones 3b	4	0	1	0
McGriff 1b	4	1	1	0
Justice rf	4	0	0	0
Klesko dh	4	2	2	2
Lemke 2b	4	0	0	0
O'Brien c	1	0	0	0
Lopez ph-c	1	0	0	0
Belliard ss	1	0	0	0
Smith ph	0	0	0	0
Mordecai ss	1	0	1	0
TOTAL	32	4	7	4

	IP	H	R	ER	BB	SO
Maddux (L)	7	7	4	4	3	4
Clontz	1	1	1	1	0	1

CLEVELAND

	AB	R	H	RBI
Lofton cf	4	0	0	0
Vizquel ss	3	1	1	0
Baerga 2b	4	1	1	0
Belle lf	3	2	1	2
Murray dh	3	0	0	0
Thome 3b	4	1	2	2
Ramirez rf	3	0	1	1
Perry 1b	1	0	0	0
Sorrento 1b	3	0	0	0
Kirby rf	0	0	0	0
Alomar c	3	0	2	0
TOTAL	31	5	8	5

	IP	H	R	ER	BB	SO
Hershiser (W)	8	5	2	1	1	6
Mesa (Sv)	1	2	2	2	0	1

Attendance: 43,595

#35

INDIANS 3, DETROIT TIGERS 2
SEPTEMBER 18, 1954

Greater Than Anybody Knows

After three straight second-place finishes, the Indians' hour was finally at hand.

Cleveland was on the cusp of ending the greatest run in baseball history after clinching a tie for first place with a 6–3 win at Detroit's Briggs Stadium to kick off a three-game weekend series. With one more triumph, the 1954 Tribe would secure the American League pennant and end the New York Yankees' incredible run of consecutive World Series titles at five.

Entering the Saturday-matinee contest with the Tigers, the Indians held baseball's best record at 106–40, already establishing themselves as one of the finest teams in American League history. Since first nesting atop the standings in mid-May, only four times all summer had Cleveland not held the top spot to itself. The key to the Tribe's success had been its ability to mop up on the AL's lesser teams, racking up records of 18–4 against last-place Philadelphia, 18–4 against sixth-place Washington, 19–3 against seventh-place Baltimore, and a whopping 20–2 against fourth-place Boston. But to secure their first pennant in six years, the Indians would have to knock off a team that had defeated them six times during the season.

On a gloomy, overcast afternoon in the Motor City, the Tigers crept to a 1–0 lead in the third, and with the Cleveland bats silent for much of the day, it appeared the victory celebration would have to wait. The game was delayed twice as heavy rain pelted downtown Detroit, and the Tribe was running out of chances. However, in the seventh inning, it was as if the stars aligned and maneuvered the ghosts of the Indians' last pennant into clinching the next.

Right fielder Dave Philley started the rally with a one-out walk from Detroit pitcher Steve Gromek, who had spent thirteen years in Cleveland and won a critical game in the '48 World Series. With a hard rain continuing to

On a rainy Saturday afternoon in Detroit, longtime Tribe catcher Jim Hegan, nearing the twilight of a marvelous career, is congratulated by his teammates after hitting the home run that clinched the 1954 pennant. Cleveland State University Library's *Cleveland Press* Collection.

fall, Cleveland manager Al Lopez replaced shortstop George Strickland with little-used veteran Dale Mitchell, another hero of 1948 and one of just five remaining players from that championship team. Mitchell smashed his former teammate's second pitch into the right-field stands for his first home run of 1954 (and what would prove to be the last of his career) to give the Indians a 2–1 lead. Then, to cement the deal, Cleveland catcher Jim Hegan—another stalwart of the '48 team—followed with a homer of his own on Gromek's first pitch. Though the game would continue through the rain, for all intents and purposes it could have stopped right there. The fates were finally smiling on the Cleveland Indians.

The Tigers added a meaningless run in the bottom of the seventh, then Ray Narleski came on to close out the game for Early Wynn, who would pick up his twenty-second victory of the year. With two out and a runner on first in the bottom of the ninth, Cleveland shortstop Sam Dente went down on one knee to field a wobbly Fred Hatfield grounder off the muddy infield and cautiously flipped the ball to Bobby Avila, who touched second base with extreme care. "That was the final out," wrote the *Plain Dealer*'s Harry Jones, "the end of a memorable pennant race, an American League championship for Cleveland's beloved Indians, who brought to a close the intolerable five-year reign of terror imposed by the New York Yankees."

As soon as Avila touched second, the Cleveland players poured onto the field from the top step of the dugout for a massive celebration. "Ladies and gentlemen," Detroit's public address announcer noted casually, "the Cleveland Indians have just won the pennant."

The rain-soaked Indians moved their party into the clubhouse, where a teammate wrote "We're In" in lipstick atop first baseman Vic Wertz's bald scalp. Yankees manager Casey Stengel sent a congratulatory telegram to Lopez, and the Yankee players wired one to their Cleveland counterparts. In the next few hours, dozens of Hollywood stars would contact comedian Bob Hope—a minority owner of the Indians—to hit him up for World Series tickets.

While many were looking forward to the Fall Classic, the Indians were still reflecting on what a magical summer it had been. "It's been a great season," Lopez said. "This is a great team. It's a greater team than anybody knows." In fact, with a .721 winning percentage, the '54 Indians still stand as the best team in American League history. But, following their stunning sweep at the hands of the New York Giants in the World Series, Lopez's comment would take on added meaning.

Still, the 1954 Indians had their moment of glory, culminated on a rainy Saturday in Detroit which provided "a fantastic ball game that climaxed as fantastic a season as ever a team has played in all the long history of baseball," *Plain Dealer* sports editor Gordon Cobbledick wrote. "The long chase had ended, and all the tensions and frustration and disappointments were forgotten. This was their big day."

Indians	0	0	0	0	0	0	3	0	0	=3
Tigers	0	0	1	0	0	0	1	0	0	=2

CLEVELAND

	AB	R	H	RBI
Smith lf	4	0	3	0
Avila 2b	4	0	1	0
Doby cf	4	0	1	0
Rosen 3b	4	0	0	0
Wertz 1b	3	0	1	0
Glynn 1b	1	0	0	0
Philley rf	3	1	1	0
Strickland ss	2	0	0	0
Mitchell ph	1	1	1	2
Dente ss	1	0	1	0
Hegan c	4	1	2	1
Wynn p	2	0	0	0
Narleski p	0	0	0	0
TOTAL	33	3	11	3

	IP	H	R	ER	BB	SO
Wynn (W)	6⅔	8	2	2	2	6
Narleski (Sv)	2⅓	1	0	0	0	2

DETROIT

	AB	R	H	RBI
Kuenn ss	5	1	3	0
Hatfield 2b	4	0	1	0
Delsing lf	3	0	1	1
Boone 3b	3	0	1	1
Belardi 1b	4	0	0	0
Kaline rf	4	0	0	0
Tuttle cf	4	1	2	0
House c	4	0	0	0
Gromek p	2	0	0	0
Nieman ph	1	0	1	0
Bertola pr	0	0	0	0
Herbert p	0	0	0	0
Drope ph	1	0	0	0
TOTAL	35	2	9	2

	IP	H	R	ER	BB	SO
Gromek (L)	7	9	3	3	1	2
Herbert	2	2	0	0	0	1

Attendance: 6,913

#34

INDIANS 11, BALTIMORE ORIOLES 8
JUNE 10, 1959

Rocky's Four

Perhaps the only silver lining of the Indians' fall from the most dominant team in baseball in 1954 to an ordinary also-ran by the end of the decade was the emergence of a handsome slugger from New York City who quickly became one of the finest power hitters in Cleveland history.

Rocco Domenico Colavito was signed by the team prior to the 1951 season and broke through with a dazzling rookie year in 1956, smashing twenty-one home runs in 101 games, then exploded for forty-one round-trippers and 113 RBI in 1958. As Colavito's popularity grew and fan clubs dedicated to him began to spring up all over Cleveland, his legend was just beginning.

On a Wednesday evening in early June 1959, the Indians would face the Orioles at Baltimore's Memorial Stadium with plenty on the line. The O's were tied for first in the American League, with the Tribe just a game and a half back. The game started brilliantly for the Indians as left fielder Minnie Minoso blasted a two-out, three-run home run to left to provide an early lead. After Baltimore countered with a run in the bottom of the inning, the Indians struck again when second baseman Billy Martin hit a solo homer to make it 4–1 in the second. But the show didn't really begin until the third.

After Baltimore had cut the lead to one with a pair of runs, Colavito blasted a hanging slider off Orioles pitcher Jerry Walker for a two-run home run to left to make it 6–3 on the team's third homer in as many innings. The score remained 6–3 until Colavito came up in the fifth, when he crushed a high curve from Arnold Portocarrero for his second home run of the evening. An inning later, after an RBI double by center fielder Tito Francona, Colavito stepped to the plate again, once more facing Portocarrero. And again, Colavito belted a pitch—a sinking fastball this time—to left center for his third home run and a 10–3 Cleveland lead.

Though Colavito had provided historic flavor to the contest, the Indians couldn't relax. Baltimore rallied for four runs in the seventh to cut the margin to three and the next eight Cleveland batters were retired. Now facing Ernie Johnson, who hadn't allowed a home run all season, Colavito stepped in for his fifth plate appearance already satisfied with what he'd accomplished on the evening. Yet once again, the Rock slammed another—ripping an inside fastball over the left-field wall for his fourth home run of the night.

The Baltimore crowd gave Colavito a standing ovation. As Colavito approached home, he jumped into the air and landed on the plate with both feet, then casually tipped his cap to the crowd. It was a once-in-a-lifetime game for a player who had never hit more than two home runs in a major-league game. Colavito became just the eighth player in baseball history to hit four homers in a game, and only the third to do it in consecutive at-bats. He knocked in six runs, scored five times, and tied an American League record with sixteen total bases.

After the Indians' 11–8 triumph was complete, reporters swarmed Colavito in the locker room wanting to know how he'd done it. The Tribe right fielder shrugged and explained that he'd just been swinging for base hits. "Honest," he said, "I was just trying to meet the ball." Would he try for a fifth consecutive homer the next night? "Heck no," he said with a smile. "I might cross 'em up and bunt." He did neither, popping out to second.

Already the most popular athlete in Cleveland, Colavito soared into notoriety as a household name following his quadruple feature in Baltimore. "Rocky Colavito shows you how to slug home runs . . . and how to get 100% meat energy!" proclaimed an ad for Kahn's hot dogs that ran coincidentally in the following day's *Plain Dealer.* "Take an energy-building tip from Rocky."

That June evening would prove to be the highlight of his career—and the last moment of glory for Cleveland baseball in the 1950s. Though he would lead the American League with forty-two homers in 1959 and was a key component to the Indians' second-place finish, he was traded to Detroit days before the 1960 opener. With fans in an outrage, the team dropped to fourth and posted the first of five consecutive losing records. Their beloved Rocky would return in 1965 but via another ill-fated trade in which the Indians gave up pitcher Tommy John and outfielder Tommie Agee. Colavito clubbed sixty-one home runs for the Tribe over the next three seasons, finishing with 190 as an Indian.

Indians fans—whose three-decade stretch of misery began the day Colavito was traded—would always ponder what might have been had Rocky remained in Cleveland and curse general manager Frank Lane for shipping off one of the most beloved athletes in Cleveland history. However, the residue of resentment was softened by the memories of Rocky Colavito's greatest hour, when he etched his name in the record books and secured an almost mythical legacy.

Indians	3	1	2	0	1	3	0	0	1	=11
Orioles	1	2	0	0	0	0	4	0	1	=8

CLEVELAND

	AB	R	H	RBI
Held ss	5	1	1	0
Power 1b	4	1	0	0
Francona cf	5	2	2	1
Colavito rf	4	5	4	6
Minoso lf	5	1	3	3
Jones 3b	3	0	0	0
Strickland 3b	2	0	1	0
Brown c	4	0	1	0
Martin 2b	3	1	1	1
Webster ph-2b	1	0	0	0
Bell p	3	0	0	0
Garcia p	1	0	0	0
TOTAL	40	11	13	11

	IP	H	R	ER	BB	SO
Bell (W)	6⅓	8	7	7	4	3
Garcia (Sv)	2⅔	4	1	1	0	3

Attendance: 15,883

BALTIMORE

	AB	R	H	RBI
Pearson cf	3	1	2	0
Pilarcik rf	5	1	1	2
Woodling lf	5	1	3	1
Triandos c	2	0	1	1
Ginsberg c	1	1	0	0
Hale 1b	3	0	0	0
Zuverink p	0	0	0	0
Boyd ph	1	0	0	0
Johnson p	0	0	0	0
Nieman ph	1	1	1	0
Klaus 3b	5	0	2	4
Carrasquel ss	5	0	0	0
Gardner 2b	4	1	1	0
Walker p	1	1	1	0
Portocarrero p	1	0	0	0
Lockman 1b	1	1	0	0
TOTAL	38	8	12	8

	IP	H	R	ER	BB	SO
Walker (L)	2⅓	4	6	6	2	1
Portocarrero	3⅓	7	4	4	1	3
Zuverink	1⅓	0	0	0	0	0
Johnson	2	2	1	1	0	0

#33

GUARDIANS 6, NEW YORK YANKEES 5
OCTOBER 15, 2022

Jabs vs. Haymakers

Understandably for Cleveland fans, thoughts had already begun to drift to trying again tomorrow.

A promising beginning for the Guardians in Game Three of their American League Division Series against the New York Yankees on a chilly Saturday night at Progressive Field had dissolved. The visiting Yankees had gradually wrested control of the game and would take a two-run lead into the bottom of the ninth inning.

But based on the evidence, those two runs might as well have been ten. In their long and storied history, the Yankees had never lost a postseason game in which they led by two or more runs in the ninth inning or later. Not once. In each of the 167 occasions covering more than 100 years, New York had succeeded in slamming the door.

And there was little to suggest that the Guardians would snap that century-long string.

A few hours earlier, this game had been theirs for the taking. Cleveland surged to a 2–0 lead after two innings but had failed to take advantage of additional scoring opportunities that could have broken things wide open. New York starting pitcher Luis Severino settled down, and from the third inning until he was lifted in the sixth, he threw just fifty pitches without allowing a hit and retired thirteen straight Cleveland batters.

Meanwhile, the mighty Yankee bats came alive. Star hitter Aaron Judge, who'd amassed sixty-two home runs during the regular season, blasted a 449-foot homer to center that tied the game in the third. Incredibly, after a dazzling year that would earn him American League Most Valuable Player honors, it was Judge's first hit the series after being shut down in his first nine at-bats against a prepared Cleveland pitching staff.

New York left fielder Oswaldo Cabrera followed with another towering homer in the fifth that put the Yankees ahead 4–2. And after the Guardians notched a run to claw back within one, a third New York homer, this one by Harrison Bader in the seventh, appeared to pave the Yankees' path to victory. Cleveland's bats were silenced in the seventh and eighth innings, and New York was now just three outs away from taking a two-games-to-one lead in the series.

The odds grew longer when Cleveland catcher Luke Maile flew out to start the inning. But Myles Straw plopped a soft hit to left that bounced off the glove of Cabrera as he tried to field it, enabling Straw to move to second base. Leadoff hitter Steven Kwan then looped a single that moved Straw to third and got the potential tying run on base.

Clarke Schmidt was called from the New York bullpen to put out the fire, but Cleveland's Amed Rosario, hitless in four previous at-bats on the night, promptly grooved a single to left that scored Straw and cut the deficit to a run. The capacity crowd at Progressive Field was beginning to believe a miracle was possible, particularly when José Ramírez followed with a soft single just beyond the infield that loaded the bases. Schmidt hunkered down and struck out cleanup hitter Josh Naylor on three pitches for the second out. The Guardians' last hope would be rookie right fielder Oscar Gonzalez.

And considering the past week, there was nobody else Cleveland wanted in that spot. Twice in the previous six days, Gonzalez had come through with hits to provide the winning runs in narrow Cleveland triumphs, including a two-run single in the tenth inning the day before to give the Guardians a 4–2 win in New York in Game Two. It was the continuation of a remarkable debut campaign for Gonzalez, who'd provided an unexpected jolt to the Cleveland lineup after getting called up from the minors in late May, hitting .296 in ninety-one games in the regular season and then stepping up as a surprising hero in the playoffs. But the best was yet to come.

Gonzalez quickly fell behind in the count, and Cleveland was down to its final strike. On the next pitch, he laced a line drive right back up the middle and into center field, enabling Kwan to score the tying run and Rosario followed with the winning run.

The feeling in the ballpark and for Cleveland fans watching on television was as much utter shock as it was pure joy. The Cleveland players sprinted out of the dugout and mobbed Gonzalez in a sea of red jerseys. Progressive Field went bonkers, with fans screaming and cheering while trying to process what they'd just seen.

For one, they'd just witnessed a couple of big chunks of history. On the 168th attempt, the Guardians had become the first team ever to defeat the Yankees in the postseason after trailing by two in its final at-bat. And Gonzalez had become only the second player in baseball history to deliver go-ahead RBIs in the ninth inning or later of three games in the same postseason.

And the way in which they picked away in the final inning represented all that the Guardians had been about in 2022, the blueprint they'd established throughout the course of their ninety-two-win season. Five hits, four of them singles, the distance of all of which put together wouldn't have matched that of Judge's home run. Add it up and the end result was the thirteenth time in the season the Guardians won a game they'd trailed after the seventh inning.

"Because we love each other and care for each other, we know as long as we get the next guy up, someone will get the job done," explained Kwan, who'd collected three hits himself. "Unselfish baseball, moving the chains, and luckily it all worked out."

Worked out indeed, with Cleveland displaying an almost invisible dominance that typically wouldn't show up in the highlight reels. Fifteen hits to the Yankees' five. Seventeen at-bats with runners in scoring position to the Yankees' two. A no-name bullpen that kept the Guards close even after the New York bats caught fire. Small-ball David's slingshot had bested Goliath's mighty club.

Put another way by the New York Post: "The jab, jab, jab of the Guardians defeated the haymakers of the Yankees."

Yankees	0	0	2	0	2	0	1	0	0	=5
Guardians	1	1	0	0	0	1	0	0	3	=6

NEW YORK

	AB	R	H	RBI
Torres 2b	4	0	0	0
Judge rf	4	1	1	2
Rizzo 1b	3	0	0	0
Stanton dh	4	0	0	0
Donaldson 3b	4	0	0	0
Kiner-Falefa ss	4	0	0	0
Bader cf	4	2	2	1
Higashioka c	2	0	0	0
Cabrera lf	3	2	2	2
TOTAL	32	5	5	5

	IP	H	R	ER	BB	SO
Severino	5⅔	8	3	3	0	6
Trivino	⅓	1	0	0	0	0
Loáisiga	⅔	1	0	0	0	1
Peralta	1⅔	2	2	2	0	2
Schmidt (L)	⅓	3	1	1	0	1

CLEVELAND

	AB	R	H	RBI
Kwan lf	5	2	3	1
Rosario ss	5	1	1	1
Ramírez 3b	5	0	3	0
Naylor dh	5	0	1	1
González rf	5	0	1	2
Giménez 2b	4	1	1	0
Arias 1b	4	1	2	0
Hedges c	2	0	1	0
Brennan ph	1	0	1	1
Maile c	1	0	0	0
Straw cf	4	1	1	0
TOTAL	41	6	15	6

	IP	H	R	ER	BB	SO
McKenzie	5	4	4	4	1	5
Hentges	1⅔	1	1	1	1	2
De Los Santos	1⅓	0	0	0	0	1
Morgan (W)	1	0	0	0	0	1

Attendance: 36,483

#32

INDIANS 6, NEW YORK YANKEES 4
OCTOBER 8, 2007

Grit in Gotham

For every dollar the Indians spent on player salaries in 2007, the New York Yankees spent $3.25. Yet after three games in the best-of-five Division Series between the two, it was the bargain-basement Indians who were in control, capturing back-to-back wins at Jacobs Field to open the playoffs. After New York rallied from a three-run deficit to capture Game Three at Yankee Stadium, the financially bloated Bronx Bombers appeared to have halted the Tribe's momentum. Then George Steinbrenner entered stage left.

New York's infamous owner made a less-than-subtle ultimatum to manager Joe Torre through the media. Though Torre had been one of the most successful skippers in franchise history, never once missing the postseason while winning six pennants and four world titles, it wasn't enough. Steinbrenner proclaimed that if the Yanks didn't come back to defeat the Indians and advance to the American League Championship Series, Torre would be fired. Ludicrous as that logic was, the players and fans rallied around their suddenly embattled manager.

Meanwhile, the Indians had some inner drama of their own, though nowhere near as glamorous. Some fans were questioning manager Eric Wedge's decision to start pitcher Paul Byrd for Game Four rather than ace CC Sabathia on three days' rest. Byrd had enjoyed a fine season with the Tribe, winning fifteen games, but wasn't exactly a big-game pitcher. "If I was tall and threw 95, nobody would say anything," he said. "But I'm short, balding, and I throw 84." The determined Wedge saw no reason to change the routine that had worked for ninety-six wins and the AL Central Division title during the regular season and emphatically defended his decision. Not surprisingly, the desperate Yankees opted to go with ace Chien-Ming Wang on short rest, though he'd been smacked around in Game One.

Things started dramatically well for Cleveland when leadoff hitter Grady Sizemore belted a 1–1 pitch over the center-field wall for a 1–0 lead. The Tribe added another run in the inning when shortstop Jhonny Peralta ripped an RBI single, then two more in the second to make it 4–0, and Wang was taken out.

The Indians pile on top of one another in celebration after winning Game Four of the 2007 American League Division Series over the New York Yankees. It gave the Tribe a three-games-to-one triumph in the best-of-five series and proved to be the final post-season game ever played at Yankee Stadium. *Akron Beacon Journal.*

Veteran starter Mike Mussina came in and fared little better, giving up a pair of runs in the fourth on a two-run single by Cleveland catcher Victor Martinez.

Through it all, Byrd was coolly efficient, though each New York at-bat was an adventure. Rarely ever getting behind hitters, he struck out AL RBI champ Alex Rodriguez with a runner in scoring position in the first, then toughened in the second to get out of a bases-loaded, one-out jam, allowing just one run on an infield single. Byrd encountered base runners in each of the first five innings, then gave up a leadoff homer by Robinson Cano in the sixth to cut the Cleveland margin to 6–2. Byrd was replaced by Rafael Perez, who proceeded to give up back-to-back singles to put runners on the corners with one out. Then he enticed shortstop Derek Jeter to bounce into an inning-ending double play to thwart the threat. However, the Yankees kept scratching.

Rodriguez smashed a homer in the seventh to make it 6–3. Wedge then called on Rafael Betancourt in the eighth, and he delivered the Indians' first one-two-three inning of the night. Though many of the same fans who begged Wedge to start Sabathia now hoped he'd stick with Betancourt in the ninth, once again Wedge stuck to his guns and brought in the efficient yet adventurous closer, Joe Borowski, who'd saved forty-five games during the regular season, albeit with a frightening 5.07 ERA.

True to form, after retiring Jeter on a pop fly, Borowski served up a pitch to right fielder Bobby Abreu which he drove into the upper deck in right to make it 6–4. With the Yankee Stadium crowd buzzing and sensing a comeback, Tribe fans' memories flashed back to six months before in this ballpark, when Borowski gave up six runs with two out in the ninth to blow a four-run lead and lose.

Borowski rebounded to retire Rodriguez on a fly to right, then catcher Jorge Posada blasted Borowski's second pitch down the right-field line which barely went foul, inches from being another New York home run. "All year long they say I've put some drama into the game," Borowski said later, "so I guess I had to do it again." Unfazed, Borowski simply went back to work and struck Posada out on a nasty sinker, clinching Cleveland's first playoff series victory in nine years.

The players and coaches flooded out of the dugout onto the Yankee Stadium infield, and the thousands of fans who had gathered at Jacobs Field back in Cleveland to watch the game on the scoreboard screen erupted in jubilation. The Indians had become the first team in baseball history to win a playoff series from a team it had not defeated in the regular season. Not only had the Indians advanced in the playoffs, defeating their bitter rival, but they'd scored "a victory of mind over money," Bud Shaw wrote in the *Plain Dealer,* "of cost-efficiency over bloat."

Due to the Indians' gritty victory, Steinbrenner would now have to face the consequences of his smarmy public demands. Ten days later, Torre—who had received a standing ovation from the New York faithful upon making his last pitching change in the eighth inning—turned down the Yankees' lowball contract offer. Two weeks after that, Torre became manager of the Los Angeles Dodgers, taking two members of the New York coaching staff with him.

Perhaps at no other time in Yankee history had one loss delivered such a damaging blow to the structure of the storied franchise. And the long-suffering Cleveland Indians had delivered it—at a cost of pennies on the dollar.

Indians	2	2	0	2	0	0	0	0	0	=6
Yankees	0	1	0	0	0	1	1	0	1	=4

CLEVELAND

	AB	R	H	RBI
Sizemore cf	3	2	2	1
A. Cabrera 2b	4	0	1	1
Hafner dh	3	1	1	0
Martinez 1b	5	0	2	2
Peralta ss	4	0	3	1
Lofton lf	5	0	0	0
Gutierrez rf	5	1	1	0
Blake 3b	5	1	1	0
Shoppach c	3	1	2	0
TOTAL	37	6	13	5

	IP	H	R	ER	BB	SO
Byrd (W)	5	8	2	2	2	2
Perez	2	3	1	1	1	1
Betancourt	1	0	0	0	0	2
Borowski (Sv)	1	1	1	1	0	1

NEW YORK

	AB	R	H	RBI
Damon lf	5	0	1	0
Jeter ss	5	0	2	1
Abreu rf	5	1	2	1
Rodriguez 3b	5	1	2	1
Posada c	5	0	1	0
Matsui dh	2	1	0	0
Cano 2b	4	1	2	1
M. Cabrera cf	4	0	1	0
Mientkiewicz 1b	1	0	0	0
Duncan ph-1b	1	0	1	0
Giambi ph-1b	1	0	0	0
TOTAL	38	4	12	4

	IP	H	R	ER	BB	SO
Wang (L)	1	5	4	4	0	0
Mussina	4⅔	4	2	2	4	3
Villone	⅓	0	0	0	0	0
Farnsworth	1	1	0	0	0	2
Veras	⅓	1	0	0	1	1
Rivera	1⅔	2	0	0	0	1

Attendance: 56,315

#31

INDIANS 8, NEW YORK YANKEES 6
AUGUST 8, 1948

Sunday Best

The summer of 1948 provided Cleveland and its Indians one of those experiences a franchise may only witness once or twice a century. A four-way pennant race had begun almost immediately after opening day, with the Tribe, Yankees, Red Sox, and Philadelphia Athletics all jockeying for position and swapping places in the standings through June and July. As the dog days of summer settled in, the logjam atop the American League was becoming even more complicated. Entering the first weekend of August, the quartet of contenders was all within a game and a half of first, but because of their vast experience in pressure games, the Yankees were the odds-on favorites.

Thus, going into a Sunday doubleheader at Cleveland Stadium, the Indians very much needed a good showing. Only one more series against New York remained, and the Yanks were coming off a resounding 5–0 win over the Tribe the day before, witnessed by the largest Saturday crowd in Stadium history. From here on, every game would be critical, and once again, Cleveland would go to battle without its best hitter. Shortstop and manager Lou Boudreau had been sidelined for the previous three days with an injured shoulder, knee, and ankle sustained after a second-base collision in a win over the Washington Senators on Thursday, missing the first two games of the crucial Yankees series. He would remain in the dugout for Sunday's twin bill, during which a new major-league attendance record for a three-game series would be set.

New York's experience shone through as they gradually took control of what had been an evenly matched game. Cleveland starter Sam Zoldak and New York's Spec Shea kept both offenses at bay in the early going, and after three innings, the contest was tied at one. The Yankees plated a run in the fourth, then two more in the fifth to make it 4–1. When the New Yorkers pushed the lead to 6–1 in the seventh, many in the gargantuan crowd of 73,000-plus turned their attention to the second game, hoping the hometown Tribe could at least manage a split for the day. When Zoldak faltered, he was replaced by Ed Klieman, who got Cleveland out of the seventh. Then in the eighth, Boudreau tapped the ageless Satchel Paige, the legendary pitcher from the Negro League who had just made his major-league debut with the Indians a month before. Paige would pitch a scoreless eighth to keep the home team's fleeting hopes simmering.

Missing its leader, the Cleveland offense had been silent all day, managing a harmless three hits and a single run through the first six innings. Finally in the seventh, the Tribe started to gather momentum. After third baseman Ken Keltner reached on Shea's only walk of the game, Johnny Berardino, starting at shortstop in place of Boudreau, blasted a home run to left to cut the New York lead in half. With the crowd starting to stir, first baseman Eddie Robinson, who hadn't hit a homer in more than a month, crushed a Shea pitch over the right-field wall to make it 6–4. All of a sudden, Cleveland was right back in the game. Catcher Jim Hegan kept the inning going with a single to center, and New York manager Bucky Harris had seen enough. He replaced Shea with Joe Page, who promptly walked pinch-hitter Allie Clark. Back to the top of the order, the Indians struck again when left fielder Dale Mitchell laced a shot into the hole at short which Phil Rizzuto couldn't handle, and the bases were loaded.

With the fans on their feet and cheering, the roar softened as the public address announcer notified them the Indians would bring a pinch-hitter to the plate—Lou Boudreau would bat for center fielder Thurman Tucker, who was zero-for-three on the day. The fans were silent for one hushed moment, letting the realization sink in, and then they exploded into another cascade of cheering. "I saw Lou eyeing those bats as that rally progressed," Cleveland coach Bill McKechnie would say later. "I knew what he was going to do."

The aching Boudreau then put the pain out of his mind and focused on the task at hand as he stepped to the plate. "My shoulder was stiff when I made that first stretch I take to loosen up," he said. "But after that I forgot everything but concentrating on that base hit." Boudreau took a ball from Page, sliced a foul ball, and then took a pitch inside that was called a strike. On the next pitch, the Indians shortstop lined a shot past Rizzuto into left field, scoring two runs to tie the game as the Stadium faithful showed their appreciation. Things would only get better.

In the eighth Berardino reached on a two-out walk, then Robinson, who had gone hitless in his previous fifteen at-bats prior to his homer in the seventh, clobbered another round-tripper, this one giving the Tribe its first lead of the game at 8–6.

Paige and Russ Christopher then combined to shut down New York in the ninth, and the Indians had secured a memorable come-from-behind victory in the heat of one of the greatest pennant races in American League history. The momentum carried over to the nightcap, won by Cleveland 2–1, and when the sun set that Sunday evening, the Indians stood atop the American League by six percentage points over Philadelphia and two full games over the Yankees, thanks to a stirring weekend that saw the Tribe take two of three from the defending world champs, capped by Sunday's twin-bill special. "Not just an ordinary doubleheader," Harry Jones would write in the *Plain Dealer*, "but one from the New York Yankees, whose world-championship crown was jolted slightly askew."

Yankees	1 0 0	1 2 0	2 0 0 =6
Indians	1 0 0	0 0 0	5 2 x =8

NEW YORK

	AB	R	H	RBI
Stirnweiss 2b	5	2	2	1
Henrich rf	5	1	3	1
Lindell lf	3	1	3	1
Keller ph	1	0	0	0
DiMaggio cf	4	0	0	1
Johnson 3b	4	0	1	1
Souchock 1b	3	0	0	0
McQuinn 1b	1	0	0	0
Niarbos c	3	0	0	0
Berra c	1	0	0	0
Rizzuto ss	4	2	3	0
Shea p	2	0	0	0
Page p	0	0	0	0
Brown ph	1	0	0	0
TOTAL	37	6	12	5

	IP	H	R	ER	BB	SO
Shea	6⅔	6	5	5	1	1
Page (L)	1⅓	3	3	3	3	2

CLEVELAND

	AB	R	H	RBI
Mitchell lf	4	1	3	0
Tucker cf	3	0	0	0
Boudreau ph	1	0	1	2
Kennedy rf	0	0	0	0
Doby rf -cf	4	0	0	1
Keltner 3b	3	1	0	0
Gordon 2b	3	0	1	0
Berardino ss	3	2	1	2
Robinson 1b	4	2	2	3
Hegan c	4	1	1	0
Zoldak p	2	0	0	0
Klieman p	0	0	0	0
Peck ph	0	0	0	0
Clark ph	0	0	0	0
Lemon pr	0	1	0	0
Paige p	0	0	0	0
Christopher p	0	0	0	0
TOTAL	31	8	9	8

	IP	H	R	ER	BB	SO
Zoldak	6⅓	10	6	6	1	2
Klieman	⅔	0	0	0	0	0
Paige (W)	1⅔	2	0	0	0	0
Christopher (Sv)	⅓	0	0	0	0	0

#30

INDIANS 9, NEW YORK YANKEES 8 (13 INNINGS)
OCTOBER 6, 2017

Long Day's Journey into Night

It didn't take long for the plot to thicken.

While Game One of the American League Division Series between the Indians and New York Yankees had slowly and methodically unfolded into a 4–0 Cleveland victory, Game Two felt like a blockbuster movie opening with an intense action scene.

Fifteen pitches into the game—which began at 5 P.M. on a Friday just as the work week ended for most fans—the Yankees surged ahead 2–0 on a home run by catcher Gary Sanchez. Within moments they threatened to score again before Indians starting pitcher Corey Kluber struck out Aaron Hicks with runners on the corners to end the inning. It took just fourteen more pitches for the Indians to equalize matters as they loaded the bases for Carlos Santana to single in two runs off former Cleveland star pitcher CC Sabathia, who started for the Yankees. While the Indians had momentarily stolen the momentum, a twist of fate—quite literally—would shift it right back.

On the next pitch, right fielder Jay Bruce lined into a double play, which resulted in designated hitter Edwin Encarnación twisting his ankle trying to get back to second base. After laying flat on the infield dirt and receiving treatment for several minutes, Encarnación was helped off the field by Cleveland trainers and would miss the rest of the game. It was an early blow for the home team, losing its cleanup hitter who'd hit thirty-eight home runs and driven in more than 100 RBI during the regular season, and manager Terry Francona wanted to make sure it didn't shake the team's confidence. During the delay, he pulled aside shortstop and team leader Francisco Lindor. "I said, 'Hey, we can't act like we got hit in the stomach and got the wind knocked out of us,'" Francona would explain later. "I said, 'Keep 'em going.'"

Cleveland did quickly bounce back, briefly surging to a 3–2 lead in the second before the Yankees got to a struggling Kluber in the third with four runs, three on a homer by Hicks, that put New York up 6–3. Once Kluber was taken out after lasting just 2⅔ innings—marking his shortest outing of the season—a third Yankee home run in the fifth made it 8–3, and the Indians' chances for victory appeared to be waning with the daylight as the colorful autumn dusk turned to dark

Things looked even bleaker after they went down in order in the fifth and then saw two more batters quickly retired in the sixth. A walk by Santana was followed by a double from catcher Yan Gomes to put runners on second and third. After pinch hitter Lonnie Chisenhall fell behind 0–2 to New York pitcher Chad Green, the third pitch angled inside and appeared to hit Chisenhall's hand before settling into Sanchez's glove. Home plate umpire Dan Iassogna declared a hit batter and Chisenhall was granted first base to load the bases, through slow-motion replays suggested that the ball may have actually hit the handle of the bat rather than Chisenhall's hand, which would have resulted in a foul tip strikeout to end the inning. But Yankees manger Aaron Boone chose not to challenge the call. For his part, Chisenhall deferred to offer an opinion. "I'm not an umpire," he would coyly remark later.

Up to the plate stepped Lindor. On the second pitch, a slider, he lifted a high, towering fly ball down the right-field line. "As soon as I saw it go up, I knew it had a chance to go out," Lindor said. "But then I was like, 'Uh oh, it might go foul.' I started blowing on it, and it came back and hit the foul pole."

That it did, ricocheting high off the pole and back down into the right-field seats for a grand slam home run—and one of the most dramatic moments in franchise history. With one swing, the five-run deficit had been trimmed to one, and it was a brand-new ballgame. Lindor had accomplished the mission his manager had tasked him with a few hours before when Encarnación's injury had taken the wind out of the Indians' sails—he'd kept his team going.

With the Cleveland bullpen continuing to silence the New York bats, the Indians remained within reach into the eighth inning. Leading off the bottom of the frame was Jay Bruce, who rocketed a 3–1 curveball into deep left-center field. It landed several rows deep in the bleachers, and Cleveland had, beyond the odds, come all the way back to tie the game at 8–8 as the sellout crowd roared in yet another incredible moment.

"Emotion overtook me when I rounded second base and saw the guys in the dugout," Bruce said later. "Because you understood at that moment what it took to get back in the game."

After the teams had lit up the scoreboard for sixteen runs over the first eight innings, the tone of the game changed as strong pitching rose to the forefront. Following a scoreless ninth, the contest stretched into the tenth, where both bullpens quelled scoring opportunities. Cleveland catcher Yan Gomes lasered a throw to second to pick off pinch-runner Ronald Torreyes and smother a Yankee threat in the eleventh, while New York reliever Dellin Betances retired six straight to cruise through the Cleveland eleventh and twelfth.

In the bottom of the thirteenth, Indians leadoff hitter Austin Jackson walked and quickly stole second, bringing up Gomes with a chance to end the marathon. After working a full count in a long, anxiety-riddled at-bat, Gomes connected on the tenth pitch, bouncing a ground ball over third base and into left field. Jackson sprinted around third and came home to score Cleveland's ninth and the game's winning run.

The Indians' long day's journey into night had become one of the most incredible postseason victories in their history. "The understatement of the year," Francona told reporters, "would be to say that there was a lot going on in that game."

Understatement indeed. In the longest postseason game in franchise history at five hours eight minutes, the Indians had achieved their greatest playoff comeback, rallying from five down to take a two-game lead in the series. It was an epic contest that had a little bit of everything, including twenty hits, seventeen runs, and five homers, all while fourteen pitchers combined to throw more than 400 pitches and rack up twenty-four strikeouts.

It was a game that drastically shifted from shootout to pitching duel, from blowout to nail-biter. And was defined by two dramatic home runs and concluded on a clutch walk-off hit.

"That," Gomes would say, "was what you call October baseball right there."

Yankees	2	0	4	0	2	0	0	0	0	0	0	0	0	=8
Guardians	2	1	0	0	0	4	0	1	0	0	0	0	1	=9

NEW YORK

	AB	R	H	RBI
Gardner lf	5	0	0	0
Judge rf	3	1	0	0
Sánchez c	6	2	2	2
Gregorius ss	5	1	0	0
Castro 2b	6	1	2	1
Bird 1b	5	2	2	2
Hicks cf	6	1	2	3
Ellsbury dh	3	0	0	0
Headley ph-dh	3	0	0	0
Frazier 3b	5	0	3	0
Torreyes pr-3b	1	0	0	0
TOTAL	48	8	11	8

	IP	H	R	ER	BB	SO
Sabathia	5⅓	3	4	2	3	5
Green	⅓	2	3	3	0	0
Robertson	1⅔	1	1	1	0	3
Kahnle	⅔	0	0	0	0	0
Chapman	2	2	0	0	1	2
Betances (L)	2	1	1	1	1	2

CLEVELAND

	AB	R	H	RBI
Lindor ss	5	2	1	4
Kipnis cf	6	0	2	1
Ramírez 2b	5	1	0	0
Encarnación dh	0	0	0	0
Brantley ph-dh	5	0	0	0
Santana 1b	5	1	1	2
Bruce rf	6	1	1	1
Jackson lf	5	2	2	0
Gomes c	5	1	2	1
Urshela 3b	1	0	0	0
Chisenhall ph	0	1	0	0
González 3b	2	0	0	0
TOTAL	45	9	9	9

	IP	H	R	ER	BB	SO
Kluber	2⅔	7	6	6	1	4
Olson	1	0	0	0	0	0
Clevinger	⅔	1	2	2	2	2
Shaw	2⅔	1	0	0	0	1
Miller	1⅓	1	0	0	0	0
Smith	⅔	0	0	0	0	1
Allen	2	1	0	0	2	1
Tomlin (W)	2	0	0	0	0	3

Attendance: 37,681

#29

INDIANS 5, BROOKLYN DODGERS 1
OCTOBER 9, 1920

A Real World's Series

"There is no city in all America that owns more red-blooded citizens than this," declared the *Plain Dealer*. "Consequently, today is a day that Clevelanders have been waiting for since 1879."

On a bright, unseasonably warm Saturday afternoon in October, the city of Cleveland would host its first World Series game, and the occasion dominated the hearts and minds of the residents of the fifth-largest city in the United States. "With office boys and bankers, waitresses and widows, business men and hobos, there was only one topic last night," the *Plain Dealer* reported. By sunset Friday, more than 500 fans stood in line outside League Park, waiting for the opportunity to buy tickets to Saturday's game. After the gates opened the following morning, the bleachers were full by 10:30—more than three hours before the first pitch. "Often it has been said that if a collection of Cleveland athletes ever figured in a blue-ribbon diamond event, the populace would go insane," wrote reporter Frank Menke. "The prophecy has come true, for tonight everything else is forgotten in the Fifth City save one thing and one thing only." Not surprisingly, the passion of the Cleveland crowd would dramatically overshadow the zeal of those that had gathered in Brooklyn.

That their beloved Indians were down two games to one to Brooklyn in the best-of-nine series mattered little. The Tribe had spent much of the 1920 season overcoming adversity, partly in holding off the White Sox and Yankees in a bitter pennant race. More notably, however, was the way the team endured after star shortstop Ray Chapman was hit in the head by a pitch in August and died a day later. Dedicating the rest of the season to their fallen teammate and wearing black armbands in his memory, the Indians rallied from a 3½-game deficit to take the pennant. Thus, trailing by one game in the World Series hardly fazed either the team or its followers. "If anyone believes we think we are beaten, they have another guess. We have just begun to fight," said player/manager Tris Speaker after the Indians dropped back-to-back heartbreakers at Ebbets Field. "You know they had us down a few times during the American League season, but they could not keep us down. Brooklyn has us down now, but it cannot keep us there." Reflecting that confidence, Indians president Jim Dunn told his traveling secretary there was no need for him to make plans for a return trip to Brooklyn. He was certain the Tribe would win all four games at home to close out the series.

The atmosphere in and around League Park that Saturday afternoon was like that of a world's fair—a particularly welcome setting after the shadow of scandal that had fallen across the previous year's World Series, thrown by the Chicago White Sox. "This," noted Boston Braves president George Grant, "is more like a real world's series." Hotels were filled with out-of-towners, including better than 200 newspaper writers. Scalpers sold bundles of tickets to the four games Cleveland would host for $100—this in a time when an average car cost $250. Ironically, Dodger pitcher Rube Marquard was arrested for offering to sell his box-seat ticket for $350, eventually getting kicked off the team for his indiscretion. Those lucky enough to acquire a seat for the contest got their money's worth.

Cleveland spitball pitcher Stan Coveleski, who had throttled the Dodgers in Game One, was equally dominant to start Game Four, retiring the first ten batters. After he told his teammates all he would need was two runs to win the game, they instantly got him the support he requested in the first inning on an RBI single by right fielder Elmer Smith and a sacrifice fly by third baseman Larry Gardner, chasing Brooklyn starter Leon Cadore. Pinch-hitter George Burns then ripped a two-run single to left in the third to make it 4–0, and Cleveland had all the offense it would need. Brooklyn scored a run in the fourth, but Coveleski settled and didn't allow a runner to reach second base for the remainder of the game. Appropriately, Coveleski scored the final run of the contest in the sixth when he singled to center, advanced to second on a wild pitch, and came home on a single by second baseman Bill Wambsganss.

The final was 5–1, and the Indians had evened the World Series at two games apiece. The hometown fans went home "satisfied that nothing short of dire misfortune can keep the Indians from winning the world's championship," Richard Harding wrote in the *Plain Dealer.* "Brooklyn was being slain to make a Cleveland holiday, and everyone there was ready to make the most of it."

"The unofficial and perhaps more exact explanation," Fred Charles wrote, "is that 20,000 Cleveland fans warmed the Indians to victory by the mere contagion of enthusiasm."

Three more memorable games would follow in the coming days, and, though there would be long respites in between, the World Series would eventually return to Cleveland five times. Yet nothing could compare with the first time around on an apple-crisp afternoon bathed in golden autumn sunshine.

"The descending sun leaves long shadows over the yard," legendary sportswriter Damon Runyan wrote. "It is a warm evening. It has been a warm day. It has been a great day for Cleveland."

Dodgers	0 0 0	1 0 0	0 0 0	=1
Indians	2 0 2	0 0 1	0 0 x	=5

BROOKLYN

	AB	R	H	RBI
Olson ss	4	0	1	0
Johnston 3b	4	1	2	0
Neis pr	0	0	0	0
Griffith rf	4	0	1	1
Wheat lf	4	0	0	0
Myers cf	3	0	0	0
Konetchy 1b	2	0	0	0
Kilduff 2b	3	0	1	0
Miller c	3	0	0	0
Cadore p	0	0	0	0
Mamaux p	1	0	0	0
Marquard p	0	0	0	0
Lamar ph	1	0	0	0
Pfeffer p	1	0	0	0
TOTAL	30	1	5	1

	IP	H	R	ER	BB	SO
Cadore (L)	1	4	2	2	1	1
Mamaux	1	2	2	2	0	1
Marquard	3	2	0	0	1	2
Pfeffer	3	4	1	1	2	1

CLEVELAND

	AB	R	H	RBI
Jamieson lf	2	0	0	0
Evans ph-lf	3	0	1	0
Wambsganss 2b	4	2	2	1
Speaker cf	5	2	2	0
Smith rf	1	0	1	1
Burns ph-1b	2	0	1	2
Gardner 3b	3	0	1	1
Johnston 1b	1	0	0	0
Wood ph-rf	2	0	0	0
Graney ph-rf	1	0	0	0
Sewell ss	4	0	2	0
O'Neill c	2	0	1	0
Coveleski p	4	1	1	0
TOTAL	34	5	12	5

	IP	H	R	ER	BB	SO
Coveleski (W)	9	5	1	1	1	4

Attendance: 25,734

#28

INDIANS 3, NEW YORK YANKEES 2
OCTOBER 5, 1997

Back from the Brink

A disappointing season was about to come to an appropriately disappointing conclusion. True, the 1997 Indians had captured their third straight American League Central Division crown, but they had done so almost by default, barely finishing above .500. Matched with the defending world-champion New York Yankees in the best-of-five Division Series, there was little doubt the Tribe would yield to the mighty Yanks, who were better in essentially every category.

The Indians threw a bit of a scare into New York, jumping to a 5–0 lead in the first inning of Game One, but the Cleveland bullpen imploded and the Yankees came back to win, 8–6. The Tribe took Game Two but then was silenced in Game Three at Jacobs Field, where the Yankees seemed to hold a trance over Cleveland. Following the win in the third game of the series, New York held a 16–5 all-time record at the Jake dating back to its opening three years before. Now, with one more victory on a balmy Sunday night in Cleveland, the Yankees would eliminate the Indians and move on to the American League Championship Series.

It appeared Cleveland caught a break when New York ace pitcher David Cone was unable to take the mound with a shoulder injury, but veteran Dwight Gooden stepped up, holding the Indians to just one run on a second-inning David Justice single. When Gooden was taken out in the sixth, the Yankee bullpen continued its mastery of Cleveland batters. After not allowing a run in the first three games of the series, New York relievers picked up where they left off and preserved the Yankees' 2–1 lead into the eighth.

In a way, it was amazing the Tribe was even that close. Orel Hershiser was battered in the first inning, giving up back-to-back doubles to Derek Jeter and Paul O'Neill to score a run, followed by a two-out RBI single by Cecil Fielder.

"They were one game away from ending the series and they approached it that way," Hershiser said. "It took me a while to get my rhythm." The Yankees were poised to stretch the margin to 3–0 when Charlie Hayes then came through with a single to left, but Cleveland outfielder Brian Giles made a fantastic throw to the plate which allowed catcher Sandy Alomar to tag out Tino Martinez and end the inning. Hershiser then settled, pitching six scoreless innings while walking none and permitting just four hits, allowing the Indians to hang around.

By the eighth, it appeared Hershiser's heroics would be wasted. New York turned to closer Mariano Rivera, on the brink of becoming the most dominant relief pitcher in baseball, and he retired Cleveland power hitter Matt Williams for the second out of the inning, moving the Yankees to within four outs of advancing.

Up stepped Alomar, who had enjoyed the finest year of his injury-riddled career. After a summer in which he rattled off a thirty-game hitting streak, hit home runs in five consecutive games, broke up a perfect-game bid by Baltimore's Mike Mussina, and blasted a homer to win the All-Star Game, Alomar now represented Cleveland's last hope to extend 1997.

He laid off a pair of pitches to get ahead 2-and-0, then Rivera fired a fastball that sailed up in the strike zone. "He was hacking," Rivera said later. "I was surprised he hit it." But hit it he did—sending a looping shot arching into right field. O'Neill followed it back to the wall and crouched in an attempt to leap after the ball, but it was no use. It cleared the wall and landed in a sea of suddenly vibrant Indians fans. O'Neill spiked his glove on the warning track in frustration as Jacobs Field came to life for the first time all night. "This was the biggest home run of my life," said Alomar, who circled the bases with his arms in the air.

Suddenly, the entire atmosphere of the game changed. Rather than a team on the brink of extinction, the Indians felt and consequently played like a charmed team. Reliever Mike Jackson cruised through the New York ninth, and the miraculous momentum carried over into the bottom of the frame. Marquis Grissom led off the inning with a bloop single to right, then Bip Roberts sacrificed him to second. It brought to the plate red-hot Omar Vizquel, who had already reached base three times on the night. Like Alomar in the eighth, Vizquel got ahead in the count 2-and-0, then laced a sinking fastball from Ramiro Mendoza right back up the middle. Destined to be a simple groundout, the ball glanced off Mendoza's glove. It then caromed on an angle through a spot in the infield vacated by Jeter, who had dashed to his left to make a play on the ball. Jeter couldn't get back in time and the baseball trickled into the outfield as Grissom rounded third and sprinted home with the winning run. The Indians had received a stay of execution, and the teams would take the diamond again Monday night for Game Five, thanks to one of the unlikeliest late-inning rallies in franchise history.

They'd tied the game on a homer off a bullpen that hadn't allowed a run in more than twelve innings of postseason play, then used two fluke base hits to beat a team that had tied a major-league record with nine consecutive postseason road victories. For one night at least, the luck that seemed to halo the Yankee franchise had swapped teams. Even O'Neill appreciated the significance. "It's one of the better games I've played in, when you take everything into consideration," he said.

The moment when the Indians stood on the brink of elimination was forgotten, bashed into the autumn night by Alomar's unforgettable home run. "The homer was big because it gave us an opportunity for tomorrow," he said. "There is always hope."

Yankees	2 0 0	0 0 0	0 0 0	=2
Indians	0 1 0	0 0 0	0 1 1	=3

NEW YORK

	AB	R	H	RBI
Raines lf	4	0	1	0
Curtis pr-lf	0	0	0	0
Jeter ss	4	1	2	0
O'Neill rf	4	1	2	1
B. Williams cf	4	0	0	0
Martinez 1b	3	0	0	0
Fielder dh	4	0	1	1
Hayes 3b	4	0	2	0
Girardi c	3	0	0	0
Sanchez 2b	4	0	1	0
TOTAL	34	2	9	2

	IP	H	R	ER	BB	SO
Gooden	5⅔	5	1	1	3	5
Lloyd	0	0	0	0	0	0
Nelson	1	1	0	0	0	0
Stanton	⅔	0	0	0	0	2
Rivera	⅔	1	1	1	0	0
Mendoza (L)	⅓	2	1	1	0	0

CLEVELAND

	AB	R	H	RBI
Roberts 2b-lf	4	0	0	0
Vizquel ss	4	0	3	1
Ramirez rf	4	0	0	0
Thome 1b	4	0	0	0
Justice dh	3	1	1	1
M. Williams 3b	4	0	1	0
Alomar c	4	1	2	1
Giles lf	2	0	1	0
Fernandez ph-2b	2	0	0	0
Grissom cf	3	1	1	0
TOTAL	34	3	9	3

	IP	H	R	ER	BB	SO
Hershiser	7	8	2	2	0	3
Assenmacher	⅔	1	0	0	0	2
Jackson (W)	1⅓	0	0	0	0	2

Attendance: 45,231

#27

INDIANS 4, FLORIDA MARLINS 1
OCTOBER 25, 1997

Up Against the Wall

As the Indians went into what was almost assuredly their final game of the 1997 season, the consensus by fans and the media was identical: it had been a good ride while it lasted.

They'd caught fire in the postseason, upsetting New York and Baltimore to reach the World Series, and showed resolve against a plucky Florida Marlins team, taking Game Two in Miami. However, after Florida took two of three amidst arctic conditions at Jacobs Field, the Tribe was in trouble. It would have to win back-to-back games at Pro Player Stadium to capture the franchise's first world title in forty-nine years. In fact, simply getting to a deciding Game Seven looked hopeless. For Game Six, the Marlins would send to the mound star pitcher Kevin Brown, who had been dominant in the regular season with a 2.69 ERA, to close out the series. While the Indians had roughed up Brown in the second game of the series, handing him his first defeat in three months, most doubted the Tribe could match its success the second time around.

Conversely, the Indians would counter with unpredictable Chad Ogea, who had failed to live up to expectations for three consecutive years, fighting through injury to post just an 8–9 record in '97 with an unimpressive 4.99 ERA. As it happened, Ogea would indeed become the story of the game—but not particularly for what he did on the mound.

On a sultry Saturday night in south Florida, the Indians posed their first scoring threat in the second, when they loaded the bases with one out. Playing in a National League park, the designated-hitter rule was suspended, and Ogea stepped into the batter's box to face the hottest pitcher in baseball with just five major-league at-bats under his belt. Rather than an easy out, Ogea

In one of the finest defensive plays in postseason history, Tribe shortstop Omar Vizquel goes airborne to snag a scorching ground ball hit by Florida catcher Charles Johnson in the sixth inning of Game Six of the 1997 World Series. The play saved two runs and secured the Indians' clutch 4–1 triumph. *Akron Beacon Journal.*

battled Brown, staying alive through six pitches. Looking uncomfortable and awkward, Ogea threw the bat at Brown's seventh pitch and bounced a single into right field, scoring Matt Williams and Jim Thome for a 2–0 Cleveland lead. The rally ended when Bip Roberts grounded into a double play, but Ogea's miraculous hit—his first since high school—had set the tone.

Aided by a dazzling running catch by center fielder Marquis Grissom with his back to home plate, Cleveland's sudden star cruised through the second, then the Indians tacked on another run in the third off an Omar Vizquel double and a sacrifice fly by Manny Ramirez. When the Indians came to bat in the fifth, Ogea had already delivered the game-changing hit, sparking a three-run lead, and had allowed only one hit himself. His performance propelled into that of legend when he sliced the first pitch of the fifth down the right-field line and rumbled awkwardly into second for a double to the shock and delight of the Indians and their fans. After a Roberts single moved him to third, Ogea scored on Ramirez's second sac fly of the game to make it 4–0, Tribe. Ogea's heroics came at a price, however. He returned to the dugout exhausted from his unexpected trip around the bases, and trainers doused him with ice and ammonia to cool him down before returning to the mound.

Battling fatigue, Ogea gave up back-to-back singles to start the Florida fifth but wiggled out of the jam after allowing just one run. When he led off the sixth with a walk to Charles Johnson, Cleveland manager Mike Hargrove replaced Ogea with reliever Mike Jackson, concluding one of the finest postseason performances by a pitcher in World Series history. Yet the Indians weren't out of the woods yet. A walk to Jim Eisenreich put Marlins on first and second with one down, but Jackson rebounded by enticing a groundout that put the runners on second and third. With momentum teetering in the balance, Charles Johnson ripped a sharp liner between second and third, destined for left field as a two-run single. But Vizquel leaped to his right to spear the baseball on the edge of the grass, then sprang up and threw to first to retire Johnson, save two runs, and end the inning. "That's the biggest play I've ever made in my career," said Vizquel, who won his fifth Gold Glove in 1997. "I've made that play before, but not in this situation." Even the partisan Florida crowd of better than 67,000 gave Vizquel a round of applause.

Jackson again got into trouble in the seventh, allowing two hits to open the inning. He rebounded to strike out a pair, then surrendered a walk to load the bases and bring the go-ahead run to the plate in third baseman Bobby Bonilla. Bloodied but not bowed, Jackson got Bonilla to pop out, and the Indians had escaped once again.

Paul Assenmacher and Jose Mesa each allowed a base runner in the final two innings but extinguished any threats before they started. After Mesa struck out Edgar Renteria, then got Gary Sheffield to ground out, stranding a runner at third, the Indians had clinched a gutsy 4–1 win, forcing the thirty-third deciding game in World Series history. "Don't put the Chief Wahoo banners and pennants away just yet," Paul Hoynes wrote. "Keep those red-and-blue knee socks pulled high. The Indians still have a game to play."

Suddenly, after five games of floundering and streakiness, the Tribe had gathered momentum and looked like a team that belonged in the World Series. With Ogea leading the way on the mound and at the plate, the rest of the team followed suit. "The Indians played almost a perfect game," Florida manager Jim Leyland said. "They were flawless." Such adjectives are hard to muster in any baseball game, let alone with an entire season hanging in the balance and fans around the planet hanging on every pitch. "This team thrives when we're up against the wall," said Tribe pitcher Brian Anderson. "I don't know what it is. We just do."

Indians	0	2	1	0	1	0	0	0	0	=4
Marlins	0	0	0	0	1	0	0	0	0	=1

CLEVELAND

	AB	R	H	RBI
Roberts 2b	3	0	1	0
Fernandez 2b	1	0	1	0
Vizquel ss	4	1	1	0
Ramirez rf	1	0	0	2
Justice lf	4	0	0	0
Williams 3b	4	1	2	0
Thome 1b	3	1	0	0
Alomar c	3	0	0	0
Grissom cf	3	0	0	0
Ogea p	2	1	2	2
Jackson p	1	0	0	0
Assenmacher p	0	0	0	0
Seitzer ph	1	0	0	0
Mesa p	0	0	0	0
TOTAL	30	4	7	4

	IP	H	R	ER	BB	SO
Ogea (W)	5	4	1	1	2	1
Jackson	2	2	0	0	2	2
Assenmacher	1	1	0	0	0	1
Mesa (Sv)	1	1	0	0	0	1

FLORIDA

	AB	R	H	RBI
White cf	5	0	3	0
Renteria ss	5	0	0	0
Sheffield rf	3	0	0	0
Bonilla 3b	4	0	0	0
Conine 1b	2	0	0	0
Eisenreich ph-1b	1	0	0	0
Alou lf	3	1	1	0
Johnson c	4	0	2	0
Counsell 2b	4	0	1	0
Brown p	1	0	0	0
Daulton ph	0	0	0	1
Heredia p	0	0	0	0
Cangelosi ph	1	0	1	0
Powell p	0	0	0	0
Vosberg p	0	0	0	0
Floyd ph	1	0	0	0
TOTAL	34	1	8	1

	IP	H	R	ER	BB	SO
Brown (L)	5	5	4	4	3	2
Heredia	2	0	0	0	0	4
Powell	1	2	0	0	0	1
Vosberg	1	0	0	0	1	1

Attendance: 67,498

#26

INDIANS 6, NEW YORK YANKEES 1
OCTOBER 9, 1998

David Spanks Goliath

What started as another impressive campaign for the New York Yankees had gradually become one of the finest seasons in baseball history. After a 1–4 start, New York won fourteen of its next fifteen games and never looked back, winning sixty of its first eighty games and building a ten-game lead in the American League East Division by the first weekend of June. When the regular season concluded, the Yankees had set a new American League record with 114 victories, winning their division by a whopping twenty-two games, and it appeared the playoffs would simply be a victory lap for the unbeatable Bronx Bombers.

Sure enough, New York cruised past Texas in the Division Series, allowing just one run in a three-game sweep. It appeared the script would continue in the ALCS against the Indians when the Yanks scored five runs in the first inning of Game One and coasted to a 7–2 victory—their eleventh straight. But the victory parade hit some turbulence in the second game when the Tribe outlasted New York in a matinee marathon that turned on a controversial noncall of runner interference on Cleveland's Travis Fryman on a run-scoring play in the twelfth inning. The series, knotted at one game apiece, moved to Cleveland for Game Three on a crisp autumn Friday night at Jacobs Field, where most felt the jilted Yankees would return to their winning ways.

Continuing a trend established in Game One, New York got on the board in the first inning on a two-out RBI single by center fielder Bernie Williams. It had been a shaky first frame for Indians pitcher Bartolo Colon, making his second career postseason appearance after enjoying a breakthrough season in '98, winning fourteen games with a 3.71 ERA. But Colon would settle in—and make history.

Meanwhile, the Cleveland offense came into the second inning scuffling, having scored just eight runs in the previous thirty-one innings. First baseman Jim Thome ended that string with a thunderclap, blasting a 421-foot home run into the Cleveland bullpen to tie the game. Cleveland left fielder Mark Whiten—a midseason acquisition who'd begun the year playing in Mexico—followed with a double to left, then scored on a single by second baseman Enrique Wilson to give the Indians the lead at 2–1. There the score would remain through the third and fourth as Colon heated up, twice enticing inning-ending double plays to snuff out New York rallies before they started. It was shaping up as a classic pitcher's duel between Colon and New York's Andy Pettitte, but that would change in the bottom of the fifth.

The theme of the evening continued as Pettitte retired Omar Vizquel and David Justice, making it eight straight Indians retired. But left fielder Manny Ramirez tomahawked Pettitte's first pitch into the Yankee bullpen to make it 3–1, and the sellout crowd of better than 44,000 fans, already electrified, further lit up the October night. It was Ramirez's thirteenth career postseason home run, putting him within two of legendary Babe Ruth and six back of Yankee immortals Reggie Jackson and Mickey Mantle.

Fryman followed with a walk, then Thome mirrored Ramirez, crushing Pettitte's first pitch over the wall in right for his second homer of the night. With the hometown fans still delirious with joy, Whiten, released by New York fourteen months before, kept the party going. He smashed a 1–0 Pettitte pitch into the bleachers in left field for the Tribe's third home run of the inning and fourth of the night—tying an ALCS record—to make it 6–1. As he watched his first career postseason homer rocket into the night, Whiten flipped the bat into the air triumphantly. "Jacobs Field was primed for a pep rally and a bonfire," Bud Shaw wrote.

It would be all the offense Colon would need. He would go the distance, becoming the first Cleveland pitcher to throw a postseason complete game in forty-four years. Throwing harder as the game went on, Colon retired eight straight from the fifth through the eighth and didn't allow a base hit in the final four innings. Colon gave up just four hits for the game, only one over the final seven frames against New York's potent offense, while his offense put up a fireworks show. It marked the first time in eighteen games the Yankees had allowed more than five runs. "That's an awesome lineup," New York manager Joe Torre said. "They've got a lot of power. They can really beat you up."

Suddenly, the team everyone was prepared to rank with the greatest in baseball history was now down two games to one in a best-of-seven series. After a mediocre, occasionally frustrating regular season, the Indians were throwing the scare of a lifetime into the mighty Yankees. "They are taking the Yankees' heirloom season and smashing away at it," wrote Bill Livingston. Suddenly, the Cleveland bats were hot and the pitching had become dominant, allowing just two Yankee runs in the last twenty-one innings.

Asked to explain what had happened, Torre uttered words that the nearly perfect 1998 Yankees hadn't heard all year: "We got our butts kicked."

Yankees	1	0	0	0	0	0	0	0	0	=1
Indians	0	2	0	0	4	0	0	0	x	=6

NEW YORK

	AB	R	H	RBI
Knoblauch 2b	3	1	2	0
Jeter ss	3	0	0	0
O'Neill rf	3	0	0	0
Williams cf	4	0	1	1
Martinez 1b	4	0	0	0
Davis dh	1	0	0	0
Spencer lf	3	0	0	0
Brosius 3b	3	0	0	0
Girardi c	2	0	1	0
Posada ph-c	1	0	0	0
TOTAL	27	1	4	1

	IP	H	R	ER	BB	SO
Pettitte (L)	4⅔	8	6	6	3	1
Mendoza	1⅓	3	0	0	0	0
Stanton	2	1	0	0	1	3

CLEVELAND

	AB	R	H	RBI
Lofton cf	5	0	0	0
Vizquel ss	4	0	3	0
Justice dh	5	0	0	0
Ramirez rf	4	1	3	1
Fryman 3b	3	1	1	0
Thome 1b	4	2	2	3
Whiten lf	3	2	2	1
Alomar c	4	0	0	0
Wilson 2b	4	0	1	1
TOTAL	36	6	12	6

	IP	H	R	ER	BB	SO
Colon (W)	9	4	1	1	4	3

Attendance: 44,904

#25

INDIANS 5, NEW YORK YANKEES 3
APRIL 8, 1975

Storybook Stuff

One week shy of the twenty-eighth anniversary of Jackie Robinson's major-league debut, another barrier in baseball would be broken. History would be made on a frosty opening day at Cleveland Stadium when Frank Robinson (no relation) would become the first African American to manage a Major League Baseball team.

Throughout spring training, the national media swarmed to Robinson as he not only tried to prepare the Indians for 1975 but also to ready himself as player/manager for what would be the twentieth season of his illustrious career. Not surprisingly, Robinson's individual preparation took a backseat to the hoopla surrounding his historic position and trying to put a team together. "I'm probably about fifteen or twenty at-bats away from being really ready," Robinson said on the eve of the opener, "although I'm not hitting the ball too badly."

Spring training got off to a rocky start on the first day of practice when Robinson got into a publicized squabble with star pitcher Gaylord Perry, who'd won the American League Cy Young Award three years before. It was the first challenge of Robinson's authority by a veteran who was set in his ways, and reporters kept an eye on the situation throughout the month of March to see if the embers of tension would spread into a full-blown controversy. Though the spotlight was clearly pointed at him, Robinson deflected it. "Pressure is something a person creates within himself," he said, "and I won't do it." Further, while appreciating its importance, Robinson downplayed his role in history, explaining that Jackie Robinson's 1947 debut was a much more significant event. Whereas Jackie Robinson would do little on the field on that fateful opening day, Frank Robinson would steal the show.

Frank Robinson (*right*) is greeted by John Lowenstein after hitting a dramatic home run in his first at-bat as baseball's first black manager on April 8, 1975. Cleveland State University Library's *Cleveland Press* Collection.

The bright promise of opening day began with Cleveland general manager Phil Seghi needling Frank Robinson before the game. The manager wasn't going to put himself in the lineup, but Seghi convinced him otherwise. Even if he didn't feel he was ready, Seghi said, he simply had to play. History demanded it. Once he'd convinced Robinson, he then suggested that he might as well go out and hit a home run. Robinson laughed it off.

It was sunny but just thirty-six degrees when the Indians took the field after Jackie Robinson's widow, Rachel, had thrown out the ceremonial first pitch. Wearing their new fire-engine-red uniforms, the Indians cruised through the first, as Perry struck out Lou Piniella and Bobby Bonds. Cleveland left fielder Oscar Gamble started the Indians season by popping out, bringing Robinson to the plate. Though he'd joined the Indians the previous September and appeared in fifteen games, his at-bat had all the earmarks of not only a fresh start but that of a rookie making his professional debut. He thought he'd be able to keep his emotions in check, but Robinson felt numb as he stepped into the box. Mentally unbalanced, he fell behind 0-and-2 to Yankee pitcher Doc Medich, then barely fouled off a third pitch before zeroing in. He fouled off another, then took a pair outside as he settled into the situation. Medich tried to put Robinson away with a 2–2 fastball over the outside corner.

Robinson's bat met the ball and sent it searing into the clear April sky. It floated over the fence in left field as the crowd of better than 56,000 roared, having witnessed not only the 575th home run of Robinson's career but one of the most dramatic in baseball history. "At first, there was nothing running through my mind, really," Robinson would say later. "But by the time I got to third base, I thought to myself, 'Wow—will miracles never cease to happen?'" As he neared home plate, Robinson tipped his cap to his wife Barbara, and *Plain Dealer* columnist Hal Lebovitz described the moment: "Even if you were frozen, the heart pounded faster and the blood flowed quicker from the thrill." Adding to the fiction-feel of the moment, the first player out of the Cleveland dugout to offer congratulations to his manager was Gaylord Perry. "Any home run is a thrill," Robinson would say, "but I've got to admit, this one was a bigger thrill."

Robinson's wonderful moment faded somewhat in the second when New York began battering Perry, stroking four hits and bringing three runs around to take the lead. Rather than pulling Perry, the Cleveland manager stuck with him, and his pitcher rewarded him with a dominating finish. Over the next seven innings, New York would not score again, managing just five hits. Meanwhile, after the Tribe cut the lead to 3–2 in its half of the second and tied it on a home run by newcomer Boog Powell in the fourth, the home team pulled away in the sixth. Powell, making his Cleveland debut after being acquired from Baltimore in the offseason, hit a one-out RBI double to right to put the Indians ahead, then scored on a Jack Brohamer single to center to make it 5–3.

The rivals battled through the final innings, and the Yankees had their last chance in the ninth with a runner on first and powerful catcher Thurman Munson at the plate. Again, Robinson showed faith in Perry and allowed him to stay in the game. Munson hit a soft grounder back to the mound which Perry fielded and threw to Powell at first to end the game as a tidal wave of cheering crashed onto the field. "I've never been involved in anything like that," Powell said.

The dramatics would continue. Just as Perry had been the first to congratulate Robinson in the first, Robinson was now the first to meet Perry, putting his arm around him—the spring-training spat all but forgotten. "Fiction?" Lebovitz wondered. "Storybook stuff? No, it was real."

An otherwise dismal era in Indians history had been blessed with a truly magical moment—a game "which could be classified as a lifter of spirits all around," declared a *Plain Dealer* editorial. "One victory does not mean a pennant, but there is no better way to start."

Yankees	0	3	0	0	0	0	0	0	0	=3
Indians	1	1	0	1	0	2	0	0	x	=5

NEW YORK

	AB	R	H	RBI
Alomar 2b	2	0	0	0
Johnson ph	1	0	0	0
Stanley 2b	0	0	0	0
Piniella lf	4	0	0	0
Bonds cf	4	0	0	0
Bloomberg rf	4	1	2	0
Nettles 3b	4	1	1	0
Herrman dh	4	0	1	0
White pr	0	0	0	0
Chambliss 1b	4	1	3	2
Munson c	4	0	2	1
Mason ss	3	0	0	0
TOTAL	34	3	9	3

	IP	H	R	ER	BB	SO
Medich (L)	5⅔	8	5	5	2	2
May	1⅓	0	0	0	1	1
Lyle	1	2	0	0	1	0

CLEVELAND

	AB	R	H	RBI
Gamble lf	5	0	1	0
Robinson dh	3	1	1	1
Hendrick cf	3	1	0	0
Spikes rf	4	0	0	0
Powell 1b	3	3	3	2
Ellis c	3	0	2	0
Bell 3b	4	0	0	0
Brohamer 2b	3	0	2	2
Crosby ss	4	0	1	0
TOTAL	32	5	10	5

	IP	H	R	ER	BB	SO
Perry (W)	9	9	3	3	1	6

Attendance: 56,715

#24

INDIANS 2, BOSTON BRAVES 1
OCTOBER 9, 1948

An Unlikely Ace

After enduring possibly the greatest pennant race in American League history and watching their team come away with the flag, Indians rooters seemed a bit battle-fatigued when the World Series finally arrived. Almost viewing the Fall Classic as anticlimactic, a phlegmatic crowd of better than 70,000 filed into Cleveland Stadium for Game Three on a Friday afternoon but appeared subdued and listless as the Indians coasted to a 2–0 victory to take a two-games-to-one lead in the series. It would be an entirely different story twenty-four hours later.

The largest crowd in World Series history—81,897—packed into the ballpark on the lakeshore on a cool, cloudy Saturday afternoon, and unlike Friday's throng, this one was riled and ready for action. Part of the reason for the library atmosphere of Game Three was the quiet nature of the World Series itself. Dominated by strong pitching on both sides, a total of just eight runs had been scored in the first three games, including a 1–0 Boston victory in the opener and the Tribe's 2–0 triumph in Game Three. The pitching matchup for Game Four favored the Braves, who would send to the mound twenty-four-game winner Johnny Sain three days removed from a four-hit shutout victory over the Indians in Game One. Cleveland would counter with Steve Gromek, who'd won nineteen games three years before but spent most of 1948 as a spare part trying to find a niche, starting just nine times. About to make his first start in three weeks in what would prove to be the only postseason appearance of his seventeen-year career, Gromek didn't get much sleep the night before.

He gave up a double to first baseman Earl Torgeson in the first but got cleanup hitter Bob Elliott to pop out to end the threat. The Indians instantly warmed up their bats in the bottom half of the first, as left fielder Dale Mitchell laced

Thousands of fans line up outside Cleveland Stadium to buy tickets for the 1948 World Series, which would provide some of the greatest moments in franchise history. The three games played in Cleveland drew more than 230,000 fans, shattering baseball attendance records. Cleveland State University Library's *Cleveland Press* Collection.

a leadoff single to center, then moved to second on a Larry Doby groundout. Lou Boudreau then continued his storybook season, ripping a shot down the right-field line that scored Mitchell. Yet as Boudreau tried to stretch a double into a triple, he was called out sliding into third by umpire Bill Stewart. The fans disagreed, quickly remembering Stewart's blown call in Game One on a pickoff play that turned out to be the difference in Boston's win. With boos filtering out of the stands, Sain ended the inning, and another pitching duel was under way.

Gromek cruised through the second and third, then got a boost. After Sain struck out Gromek and got Mitchell to ground out to start the bottom of the third, Doby blasted a curveball to deep right field for a home run to make it 2–0, and the crowd was roaring again. Little did the fans know the Indians were done scoring for the day—but the two runs would be all that Gromek would need.

After stranding second baseman Eddie Stanky in scoring position in the third, Gromek caught fire, not allowing a runner to reach second for the next three innings. Left fielder Marv Rickert broke up Gromek's shutout with a leadoff homer in the seventh to cut the lead to 2–1, snapping an incredible string of twenty-two scoreless innings by Cleveland pitchers. Then center fielder Mike McCormick followed with a single to left, and Tribe fans began to squirm. Gromek hunkered down, getting catcher Phil Masi to pop out to third, then Stanky to fly out to left. Sain then grounded to Gromek, and Cleveland's pitcher threw out his counterpart to end the inning. Boston would threaten again in the eighth when Torgeson hit a two-out double, but again Gromek came through, getting Elliott to pop out to catcher Jim Hegan.

Meanwhile, the Indians' hot offensive start cooled quickly as Sain settled in. After Doby's homer in the third, Sain retired sixteen of the next seventeen batters, including the last twelve in a row to keep the Braves' hopes alive. With the tension mounting on each pitch, Gromek saved his best for last. He picked up his only two strikeouts of the afternoon in the ninth, whiffing Rickert and McCormick to lead off the inning. Boston's last hope was pinch-hitter Bill Salkeld, who flied to Bob Kennedy in right to end the game and give the Indians a commanding 3–1 lead in the series after a breezy ninety-one-minute game.

Though Cleveland's dominant pitching—which was the best in the AL in 1948—figured to be an asset going into the Series, no one expected Gromek to be one of the stars. With the spotlight on inning-eaters Bob Feller, Bob Lemon, and rookie Gene Bearden, a trio which had combined for fifty-nine victories, Gromek quietly took center stage and defeated the finest pitcher in the National League. "Guess it was one of my best games," Gromek said sheepishly afterward, "considering the series excitement and all."

With the Tribe now just one win away from its first world title in nearly three decades, Cleveland was tittering with excitement and toasting its unlikely hero. Fittingly, *Plain Dealer* reporter Roelif Loveland coined a new phrase mimicking the Braves' catchy slogan "Spahn and Sain and two days of rain": "That Gromek—heck!"

Braves	0	0	0	0	0	0	1	0	0	=1
Indians	1	0	1	0	0	0	0	0	x	=2

BOSTON

	AB	R	H	RBI
Holmes rf	4	0	0	0
Dark ss	4	0	0	0
Torgeson 1b	3	0	2	0
Elliott 3b	4	0	0	0
Rickert lf	4	1	2	1
McCormick cf	4	0	1	0
Masi c	3	0	0	0
Salkeld ph	1	0	0	0
Stanky 2b	3	0	1	0
Sain p	2	0	1	0
TOTAL	32	1	7	1

	IP	H	R	ER	BB	SO
Sain (L)	8	5	2	2	0	3

CLEVELAND

	AB	R	H	RBI
Mitchell lf	4	1	1	0
Doby cf	3	1	1	1
Boudreau ss	3	0	1	1
Gordon 2b	3	0	0	0
Keltner 3b	3	0	0	0
Judnich rf	3	0	0	0
Kennedy rf	0	0	0	0
Robinson 1b	3	0	2	0
Hegan c	2	0	0	0
Gromek p	3	0	0	0
TOTAL	27	2	5	2

	IP	H	R	ER	BB	SO
Gromek (W)	9	7	1	1	1	2

Attendance: 81,897

#23

INDIANS 3, KANSAS CITY ROYALS 2 (10 INNINGS)
SEPTEMBER 14, 2017

The Streak Abides

It had come out of nowhere.

As the Indians entered the final quarter of what had been a successful—if somewhat unremarkable—2017 season, they were casually treading toward a second straight American League Central Division title. But there was little to stir any expectations of mirroring the previous season's playoff run to the World Series.

After dropping a pair of blowout defeats to Boston in late August, their division lead had shrunk to 4½ games, and even if they managed to hang on and win the division, by all appearances they'd be the weak link in the roster of teams in the AL playoffs. The following night they salvaged a split in the four-game series with the Red Sox with a 13–6 triumph. Little did anyone know what that victory had begun.

A three-game sweep of Kansas City followed—underscored by Cleveland pitchers not allowing a single run in the series. Next was a trip to New York, where the Indians swept the Yankees on their home field for the first time in twenty-eight years. They captured every contest in a Labor Day weekend series in Detroit, and suddenly, it had graduated from hot stretch to a bona fide winning streak

A sweep of the White Sox in Chicago followed, and the Indians had now set a new franchise record with fifteen straight victories—eleven of them on the road. Returning to Cleveland, they continued to break that record each day in a weekend sweep of Baltimore and inched closer to immortality with three more victories over Detroit.

The nearly incomprehensible winning streak had now stretched to twenty-one, matching the major-league record for wins in consecutive games set by the Chicago Cubs in 1935. While the 1916 New York Giants technically held the record etched in the league annals at twenty-six, that streak included a tie right in the middle that, for many historians, served as a disqualifying asterisk.

Regardless, the Indians had become a national sensation, accomplishing something no one had seen in nearly a century. Everyone knew the streak would have to end at some point, but there was something both surreal and ethereal about it that seemed to will it forward. If nothing else, it had transformed the season into something to remember. The Indians now held the best record in the American League and their lead in the division race had swelled to an insurmountable 13½ games.

While the number of consecutive wins was the only statistic that truly mattered, a closer look at the numbers behind it made the whole thing all the more impressive. While the Cleveland offense had been on fire throughout the string, averaging more than six runs per game, it was the pitching that reached heretofore unseen levels of dominance. Indians starting pitchers had won nineteen of the twenty-one games, accumulating an ERA of 1.77 along the way. With such a potent combination of excellence, the Indians had outscored their opponents by more than a hundred runs over the course of the streak and, incredibly, had trailed in only four of the 189 innings played.

Finally, on a Thursday night at Progressive Field, it appeared the spell was about to be broken. In town for the second time in a month, the Kansas City Royals took a 2–1 lead into the ninth inning. A one-out single by Cleveland outfielder Tyler Naquin was followed by a force out to retire Naquin at second, and both the Indians and their winning streak were down to their final out. Up stepped shortstop Francisco Lindor to face Kansas City closer Kelvin Herrera. With pinch-runner Erik Gonzalez ready to move on contact at first base, Lindor, batting left-handed, lifted a 2–2 pitch toward left field.

"For a second, when I hit it, I was like, 'Oh no, I went the other way,'" Lindor said later. "'I hit it to the wrong guy.'"

What at first appeared would be a wrong-way fly out continued to drift toward the wall as Royals outfielder Alex Gordon continued a backward course onto the warning track. Reaching the wall, he leapt up to catch it, but the ball glanced off the padding just above his glove and ricocheted back onto the outfield grass.

Progressive Field erupted as Gonzalez motored around the bases to come home with the tying run. Lindor cruised into second for a most unusual RBI double, marking the first time all season he'd hit a ball to the left-field wall. The Indians—and the streak—were still alive as the Royals recovered to get the final out and send the game to extra innings.

After holding Kansas City scoreless in the top of the tenth, Cleveland slugger José Ramírez led off the bottom of the inning with a hit to right center field.

Noticing the extra split-second it took Royals outfielder Lorenzo Cain to get to the baseball, Ramírez sprinted around first and made it to second with a headfirst slide for a sneaky leadoff double emblematic of both Ramírez's baseball IQ and Cleveland's overall opportunism during the streak.

Cleanup hitter Edwin Encarnación followed with a walk, bringing up right fielder Jay Bruce. In many ways, Bruce had been the match that lit the fuse of the winning streak. Acquired in a little-noticed deal with the New York Mets in early August, Bruce slid perfectly onto the roster, providing just enough protection for Encarnación and Ramírez batting ahead of him and just enough additional muscle to round out the Cleveland lineup. And the results were indisputable—from his first start with the Indians to the moment he stepped up to bat in the bottom of the tenth inning against Kansas City, the Indians' record had been 30–4.

So it came as little surprise when, on the third pitch of the at bat, Bruce laced a line drive that landed just inside the right-field line and bounced all the way to the wall. As soon as he completed his swing, Bruce dropped his bat and raised his right arm in triumph as he ran out of the batter's box. Ramírez sprinted around third to score the winning run, and the Indians flooded out of their dugout to mob Bruce, dousing him with buckets of water and tearing his jersey off.

Make it twenty-two straight.

"This streak does not want to become a cold page in history," the *Plain Dealer*'s Paul Hoynes wrote. "This streak wants to live."

Underscoring the Indians' dominance, the dramatic win marked the first walkoff victory in the string and only the fourth one-run triumph.

The streak would finally come to an end the following night when the Royals clawed out a 4–3 triumph, only to be followed by five more Cleveland victories to make it twenty-seven of twenty-eight. The Indians wound up with 102 victories for the season—second-most in franchise history—fueled by this magical string that saw them win thirty-three of their final thirty-nine games.

All symbolized by the magic that went into and came out of win number twenty-two.

"It's safe to say we're in uncharted territory," Bruce said that night. "You can't draw this stuff up, man. You really can't."

Royals	0	1	0	0	0	1	0	0	0	0	=2
Guardians	0	0	1	0	0	0	0	0	1	1	=3

KANSAS CITY

	AB	R	H	RBI
Merrifield 2b	5	0	1	0
Cain cf	4	0	0	0
Cabrera	4	1	0	0
Hosmer 1b	3	1	1	1
Perez c	3	0	2	0
Bonifacio ph	1	0	0	0
Butera c	0	0	0	0
Moustakas 3b	4	0	1	0
Moss dh	4	0	1	0
Escobar ss	4	0	3	0
Gordon lf	4	0	0	0
TOTAL	36	2	9	1

	IP	H	R	ER	BB	SO
Junis	5⅔	7	1	1	1	1
Minor	1⅓	0	0	0	1	2
Buchter	1	1	0	0	2	0
Herrera	1	2	1	1	0	0
Maurer (L)	0	2	1	1	1	0

CLEVELAND

	AB	R	H	RBI
Lindor ss	5	0	1	1
Chisenhall lf	2	0	1	1
Allen cf	1	0	0	0
Jackson ph-lf	1	0	0	0
Ramírez 2b	4	1	4	0
Encarnción dh	3	0	1	0
Bruce rf	4	0	1	1
Santana 1b	4	0	2	0
Díaz 3b	4	0	0	0
Almonte cf-lf	2	1	1	0
Guyer ph-lf	1	0	0	0
Naquin ph-cf	1	0	1	0
Gomes c	3	0	0	0
Mejia ph	1	0	0	0
González pr	0	1	0	0
Pérez c	0	0	0	0
TOTAL	36	3	12	3

	IP	H	R	ER	BB	SO
Tomlin	5⅔	6	2	2	1	4
Smith	⅓	0	0	0	0	0
Miller	1	2	0	0	0	1
Goody	⅔	0	0	0	0	0
Olson	1⅓	0	0	0	0	0
Allen (W)	1	1	0	0	0	1

Attendance: 30,874

#22

INDIANS 2, BALTIMORE ORIOLES 1 (12 INNINGS)
OCTOBER 11, 1997

Not of This World

"It's hard to believe all the things that happened out there," Indians relief pitcher Paul Assenmacher would say when it was all over. "You say it over and over in baseball—that just when you think you've seen everything, you haven't. That sums up what happened today."

It began on a golden October Saturday afternoon at Jacobs Field before a wired crowd of 45,047 that was screaming long before the first pitch, fueled by sudden optimism after the Indians had split the first two games of the 1997 American League Championship Series in Baltimore against the heavily favored Orioles. A big reason for Baltimore's apparent advantage was its dominant pitching staff, anchored by All-Star Mike Mussina, who had simply dominated Cleveland in '97. In sixteen innings and two Baltimore triumphs over the Tribe, Mussina had allowed just three runs while striking out nineteen batters. He nearly made history in late May when he retired the first twenty-five Cleveland batters before Sandy Alomar broke up his bid for a perfect game with a single in the ninth. Not only was Mussina enjoying the finest season of his career, he clearly had the Indians' number. Thus, the home team had little margin for error when Mussina took the mound for Game Three of the ALCS.

Not surprisingly, Mussina's dominance would continue. Aided by the peculiar shadow patterns enveloping Jacobs Field in the autumn twilight, he struck out the side in the first inning, then again in the third and sixth. When Manny Ramirez whiffed to start the seventh, he represented Mussina's fifteenth strikeout. Through the first six innings, the Indians had managed just one hit, and the only runner to reach second did so on a Baltimore throwing error.

Luckily for the Tribe, veteran Orel Hershiser was matching Mussina clutch pitch for clutch pitch in what would be the final masterpiece performance of his stellar career. The Orioles could manage just two hits through the first six frames as Hershiser struck out six himself. The classic pitchers' duel toiled scoreless into the falling dusk until the Indians finally broke through in the seventh.

After Ramirez's leadoff strikeout, Jim Thome reached on Mussina's second walk of the afternoon and took second on Cleveland's first hit since the fourth inning, a single by David Justice which Baltimore center fielder Brady Anderson lost in the clouds. Veteran third baseman Matt Williams then delivered the first clutch hit of the day, pushing a single through the infield to center to score Thome and give the Indians a precious 1–0 lead. Cleveland relievers Assenmacher and Mike Jackson cruised through the eighth, and closer Jose Mesa was brought on for the ninth to close out the victory.

He hit instant turbulence when catcher Chris Hoiles knocked a single to right center. Jeff Reboulet substituted for Hoiles as a pinch runner and advanced to second on a groundout by pinch-hitter Jeffrey Hammonds. Mesa then got Indian-killer Anderson to send a soft fly to center for what appeared would be the critical second out. Tribe outfielder Marquis Grissom saw the ball clearly come off Anderson's bat but then lost it in the darkening sky—just as Anderson had done with Justice's hit in the seventh. It landed thirty feet behind a confused Grissom for a double, scoring Reboulet to tie the game and stun the capacity crowd ready to celebrate a hard-earned victory. Mesa rebounded to get Eric Davis to pop out, then struck out Rafael Palmeiro with the go-ahead run at second base, but the Orioles had been given new life. And even with Mussina out of the game, the Cleveland offense remained ineffective.

Ramirez led off the bottom of the ninth with a walk but was picked off first. The miscue proved to be immense when Thome followed with another walk and Williams hit a single that could have proved to be the game winner. Instead, with two down and the winning run at second, Sandy Alomar grounded out, and the game plunged into extra innings.

Both teams went down in order in the tenth, then squandered scoring opportunities in the eleventh. After obscure Cleveland reliever Jeff Juden struck out the first two batters in the eleventh, he walked Anderson, who then stole second and took third on an infield single by substitute catcher Lenny Webster. With the bases loaded, new pitcher Alvin Morman struck out Palmeiro on four pitches, and the game remained tied. The Indians blew an even better chance in the bottom of the inning when Omar Vizquel led off with a walk, then Ramirez hit a single to move him to second. On a wild pitch by Baltimore's Arthur Rhodes, Vizquel moved to third with nobody out, and the Tribe was again poised to win. Randy Myers replaced Rhodes and got pinch-hitter Kevin Seitzer to ground out to Cal Ripken at third, with Vizquel unable to score. Justice then hit a line drive to left, though right at the Orioles' B. J. Surhoff and not deep enough for Vizquel to tag up. After Williams walked, Alomar struck out swinging, and the marathon game would continue. "Like an old trash can put out on the curb for pickup," Bud Shaw would write of the contest, "it proved impossible to throw away."

Once again in the twelfth, Cleveland was presented a golden opportunity to win the game. Grissom, who was zero-for-four with four strikeouts, reached on a one-out walk, then motored into third on a single to right by second baseman Tony Fernandez. With Vizquel at the plate, the wheels began turning in Cleveland manager Mike Hargrove's head. "I started thinking squeeze right away," he said. "There are certain players you can do certain things with." With Vizquel, one of the best bunters in baseball, at the plate and a speedy runner at third in Grissom, the stage was set for perhaps the most exciting play in baseball: the suicide squeeze.

After falling behind 2-and-1, Myers wound up the fourth pitch. Grissom began running toward the plate, and it was up to Vizquel to bunt the ball into play and allow Grissom to score. The Cleveland shortstop framed himself to bunt when the unthinkable happened: Vizquel missed the ball. For an instant, it looked as though the Indians had blown yet another chance to win the game. With Grissom already halfway to the plate, all Lenny Webster had to do was catch the pitch, stand up, and tag out Grissom to end the threat.

But just as Vizquel failed to make contact, Webster failed to grab hold of the baseball. It glanced off his glove and rolled softly into the dirt beside home plate. Thinking Vizquel had made contact and it was simply a foul ball, Webster slowly stood up and made no effort to retrieve the baseball. At that moment, Grissom cruised across home plate and umpire John Hirschbeck threw his arms sideways to signal he was safe.

After four hours and fifty-one minutes, and day long since turned to night, the game was finally over, and the controversy began.

Technically, Grissom had stolen home on a passed ball. But Webster insisted that Vizquel had made contact, making the ball foul and dead, thereby ending the play. "He definitely tipped the ball and deflected it off my glove," Webster said. "I saw contact. I heard contact. When Hirschbeck gestured, I thought he meant it was a foul ball. That's why I didn't run after it." In fact, Hirschbeck gestured to indicate that Vizquel had offered at the pitch, therefore it was a strike.

Conversely, Vizquel was just as adamant that he hadn't made contact. "I never tipped it. You can feel it if you tip it," he said. "I was going to get ready to kill myself, then I saw Marquis cross the plate." As he did, pandemonium ensued. "Once I touched home plate and the guys came around me," said

Grissom, who hadn't forgotten his muffed play in the ninth, "I think I was the happiest man in the world, not just Cleveland."

Players, coaches, fans, and members of the media all tried to recall a game ending in such a fashion. No one could. Adding to the "believe-it-or-not" atmosphere, nine records were either tied or broken, including the most combined strikeouts in a postseason game (thirty-three) and most pitchers used in the longest game in league championship series history. Fittingly, it had an equally amazing ending. "That was craziness at its peak," said Cleveland second baseman Bip Roberts, a comment that covered not only the finish but the entire event.

"It's obvious by now that this team is touched by something not of this world," wrote Shaw, adding that the Indians' bizarre playoff run had now "bypassed phenomenal and gone straight to inexplicable phenomenon."

Orioles	0 0 0	0 0 0	0 0 1	0 0 0	=1
Indians	0 0 0	0 0 0	1 0 0	0 0 1	=2

BALTIMORE

	AB	R	H	RBI
Anderson cf	4	0	2	1
R. Alomar 2b	3	0	1	0
Davis rf	4	0	0	0
Webster c	1	0	1	0
Palmeiro 1b	5	0	1	0
Surhoff lf	5	0	0	0
Ripken 3b	5	0	0	0
Baines dh	1	0	1	0
Berroa ph-dh	3	0	1	0
Hoiles c	3	0	1	0
Reboulet pr-ss	2	1	0	0
Bordick ss	2	0	0	0
Hammonds ph-rf	2	0	0	0
TOTAL	40	1	8	1

	IP	H	R	ER	BB	SO
Mussina	7	3	1	1	2	15
Benitez	1	0	0	0	1	1
Orosco	⅔	0	0	0	1	1
Mills	⅓	1	0	0	0	0
Rhodes	1	1	0	0	1	2
Myers (L)	1⅓	1	1	0	2	2

CLEVELAND

	AB	R	H	RBI
Roberts 2b	3	0	0	0
Fernandez 2b	3	0	1	0
Vizquel ss	4	0	0	0
Ramirez rf	4	0	2	0
Thome 1b	1	1	0	0
Seitzer ph-1b	1	0	0	0
Justice dh	5	0	1	0
Williams 3b	4	0	2	1
S. Alomar c	5	0	0	0
Giles lf	5	0	0	0
Grissom cf	4	1	0	0
TOTAL	39	2	6	1

	IP	H	R	ER	BB	SO
Hershiser	7	4	0	0	1	7
Assenmacher	⅔	0	0	0	0	1
Jackson	⅓	0	0	0	0	0
Mesa	2	2	1	1	1	1
Juden	⅔	1	0	0	2	2
Morman	⅔	0	0	0	0	1
Plunk (W)	⅔	1	0	0	0	0

Attendance: 45,047

#21

INDIANS 1, CALIFORNIA ANGELS 0
MAY 30, 1977

Memorial Day

As Clevelanders gathered around grills and bonfires on Memorial Day evening to celebrate the arrival of summer, very few had their radios tuned in to the Indians game in the background. Though the season wasn't quite two months old, the Tribe was already in deep trouble, wandering in fifth place four games below .500 with tension seeping into the clubhouse. Manager Frank Robinson, whose debut had brought such promise two years before, was now under fire from the front office and would be dismissed before the season was complete. Five days after the first chapter of George Lucas's space opera *Star Wars* exploded into theaters across the nation as a symbol of hope and change, the Indians were desperately seeking a similarly dramatic event. As the three-day weekend came to a close that Monday night, they got it.

Robinson sent a promising young right-hander with a peculiar sidearm delivery named Dennis Eckersley to the mound to face the California Angels five days after a dazzling twelve-inning, five-hit, one-run performance in a win over the expansion Seattle Mariners during which the twenty-two-year-old hurler held Seattle scoreless for the final nine innings. Prior to the game, Eckersley didn't think he'd be anywhere close to as good as he was in his last start. "I didn't have very good stuff warming up in the bullpen," he said, "but I guess that's a good sign. When you warm up bad, you pitch good, and that's a good sign." He picked up where he left off the previous Wednesday, retiring the first two California batters before walking first baseman Tony Soliata. Eckersley rebounded to entice Joe Rudi into a flyout to end the inning. It was the closest the Angels would come to scoring on the night.

Cleveland provided all the offense its young pitcher would need in the bottom of the first when second baseman Duane Kuiper rifled a triple to center, then scored on a squeeze bunt by right fielder Jim Norris. California pitcher Frank Tanana, who was coming off a nineteen-win season in '76 and had already won eight games in the young 1977 season, would handcuff the Tribe for the remainder of the night, allowing only three hits after the first inning. Yet he would be dramatically overshadowed.

After the walk to Soliata, Eckersley retired the next nineteen batters. As the evening progressed, the miniscule crowd began to realize what was happening, that with each out Eckersley drew one step closer to the fourteenth no-hitter in Indians history. Even Eckersley noticed. "I had a real good feeling for a no-hitter along about the fifth inning," he said, "though I knew I needed a lot of luck. You always need luck to get a no-hitter. Then, along about the seventh inning, I started to get some chills." Trying to lighten the mood was Kuiper, who went against usual baseball custom and teased Eckersley about his quest for history all night until the pitcher finally yelled at him to shut up. Up in the radio booth, Tribe broadcasters Joe Tait and Herb Score were careful not to speak of the potential no-hitter. All they said was that no Angels had reached base.

As realization dawned and the pressure mounted, Eckersley maintained the same routine through each inning. He would return to the dugout and sit in the middle of the bench. He'd take off his cap and then get up and take a drink from the water fountain and spit it out. Then he'd return to the bench and put his cap back on. He did this eight times.

Just after Eckersley started getting his chills, he endured a spine-tingling moment in the eighth. Leadoff hitter Bobby Bonds ripped a 2–2 pitch down the line which appeared would sail over the fence for not only the history-shattering hit but also the game-tying home run. At the last moment, it hooked foul, and Eckersley was given new life. He came back to strike out Bonds, but the final pitch got by Cleveland catcher Ray Fosse and Bonds hustled down to first base. Tiring and his momentum now shattered, Eckersley had to face power-hitting designated hitter Don Baylor, still with just a one-run lead. Baylor slapped a grounder to short, where Frank Duffy scooped up the baseball, tossed to Kuiper at second for one out, then Kuiper fired on to Bruce Bochte at first for the second out on a close call. Energized, Eckersley whiffed third baseman Dave Chalk to end the inning and increase the pressure.

After Fosse flew out to Rudi to end the eighth, Eckersley took the field and waited for Rudi to toss him the ball. Seeing Eckersley and knowing what was at stake, Rudi decided to have a little fun. He smiled at the Cleveland pitcher, kissed the baseball, then flipped it to him. Eckersley shrugged off the good-natured hex attempt to strike out shortstop Bobby Grich to start the inning—his twelfth strikeout of the game. Pinch-hitter Willie Aikens was next, flying out to Paul Dade in left. Now Angels center fielder Gil Flores was all that stood between Eckersley and immortality. The crowd of 13,400 was on its feet roaring for one more out.

The first pitch missed for a ball, then Eckersley came back with back-to-back strikes to go ahead 1-and-2 and the tension became almost unbearable. As a stalling technique, Flores stepped out of the batter's box, and Eckersley yelled at him to get back in. On the fourth pitch, Flores started to swing, then tried to hold back as the ball fluttered out of the strike zone. He couldn't do it. Home-plate umpire Bill Deegan called Flores out, and the celebration began. Fosse raced to the mound, and Eckersley leaped into his arms as his teammates sprinted to mob him. "This is it," Eckersley would say later, "this is the max."

It would go down as one of the most dominating pitching performances in Cleveland history. Eckersley faced just twenty-eight batters, throwing 114 pitches—seventy-nine of which were strikes—each of which took an added meaning through the night. "The pressure builds with each pitch and each play," Robinson said in the jubilant locker room. "I feel sky-high, like I'm in outer space, like I'm in orbit." With a second straight dominating performance, Eckersley had now not allowed a run in more than eighteen innings and hadn't allowed a *hit* for the last 16⅔. Team president Ted Bonda and general manager Phil Seghi met Eckersley in the locker room and promised him a well-deserved $3,500 bonus, along with a $1,500 stipend for Fosse for calling the game.

Unfortunately, that Memorial Day would be the only true moment of glory Eckersley would achieve in a Cleveland uniform. With personal issues rising between potential stars Eckersley and center fielder Rick Manning (Eckersley's wife had left him for Manning), the Indians decided they had to trade one or the other. They chose to part with Eckersley, partly because the general consensus was that his awkward sideways delivery would lead to arm troubles and a shortened career. Days before the 1978 season began, Eckersley was dealt to Boston, where he won twenty games and led the Red Sox to the brink of the AL East title. After another impressive seventeen-win season in '79, it appeared the Indians' predictions would be correct, as Eckersley's victory totals dropped and he became little more than an effective inning-eater with the Red Sox and Chicago Cubs.

Yet his career took a dramatic turn in 1987 when the Cubs traded him to Oakland, where he was shifted to the bullpen. There he became arguably the greatest closer in the history of the game, four times racking up forty-plus saves in a season, including a record fifty-one in 1992 as he took home the Cy Young Award. He would finish his twenty-four-year, Hall-of-Fame career with 390 saves and 197 victories—the greatest of which came, appropriately enough, on Memorial Day.

Angels	0	0	0	0	0	0	0	0	0	=0
Indians	1	0	0	0	0	0	0	0	x	=1

CALIFORNIA

	AB	R	H	RBI
Flores cf	4	0	0	0
Remy 2b	3	0	0	0
Solaita 1b	2	0	0	0
Rudi lf	3	0	0	0
Bonds rf	3	0	0	0
Baylor dh	3	0	0	0
Chalk 3b	3	0	0	0
Grich ss	3	0	0	0
Humphrey c	2	0	0	0
Aikens ph	1	0	0	0
TOTAL	27	0	0	0

	IP	H	R	ER	BB	SO
Tanana (L)	8	5	1	1	1	6

CLEVELAND

	AB	R	H	RBI
Manning cf	3	0	0	0
Kuiper 2b	3	1	1	0
Norris rf	2	0	0	1
Carty dh	3	0	2	0
Bochte 1b	3	0	1	0
Blanks ss	3	0	0	0
Duffy ss	0	0	0	0
Bell 3b	2	0	0	0
Dade lf	3	0	1	0
Fosse c	3	0	0	0
TOTAL	25	1	5	1

	IP	H	R	ER	BB	SO
Eckersley (W)	9	0	0	0	1	12

Attendance: 13,400

#20

INDIANS 3, BROOKLYN DODGERS 0
OCTOBER 12, 1920

On the Baseball Map

It was a day that commemorated one of the most incredible moments in the history of the world. And on the 428th anniversary, that date would take on even more meaning for the citizens of Cleveland, Ohio. "The better the day," *Plain Dealer* sports editor Henry P. Edwards wrote, "the better the deed."

Like a teenager on his first date, the city had gone utterly bananas as its beloved Indians reached their first World Series in 1920, packing into League Park four consecutive days and creating a carnival atmosphere that surprised even longtime baseball dignitaries and reporters. The celebration grew with each day as the Indians won three consecutive games on their home field in the best-of-nine confrontation to wipe out a two-games-to-one Brooklyn advantage and pull within a victory of capturing their first championship. On Tuesday, October 12—Columbus Day—better than 27,000 fans filed through the turnstiles at League Park, hoping to witness history on another strangely hot autumn afternoon.

Already being treated as legends, several Cleveland players were showered with gifts prior to the game in appreciation for their on-field heroics. Elmer Smith, who had belted the first grand slam in World Series history in Game Five, was given an automobile. Another of those heroes was pitcher Stan Coveleski, a former Pennsylvania coal miner who had been almost unhittable in his first two appearances in the series, permitting just two runs in eighteen innings. Two days after a dominant performance in a Game Four victory, a tired Coveleski would return to the hill for Game Seven. It was a gamble on the part of Cleveland player/manager Tris Speaker, one that, if it failed, could have swung the series momentum back to Brooklyn. Yet in the early going,

Coveleski looked anything but fatigued, cruising through the first two innings without allowing a hit as the Cleveland offense settled in.

After the Dodgers put runners on first and second with one out in the third, thanks to a single and a Cleveland error, Coveleski and the Indians caught a break. Brooklyn third baseman Jack Sheehan ripped a grounder between first and second that was bound for right field and likely would have scored pitcher Burleigh Grimes from second. But the baseball hit Dodger shortstop Ivy Olson as he dashed toward second. By rule, the play was dead, Olson was out, and Grimes had to stop at third. Now with two down, right fielder Tommy Griffith flied out to right to end the inning. It was the only piece of luck Coveleski would need. He would retire the side in the fourth on a mere four pitches.

The game was still scoreless in the bottom of the fourth when Tribe third baseman Larry Gardner and first baseman Doc Johnston hit back-to-back one-out singles, Johnston's sending Gardner to third. Shortstop Joe Sewell then flied out, and Brooklyn was one out away from escaping the threat. But when Johnston broke to second on a delayed double steal, Grimes's throw went astray, allowing Gardner to scamper home from third to the delight of the ecstatic crowd.

The fireworks continued in the fifth when left fielder Charlie Jamieson reached on a one-out infield single, then stole second and scored when Speaker lined a two-out triple down the right-field line. After two more easy innings for Coveleski, he scored Cleveland's final run when he reached on a fielder's choice and scampered home on a Jamieson double. Appropriately, Coveleski breezed through the eighth. Then after giving up a one-out single to left fielder Zack Wheat, he enticed two straight ground balls to shortstop which Sewell flipped to Bill Wambsganss covering second. At 3:57 P.M., the Cleveland Indians became world champions, giving Cleveland its first title after forty-two professional baseball seasons. "It was a long time to wait," Edwards wrote, "but the prize was worth waiting for."

The capacity crowd also appreciated the historical significance of what it had just witnessed. Fans rushed the field and swarmed the players, Speaker in particular, and he dashed toward the clubhouse the instant the final out was recorded and fought his way through the crowd to avoid being mobbed. Women had tears in their eyes, including Speaker's mother, who was sitting in a private box with Indians owner James Dunn. Speaker eventually clawed his way back through the throng to the box and gave his mother a triumphant hug. Meanwhile, thousands of fans gathered around the box and finally trapped their beloved manager. In the next hour, Speaker would drain two fountain pens signing autographs. "It has been a long time Cleveland has been waiting for its first pennant-winner,"

Speaker said, "and I am happy that the honor was reserved for me and that I and my boys also were able to bring a world's championship here."

Moved by the moment, Dunn rose and began to speak. "I am the happiest man in the whole world today," he told the crowd. "I know you are happy, too. After all, it is your team; it is Cleveland's team more than it is mine. I thank you for your enthusiasm and for your loyalty." Shortly after, Brooklyn owner Charles Ebbets arrived at the box to congratulate Dunn, noting that the better team had indeed won. The *Plain Dealer*'s Frank Menke went a step further, saying the Indians had taken a good Brooklyn team "and battered it to a mushy pulp." Dodger manager Wilbert Robinson was equally frank: "No alibi to offer. A better ball team beat us—that's the story."

With a five-hit shutout, Coveleski had put the cap on one of the most incredible individual performances in World Series history: twenty-seven innings pitched, two runs allowed, three victories earned. "I guess I did look fairly good out there today," a humble Coveleski would say, "but I didn't feel much that way. My arm felt dead." Helping alleviate the problem, he would throw just ninety pitches for the day, sixty-nine for strikes. By comparison, Brooklyn's two pitchers combined to throw 135 pitches in eight innings.

A half hour after the game was over, better than 4,000 fans frolicked on East 66th Street, cheering and refusing to go home, hoping for one more glimpse at the players who had delivered such jubilation. A *Plain Dealer* editorial called for Columbus Day to be named a civic Cleveland holiday, linking Christopher Columbus's defining moment in 1492 with the Indians' in 1920. "Cleveland's baseball team has at last put Cleveland on the baseball map," it said, "and has writ her name so large that it will not soon be erased.

"Cleveland is altogether satisfied."

Dodgers	0	0	0	0	0	0	0	0	0	=0
Indians	0	0	0	1	1	0	1	0	x	=3

BROOKLYN

	AB	R	H	RBI
Olson ss	4	0	0	0
Sheehan 3b	4	0	1	0
Griffith rf	4	0	0	0
Wheat lf	4	0	2	0
Myers cf	4	0	0	0
Konetchy 1b	4	0	1	0
Kilduff 2b	3	0	0	0
Miller c	2	0	0	0
Lamar ph	1	0	0	0
Krueger c	0	0	0	0
Grimes p	2	0	1	0
Schmadt ph	1	0	0	0
Mamaux p	0	0	0	0
TOTAL	33	0	5	0

	IP	H	R	ER	BB	SO
Grimes (L)	7	7	3	2	4	2
Mamaux	1	0	0	0	0	1

CLEVELAND

	AB	R	H	RBI
Jamieson lf	4	1	2	1
Wambsganss 2b	4	0	1	0
Speaker cf	3	0	1	1
Smith rf	3	0	0	0
Gardner 3b	4	1	1	0
Johnston 1b	2	0	1	0
Sewell ss	4	0	0	0
O'Neill c	4	0	1	0
Coveleski p	3	1	0	0
TOTAL	31	3	7	2

	IP	H	R	ER	BB	SO
Coveleski (W)	9	5	0	0	0	1

Attendance: 27,525

#19

FLORIDA MARLINS 3, INDIANS 2 (11 INNINGS)
OCTOBER 26, 1997

October Nightmare

After twenty-six days of stomach-churning, nerve-rattling playoff games—and forty-nine frustrating years—the Cleveland Indians faced the most dramatic moment in franchise history.

Following a stunning Game Six victory that tied the 1997 World Series at three games apiece, they would face the Florida Marlins again, this time with one game to decide the world champion on a warm Sunday night in Miami. "The season, this wonderful, anxiety-laced, out-of-nowhere season, has come down to twenty-seven outs tonight in Pro Player Stadium," Paul Hoynes wrote.

After almost a month of endless nights watching tension-packed contests that dragged into the wee hours of the morning, then either rejoicing or coping with crushing defeat, win or lose in Game Seven, the city of Cleveland was on the verge of an emotional breakdown. Game Seven would mark the fourth time in three weeks a loss would end the Indians' season. They'd won the previous three, each in dramatic fashion. Accordingly, the Cleveland Free Clinic set up a "Togetherness Hotline" to take calls from Tribe fans on the brink of frenzy. "The Cleveland Indians' forty-nine-year quest for a championship is one of the longer running epics in baseball," wrote the *Plain Dealer*'s Joe Dirck, "and an epic, by definition, has to go the distance." This one would. And then some.

Adding an intriguing subplot to the already drama-filled showdown was Cleveland manager Mike Hargrove's decision to start twenty-one-year-old rookie pitcher Jaret Wright on three days' rest over established veteran Charles Nagy. While Nagy had struggled to maintain his consistency in the postseason, Wright caught fire, winning a pair of games over the Yankees in the Division Series, then another in Game Four of the Fall Classic. A cocky fireballer who had started the season with the double-A Akron Aeros and only four years removed from Katella High School in Anaheim, California, Wright would get a chance to etch his name in baseball history. "It's not the playoffs you dream about," Wright noted. "It's the seventh game of the World Series."

Plus, not only would the game be played on Hargrove's forty-eighth birthday, it would also mark the conclusion of a legendary career. It would be the final game for longtime radio broadcaster Herb Score. The silver-haired Cleveland icon who had followed the team through decades of miserable play in meaningless games would call his final game on baseball's most important stage.

With many fans sludging through the day after another late night, pastors and priests dedicated sermons to the Indians that morning, as thousands of Clevelanders prayed for the end of a drought of biblical proportions. At 7:55 that evening, millions were tuned in to their television sets to see if this was the night they'd been waiting their entire lives for.

Wright instantly got into trouble in the first, giving up a one-out double to shortstop Edgar Renteria, then walking Gary Sheffield. But the Cleveland youngster snapped back into form, getting first baseman Darren Daulton to ground into a double play to end the inning. Wright then cruised through the second and came through at the plate in the third, successfully sacrificing Jim Thome to third and Marquis Grissom to second after they'd reached base to start the inning. Omar Vizquel then popped up to shortstop for the second out, and Florida was on the brink of extinguishing the threat. Then Tony Fernandez, the veteran second baseman who'd joined the Indians in the offseason and played a crucial role all season, ripped a single to center field to score both Thome and Grissom. Fans back in Cleveland looked at one another in amazement—their team now had a two-run lead in the seventh game of the World Series. And a half century of heartbreak would now fall on the shoulders of a twenty-one-year-old kid.

Wright proved up to the task. Never dominating, he skillfully maneuvered out of tricky situations. After he walked a pair of Marlins in the third, he enticed Sheffield into an inning-ending pop-up. When Daulton reached third base on an error by Manny Ramirez with two out in the sixth, Wright retired Indian-killer Moises Alou on a fly out. Young enough and confident enough not to carry the weight of the franchise's many failures, Wright was writing himself into Cleveland lore.

Meanwhile, however, his offense was letting him down. Vizquel singled and stole second and third in the fifth, but Fernandez and David Justice both struck out, leaving Vizquel stranded in scoring position. Thome grounded into a rally-killing double play in the seventh but came through in the ninth when the Tribe had another perfect opportunity to add to its precarious lead.

Matt Williams led off with a walk, then was forced out on a fielder's-choice grounder by Sandy Alomar. Thome came through with a single to right that moved Alomar to third with one down, and with the versatile Grissom coming up, Cleveland manager Mike Hargrove considered attempting a squeeze bunt to bring Alomar home. Instead, Grissom hit a grounder to Renteria at shortstop, as Alomar bolted for the plate. Renteria threw to catcher Charles Johnson, who tagged out Alomar to spoil the opportunity. The Indians still had a chance to score with Thome at second, but pinch-hitter Brian Giles flied out to left to end the inning. Unable to pad the advantage, the Indians were still just three outs away from exorcising a half-century curse.

As he'd done regularly for three years, Hargrove turned to closer Jose Mesa to shut the door on the world championship. The Cleveland bullpen had been marvelous in both Game Six and Seven. When Wright tired in the seventh, allowing a leadoff homer by third baseman Bobby Bonilla, Paul Assenmacher came on to retire back-to-back hitters. Now leading 2–1, Mike Jackson retired the first two batters in the eighth, then Geneva, Ohio, product Brian Anderson got Jeff Conine to foul out, leaving everything to Mesa in the ninth. NBC staffers had erected a stage and podium in the Cleveland locker room in preparation for the victory celebration that was now just three outs away. Plastic sheets had been draped over the lockers to protect the contents from the champagne about to be sprayed. The championship trophy sat on a cart just outside the door. Then, as Vizquel would say later, "Weird things started to happen."

Florida caught a break when Alou blooped Mesa's third pitch into center for a leadoff single. With the tying run now on base, Mesa bounced back to strike out Bonilla, and the Indians were a double play away from a world title. Johnson stepped into the box for the critical at-bat of the inning. On a 1-and-2 count, Mesa shook off Alomar's call for a fastball, his strongest pitch, and tried to slip a slider past Johnson on the outside corner. He lined a single through the right side and Alou moved to third, ninety feet away from tying the contest. Fans back in Cleveland held their heads in their hands, knowing the conclusion their team was spiraling toward. Up stepped second baseman Craig Counsell, who lofted Mesa's third pitch to right, and, for a horrifying instant, it appeared as though the ball would sail over the fence to end the game. But Ramirez caught up with the ball and snared it just in front of the warning track for the second out, deep enough to allow Alou to score from third. The Marlins had tied the game and the sellout crowd at Pro Player Stadium roared. After Mesa (who had tallied his third blown save of the postseason) got Jim Eisenreich to ground out, for just the fourth time ever, the seventh game of the World Series plunged into extra innings.

The Indians' bats remained anemic. Florida closer Robb Nen struck out the side in the tenth. Then after Williams walked to lead off the eleventh, Alomar's sacrifice bunt was a dud, allowing pitcher Jay Powell to throw to second to retire Williams. The misery continued when Thome followed by grounding into a double play. The Indians had run out of chances and the tension was becoming unbearable. "Sitting on the bench," Wright said, "your stomach is churning and you feel like you're going to throw up."

Defensively, they managed to dodge a pair of bullets in the tenth. Center fielder Devon White led off with a low liner that bounced off Mesa's leg but caromed right to Vizquel, who threw him out. Renteria followed with a single to left, and Sheffield reached on an infield hit. Mesa rallied to strike out pinch-hitter John Cangelosi, then was replaced by Charles Nagy, who was originally supposed to start Game Seven and now made his first relief appearance in seven years. He got Alou to fly to right, and the threat was over. But there would be another.

As he did in the seventh, Bonilla led off successfully in the eleventh, sending an 0–2 pitch up the middle and into center field. Gregg Zaun popped out to Nagy on a bunt attempt for the first out, then Counsell hit a dribbling grounder toward second that Fernandez charged, thinking he'd be able to throw out the slow-footed Bonilla at second. Instead, the ball rolled beneath his glove and into the outfield, allowing Bonilla to motor into third. It turned the tide of the inning. "That's a play any second baseman should make," Fernandez would say later. "I won't make an excuse. I just missed the ball."

With the entire sports world now hanging breathlessly on each pitch, Eisenreich was walked intentionally to load the bases and set up a force at each bag. "You guys have no idea," Vizquel later told reporters, "to be in the seventh game of the World Series, what it's like to be on the field, with guys on base. You prepare yourself, you dream about it, but there's no way you can know what we feel to feel it slipping away." White hit a grounder to second, which Fernandez handled this time, and threw to Alomar to get the force at the plate. The Indians were now one out away from escaping the inning and getting another chance at salvaging what had become a nightmare. But on Nagy's second pitch, Renteria hit a soft liner that floated just above Nagy's glove and dribbled into center field. Counsell sprinted home from third and leaped into home plate. At 12:06 Monday morning, the Florida Marlins were world champions, and the Indians had suffered the most heartbreaking loss in team history.

The stage and podium were quickly dismantled. The plastic sheets were taken off the lockers. The trophy was wheeled to the other side of the stadium. "I can't tell you how disappointed I am," Hargrove said. "You only get these chances so many times. But I'm proud of my players. No one gave us a chance to be here."

"After they tied it up," Vizquel said, "everything was a nightmare. Every pitch. Every ball that was hit. It's hard to believe."

While the entire October run had been a wildly unexpected surprise, the good times were dramatically overshadowed by the climax. "Not even reaching the World Series on a season of charms makes up for this disappointment," Bill Livingston wrote. Adding insult to injury, the long-suffering Indians had lost to a proverbial toddler—the Marlins were only in their fifth season of existence and had never even posted a winning record prior to 1997. "This is harder to take than in 1995, absolutely," Thome said, "because we had that game won and we were destined to win." Grissom echoed the statement: "I could see if we got flat-out beat by a better team, but we had the opportunities to get it done."

The longest day in Tribe history ended at 4:30 A.M. when the team landed back in Cleveland and was welcomed by a huge crowd that had braved rainy and windy conditions to express the city's appreciation. Though the ending would provide scars that even time couldn't heal, the Indians had given their fans an ethereal experience, capped by one of the most memorable World Series games ever played.

"That was a great ballgame," Hargrove said, "and I don't think we have anything to be ashamed of."

Indians	0 0 2	0 0 0	0 0 0	0 0	=2
Marlins	0 0 0	0 0 0	1 0 1	0 1	=3

CLEVELAND

	AB	R	H	RBI
Vizquel ss	5	0	1	0
Fernandez 2b	5	0	2	2
Ramirez rf	3	0	0	0
Justice lf	5	0	0	0
Williams 3b	2	0	0	0
Alomar c	5	0	1	0
Thome 1b	4	1	1	0
Grissom cf	4	1	1	0
Wright p	2	0	0	0
Assenmacher p	0	0	0	0
Jackson p	0	0	0	0
Anderson p	0	0	0	0
Giles ph	1	0	0	0
Mesa p	0	0	0	0
Nagy p	0	0	0	0
TOTAL	36	2	6	2

	IP	H	R	ER	BB	SO
Wright	6⅓	2	1	1	5	7
Assenmacher	⅔	0	0	0	0	1
Jackson	⅔	0	0	0	0	1
Anderson	⅓	0	0	0	0	0
Mesa	1⅔	4	1	1	0	2
Nagy (L)	1	2	1	0	1	0

FLORIDA

	AB	R	H	RBI
White cf	6	0	0	0
Renteria ss	5	0	3	1
Sheffield rf	4	0	1	0
Daulton 1b	3	0	0	0
Conine ph-1b	1	0	0	0
Nen p	0	0	0	0
Cangelosi ph	1	0	0	0
Powell p	0	0	0	0
Alou lf	5	1	1	0
Bonilla 3b	5	1	2	1
Johnson c	4	0	1	0
Zaun pr-c	1	0	0	0
Counsell 2b	3	1	0	1
Leiter p	0	0	0	0
Cook p	0	0	0	0
Floyd ph	0	0	0	0
Abbott ph	1	0	0	0
Alfonseca p	0	0	0	0
Heredia p	0	0	0	0
Eisenreich 1b	1	0	0	0
TOTAL	40	3	8	3

	IP	H	R	ER	BB	SO
Leiter	6	4	2	2	4	7
Cook	1	0	0	0	0	2
Alfonseca	1⅓	0	0	0	1	1
Heredia	0	1	0	0	0	0
Nen	1⅔	1	0	0	0	3
Powell (W)	1	0	0	0	1	0

Attendance: 67,204

#18

GUARDIANS 7, DETROIT TIGERS 3
OCTOBER 12, 2024

The Biggest Swing in the Biggest Moment

Do or die. Winner take all. No tomorrow.

Pick the cliché you like. The Guardians' entire 2024 season hung in the balance on a sunshiny October Saturday in downtown Cleveland as they faced the Detroit Tigers in the decisive Game Five of the American League Division Series.

While the Guardians certainly entered the game with high hopes, they also brought with them a sense of genuine appreciation—bordering on sheer wonder—to have even made it this far. After finishing ten games below .500 the year before, the team had charged out of the starting gate under first-year manager Stephen Vogt. They won eight of their first ten games and never looked back, surging to a nine-game lead in the American League Central Division and then holding on through the second half of the season to capture the division crown.

Yet after a 7–0 blowout win over Detroit in the first game of the best-of-five series, Cleveland went cold. It failed to score a run in the next two games as the Tigers surged into control. And indeed, Detroit crept to within seven outs of advancing to the league championship series when it took a 3–2 lead into the seventh inning of Game Four. Cleveland slugger David Fry flipped the script with a clutch two-run homer that put the Guardians ahead and paved the way for a narrow victory to force a return trip to Cleveland, where the teams would play one more game for all the marbles.

While the Guardians would have the home-field advantage, they'd also have to overcome some troubling recent history. They hadn't won a winner-take-all postseason game in twenty-seven years, losing eight straight, including four in their own ballpark.

Even more discouraging for Cleveland, the Tigers had an ace up their sleeve. Taking the mound for Game Five would be star pitcher Tarik Skubal, who'd won eighteen games during the season on his way to the American League Cy Young Award. He'd also muzzled the Cleveland bats in Game Two five days earlier, holding the Guards scoreless with only three hits in seven innings in a 3–0 Detroit victory. To be fair, it wasn't just the Guardians who couldn't touch Skubal. He hadn't allowed a run in thirteen innings in the 2024 postseason, a scoreless string that, including the final weeks of the regular season, stretched to a whopping twenty-four innings.

The Guardians entered the game expecting runs to be at a premium, and as expected, neither team scored through the first four innings. Cleveland had a chance to get on the board in the third when a single, an error, and an intentional walk of star third baseman José Ramírez loaded the bases. But cleanup hitter Lane Thomas, looking for an offspeed pitch from Skubal, popped up a fastball for the third out.

When Detroit scratched out a single run in the top of the fifth, it felt like a much deeper hole for Cleveland. But in the bottom of the inning, everything changed.

Taking what they could get off Skubal, second baseman Andrés Giménez, left fielder Steven Kwan, and Fry all poked singles to load the bases with one out. It brought up Ramírez, who was hit on the left hand by Skubal's second pitch, which sent him to first and drove home Giménez to tie the game. With the home crowd now ignited, Thomas stepped to the plate for the second time. Acquired by Cleveland at the trading deadline two months earlier, Thomas initially struggled, getting just four hits in his first fifty-five at-bats in a Cleveland uniform. But he'd caught fire in September, hitting seven homers and driving in twenty runs in helping the Guards secure the division crown. As notable as Thomas's late-season performance had been, it would all be overshadowed by his next swing.

Skubal's first pitch was a 97 miles-per-hour fastball, and this time, Thomas was ready for it. He catapulted the ball to deep center field. With the already buzzing crowd swelling to crescendo, it cleared the outfield wall. At 2:48 P.M. on that Saturday afternoon, the Guardians suddenly had a 5–1 lead, and Progressive Field literally shook in the aftermath of one of the most dramatic moments in team history.

The more granular details made the whole thing seem even more surreal. It was the first hit Thomas had ever gotten off Skubal, while also snapping Skubal's scoreless string at twenty-eight innings and marked the first home run he'd allowed in thirty-two. It was also the first grand slam Skubal had ever allowed at any level of his professional career and perhaps the last thing anyone would have predicted.

"You dream of at-bats like that as a little kid," Thomas would say later.

For as dream-like as the moment was, nothing was won yet, and there was still plenty of baseball left to play.

The Tigers fought back—plating a run in each of their next two at-bats to cut the margin to 5–3—and were poised to inch even closer with a runner on second and just one out in the seventh. Cleveland relief pitcher Eli Morgan entered the game and promptly struck out the next two batters to quell the threat. In the bottom of the frame, Thomas came through again, slicing an infield single that scored another run, and an inning later, Brayan Rocchio did the same with an RBI hit to center to extend Cleveland's lead to a much more comfortable 7–3.

Closer Emmanuel Clase, who'd struggled in the series after a dominant regular season, was called upon in the eighth. After allowing runs in both of his previous appearances in the playoffs, he cruised through the final two innings, retiring all six batters he faced. And fittingly, with two out in the ninth, Detroit's Colt Keith hit a ground ball to first baseman Josh Naylor, who fielded it and flipped the ball to Clase covering first to close out the victory.

The players piled out of the dugout to celebrate on the field as the fans soaked in a long-awaited triumph. For the first time in nearly three decades, Cleveland had won a decisive postseason contest by coming up big when it mattered most.

"They only had opportunities in three or four innings," Detroit manager A. J. Hinch said afterward. "We had them in seven or eight. But they got the biggest swing in the biggest moment with the most at stake."

Tigers	0 0 0	0 1 1	1 0 0	=3
Guardians	0 0 0	0 5 0	1 1 X	=7

DETROIT

	AB	R	H	RBI
Malloy dh	1	0	0	0
Carpenter ph-dh	3	0	1	1
Vierling 3b	5	0	0	0
Greene lf	4	1	1	0
Ibañez 2b	1	0	0	0
Keith ph-2b	4	0	1	1
Pérez rf	4	0	0	0
Torkelson 1b	4	1	2	0
Meadows cf	1	0	1	0
Rogers c	4	0	1	1
Sweeney ss	2	1	0	0
TOTAL	33	3	7	3

	IP	H	R	ER	BB	SO
Skubal (L)	6	6	5	5	1	6
Vest	⅓	3	1	1	0	1
Holton	1⅓	2	1	1	0	3
Brieske	⅓	0	0	0	0	0

CLEVELAND

	AB	R	H	RBI
Kwan lf	5	2	3	0
Fry dh	5	1	1	0
Ramírez 3b	2	1	1	1
Thomas cf	4	1	2	5
Naylor 1b	4	0	0	0
Noel rf	4	0	0	0
Naylor c	3	0	0	0
Hedges c	1	0	0	0
Giménez 2b	4	2	2	0
Rocchio ss	4	0	2	1
TOTAL	36	7	11	7

	IP	H	R	ER	BB	SO
Boyd	2	1	0	0	1	5
Smith	1⅔	1	0	0	0	3
Sabrowski	⅓	0	0	0	1	0
Walters	⅓	1	1	1	1	1
Herrin (W)	1⅓	1	1	1	1	1
Gaddis	⅔	3	1	1	1	2
Morgan	⅔	0	0	0	1	2
Clase (Sv)	2	0	0	0	0	2

Attendance: 34,105

#17

BLUES 14, WASHINGTON SENATORS 13
MAY 23, 1901

Never Too Late to Win

Cleveland's birth into the brand-new American League had been loaded with complications. Over the first month of the inaugural season in 1901, the Blues (cleverly named because of the hue of their uniforms) had established themselves as the worst team in the league, starting with a miserable 8–2 loss to Chicago on opening day and echoed by an eleven-game losing streak in mid-May. After squeaking out a 6–5 win over a solid Washington team on May 22, the Blues still held the worst record in baseball at 7–18, ten games behind front-running Detroit.

While the first four weeks in franchise history had been decidedly uninspiring, the Blues were poised to deliver what would stand for the next century and beyond as one of the most incredible finishes ever seen in baseball.

For much of that afternoon at League Park, Cleveland followed a painfully familiar script. The Senators surged to a 5–0 lead in the second inning, then stretched it to a nine-run margin in the fifth. The Blues showed signs of life when they plated four runs in the bottom of the frame, but it already seemed a lost cause, particularly when Washington tacked on three more runs to start the seventh and another pair in the ninth to make it 13–5. Much of the modest crowd of just over 1,200 had long since departed, and those who stayed did so primarily to jeer their embarrassing home team. Cleveland had added a run in the eighth, but the effort seemed almost comical at this point. Going into their final at-bat, the Blues were bound for yet another humiliating defeat.

Cleveland pitcher Bill Hoffer, who had been rocked for much of the game, led off the final frame by striking out, then Ollie Pickering grounded out to pull the Senators within one out of victory. The remaining fans gathered up their coats and belongings and began to head toward the exits, mumbling about the incredible ineptitude of their new team. Few took notice when left fielder Jack McCarthy delayed the inevitable with a single to right, or when third baseman Bill Bradley followed that up with another hit. The *Plain Dealer* would note, "The opinion was that the players were only trying to help their batting averages."

The Blues were down to their final strike when first bagger Candy LaChance quickly fell behind in the count but then lined a single to center to score McCarthy. The crowd cheered sardonically. But when catcher Bob Wood was hit by a pitch from Washington's Casey Patten to load the bases, suddenly the atmosphere began to shift. Something was happening.

Still just one out away from victory, Washington couldn't shut the door. Cleveland shortstop Frank Scheibeck ripped a double to score two runs, then center fielder Frank Genins brought home two more with a single. While the miniscule crowd was now actively participating and the Blues had come through on six consecutive at-bats to score five runs, the deficit was still imposing at 13–10, and there were still two out. Patten was removed for Watty Lee, who promptly walked Truck Eagan. Pinch-hitter Erve Beck batted for Hoffer, now representing the tying run, and continued the unlikely hit parade with another double to score both Genins and Egan and make the score 13–12. Up stepped Pickering, who'd made the second out of the inning on a groundout what seemed like hours before. This time, Pickering knocked a single to score Beck and tie the game. "By this time," the *PD* reported, "the audience gave a life-sized picture of pandemonium out for recess."

Everything within fans' reach was tossed jubilantly into the air—hats, umbrellas, canes, seat cushions. A few rowdy spectators even spilled out onto the field, forcing play to be interrupted. Once order had been restored, Pickering took second on a passed ball. Then, after perhaps the most bizarre string of at-bats in the history of the game, the inevitable occurred. McCarthy stroked a single to left, and Pickering raced around third and across the plate to win the game. The premature celebration moments before paled to the massive display that followed inside League Park after Pickering scored. Fans stormed the field again, mobbing players and trying to convince themselves to believe what had just happened. "The demonstration that followed may be imagined," the *Plain Dealer* declared, "it cannot be described."

Down by eight runs in the ninth inning, the Blues had put together a rally for the ages to win, 14–13. Ten consecutive Cleveland batters reached base: eight hits, one walk, one hit by pitch, nine runs—all with two out. The *PD* headline the next day said it all: "Never Too Late To Win."

"Never in the history of the national game has there been a more sensational finish than the one that the Cleveland team made yesterday," the paper reported. "It was a case of hopeless defeat turned into glorious history."

Senators	0	5	0	1	3	0	2	0	2	=13
Blues	0	0	0	0	4	0	0	1	9	=14

WASHINGTON

	AB	R	H	RBI
Farrell cf	6	1	1	3
Dungan rf	4	0	1	2
Quinn 2b	5	1	2	0
Foster lf	5	1	3	0
Everett 1b	3	1	0	0
Grady c	4	2	2	1
Clingman ss	4	2	2	0
Coughlin 3b	3	3	2	2
Patten p	4	2	2	3
Lee p	0	0	0	0
TOTAL	38	13	14	11

	IP	H	R	BB	SO
Patten	8⅔	16	11	2	2
Lee (L)	0	3	3	1	0

CLEVELAND

	AB	R	H	RBI
Pickering rf	6	1	1	1
McCarthy lf	5	2	2	1
Bradley 3b	5	2	4	1
LaChance 1b	5	1	3	2
Wood c	4	1	1	0
Scheibeck ss	5	2	4	4
Genins cf	4	1	1	1
Eagan 2b	4	2	1	0
Hoffer p	4	1	1	1
Beck ph	1	1	1	2
TOTAL	43	14	19	13

	IP	H	R	BB	SO
Hoffer (W)	9	14	13	3	0

Attendance: 1,250

#16

INDIANS 4, NEW YORK YANKEES 3
OCTOBER 6, 1997

Take That, New York!

Jose Mesa had been here before.

Ninth inning, two outs, Indians clinging to a one-run lead. Runner on second and the opposition's best hitter at the plate. With an out, Cleveland would close out the game and move on. A hit and the game would continue.

One year and one day earlier, Mesa had stood in this identical spot facing the same situation and had surrendered a two-strike single to Baltimore's Roberto Alomar that scored a run and tied Game Four of the American League Division Series. From the cusp of victory, the Indians toiled into extra innings, where Alomar twisted the knife with a twelfth-inning homer that ended Cleveland's season.

The painful memory hung like a specter over Jacobs Field on this warm autumn evening with the clock ticking toward midnight as Mesa took the mound looking to exorcize his ghost. Considering the events of the previous twenty-four hours, such a symbolic fate seemed only appropriate.

Cleveland's upstart Indians had gone from the very brink of elimination to the verge of one of the all-time highs in franchise history. After rallying from a deficit in the eighth inning for a walk-off victory in Game Four of their best-of-five Division Series with New York, the Tribe had extended its season by one more night. With another win the following evening, the Indians could eliminate the defending world champions, move on to the American League Championship Series, and lift the hearts of every Clevelander.

The momentum of Sunday night's miracle carried over to Monday. Twenty-one-year-old Jaret Wright, who the previous October had been pitching in the Florida Instructional League, took the mound knowing a typical rookie performance would end the Indians' season. Pitching on three days' rest for the first time, it looked like he might be in for a rough night when he allowed a leadoff single by left fielder Tim Raines, who then promptly stole second and moved to third on a groundout. Now facing the heart of the Yankee order with two out, Wright walked cleanup hitter Bernie Williams on four pitches but then got first baseman Tino Martinez to pop out to get out of the inning. Wright allowed another leadoff single in the second but enticed third baseman Charlie Hayes into a double play to end the threat. He then struck out Williams with a runner on to end the third. The brash rookie—who'd mentally prepared for the game by watching *Saved by the Bell* in the clubhouse—was clearly not intimidated by his surroundings. And he was about to get some help.

Back-to-back one-out singles by Marquis Grissom and Bip Roberts started the ball rolling in the bottom of the third. After Omar Vizquel grounded into a fielder's choice for the second out, Cleveland's wily shortstop stole second, setting the table for Manny Ramirez. Hitless in his previous thirteen at-bats, Ramirez blasted Andy Pettitte's third pitch to center, where it bounced off the warning track and over the wall for a ground-rule double to score Grissom and Vizquel. Matt Williams followed by ripping a single to left to score Ramirez from second to make it 3–0, and the capacity crowd was rocking.

The magic continued in the fourth when Sandy Alomar led off with a double to center. The incredibly unlikely sight of beefy power hitter Jim Thome bunting would follow, and, though it marked just the second sacrifice of his career, Thome looked like an old pro, casually advancing Alomar to third. Tony Fernandez then sent a line drive to right to score Alomar and give Cleveland a 4–0 lead. A blowout appeared imminent, but for the rest of the night the Indians would cling to the lead by their fingernails.

Aided by two Cleveland errors, New York cut the lead in half in the fifth on a two-out, two-run single by Bernie Williams; then a leadoff double by designated hitter Mike Stanley in the sixth led to another run to make it 4–3. With Pettitte settled, the Cleveland bats fell silent, at one point going through thirteen consecutive batters without recording a hit. Meanwhile, the Yankees kept creeping. Shortstop Derek Jeter led off the seventh with a single and appeared headed for third when Paul O'Neill ripped a grounder toward right field. Yet for the second time on the night, Thome came through with an uncharacteristic play, diving to his right to snare the grounder and, lying on his chest, threw out Jeter at second. Relief pitcher Paul Assenmacher then got Bernie Williams to bounce into an inning-ending double play. New York would threaten again in the eighth when back-to-back two-out singles put runners on the corners. Mesa, called on early, got Jorge Posada to ground out to end the inning, and it all came down to the ninth.

With the fans on their feet and on the brink of a mass nervous breakdown, Mesa recorded two outs on three pitches as Raines grounded out to second and Jeter rolled another to third. One out away from elimination, O'Neill rifled Mesa's first pitch to right center. On contact, Mesa grimaced, thinking the ball would leave the park. It came three feet short, bouncing high off the outfield wall and caroming back into play, where Grissom snared it with his bare hand and fired a perfect throw back to the infield. The ball and a sliding O'Neill arrived at second at the same instant, and O'Neill was safe, though the hard landing from his kamikaze head-first slide knocked him out of the game. With pinch-runner Scott Pose now representing the tying run, Mesa would face Bernie Williams with familiar stakes—the entire season hanging in the balance.

The suspense didn't last long. Williams hit Mesa's first pitch—just his fifth in the inning—to left field, where Brian Giles motored beneath it. It settled into his glove and Jacobs Field erupted. Fans embraced one another as Mesa's teammates piled atop him in the infield, his failure of 366 days earlier now forgotten. After one thousand losses and seventy-five years of being overshadowed, the Indians had finally proved themselves better than the Yankees—and done so dramatically.

It was a night filled with stars. Ramirez snapped his slump to knock in two runs and score another. Thome twice sacrificed himself for the good of the team. The beleaguered Indians bullpen didn't allow a run in three-plus innings. But the brightest of them all was Wright, who'd allowed two earned runs and struck out five in 5⅓ innings for his second win of the series. "I don't care if he's twenty-one or thirty-one, if he's pitching for two months or ten years," said Cleveland's Kevin Seitzer. "What he did in this series was unbelievable."

That disbelief carried into the streets of downtown Cleveland in a massive celebration. The hated Yankees, who had publically proclaimed their preference to play the Indians in the first round of the playoffs, had been conquered by their long-suffering rival. The jubilantly screaming headline of Tuesday's *Plain Dealer* captured the surprise and poetic justice in four small words: "Take That, New York!"

Yankees	0 0 0	0 2 1	0 0 0	=3
Indians	0 0 3	1 0 0	0 0 x	=4

NEW YORK

	AB	R	H	RBI
Raines lf	4	1	1	0
Jeter ss	5	0	1	0
O'Neill rf	4	1	2	0
Pose pr	0	0	0	0
B. Williams cf	4	0	1	1
Martinez 1b	4	0	0	0
Stanley dh	4	1	3	0
Hayes 3b-2b	4	0	2	0
Fox pr-2b	0	0	0	0
Girardi c	2	0	0	0
Boggs ph-3b	2	0	2	1
Sanchez 2b	2	0	0	0
Posada ph-c	2	0	0	0
TOTAL	37	3	12	2

	IP	H	R	ER	BB	SO
Pettitte (L)	6⅔	6	4	4	0	2
Nelson	1	1	0	0	1	0
Stanton	⅓	0	0	0	0	1

CLEVELAND

	AB	R	H	RBI
Roberts lf	3	0	2	0
Giles lf	1	0	0	0
Vizquel ss	3	1	1	0
Ramirez rf	4	1	1	2
M. Williams 3b	3	0	1	1
Justice dh	4	0	0	0
Alomar c	3	1	1	0
Thome 1b	2	0	0	0
Fernandez 2b	2	0	0	1
Grissom cf	3	1	1	0
TOTAL	28	4	7	4

	IP	H	R	ER	BB	SO
Wright (W)	5⅓	8	3	2	3	5
Jackson	⅔	1	0	0	0	1
Assenmacher	1⅓	0	0	0	0	0
Mesa (Sv)	1⅔	3	0	0	0	1

Attendance: 45,203

#15

NAPS 1, CHICAGO WHITE SOX 0
OCTOBER 2, 1908

Battle of Aces

"The decks are now cleared for the greatest baseball battle in the history of the American League."

So declared the *Plain Dealer* on the first day of October 1908. And though the American League was a mere seven years old at the time, that fall's AL pennant race would stand as one of the finest through the century and well into the next. With six games to play, the Cleveland Naps trailed the Detroit Tigers by a half game, four-hundredths of a percentage point. The Chicago White Sox were right behind in third, a game back of Cleveland, with the St. Louis Browns still mathematically alive in fourth. Incredibly, the quartet of contenders would square off in the final two series of the season, with the Naps facing the White Sox twice at League Park and then the Browns in a crucial four-game set at Sportsman's Park in St. Louis. With all four teams gunning for the flag, nothing would come easy over the season's final five days. "Games?" Henry Edwards wrote. "No—battles, strenuous combats in which the contesting teams will figuratively fight to the last pitch."

To begin this stirring final stanza, Cleveland and Chicago would enact perhaps the finest pitchers' duel in baseball history.

Fans who filed into League Park on that Friday afternoon certainly weren't expecting a slugfest. While Chicago would send eventual forty-game winner Ed Walsh to the mound as he wrapped up one of the game's most amazing individual campaigns, Naps player/manager Napoleon Lajoie handed the ball to veteran Addie Joss, who'd posted his fourth consecutive twenty-win season, three times posting an ERA under two. For as dominant as Walsh had been all year, he'd struggled against the scrappy Naps, losing four of seven decisions, including three defeats to Joss, who'd gone 5–1 against Chicago in

'08. Anticipating a close game that might toil into extra innings, Cleveland team officials moved the starting time up thirty minutes from its usual 3 P.M. standard to prevent the game from being called on account of darkness. While the game was indeed close, it did not last long.

With a crowd of better than 10,000 hanging on each pitch, Joss set the tone early, setting down the Sox in order in the first. Walsh came out equally dominant, striking out Cleveland hitters with a vengeance. With both pitchers absolutely dominating, it was clear in the opening frames that the game would be won by whoever caught the first break. And the game's first and only break went to the home team.

Cleveland left fielder Joe Birmingham led off the bottom of the third with a bloop single, but it appeared for naught when the White Sox caught him in a potential rundown when he dashed for second just as Walsh threw to first. The ensuing throw to second hit Birmingham in the head and the ball rolled into center field, allowing him to motor into third. With the crowd buzzing, anticipating the Naps taking the lead, Walsh buckled down. Shortstop George Perring grounded out, keeping Birmingham at third, then Joss struck out. With right fielder Wilbur Good coming up, it appeared Walsh might wiggle out of the jam, especially when he picked up two quick strikes. Then he fired a wild pitch past catcher Ossee Schreckengost, and Birmingham scampered home to give Cleveland a 1–0 lead. From then on, the game became a simple battle between two men: Joss vs. Walsh.

While not as dominating as Walsh in terms of strikeouts, Joss was aided by some spectacular defense. Lajoie, playing with a nasty cold he'd caught working out in the rain the day before, played the game of his life in the field, while Joss helped his own cause in the fifth when he fielded a Freddy Parent grounder near third and whirled to throw him out. As he took the field in the seventh inning, Joss suddenly realized what many in the crowd had already noticed: not a single Chicago batter had reached base. Joss was pitching a perfect game—long before the term had even been coined. "No one on the bench dared breathe a word to that effect," the pitcher would say later. "Had he done so, he would have been chased to the clubhouse."

His date with destiny appeared ready to waver with one out in the seventh when he fell behind Fielder Jones 3-and-1, but he came back to fire two strikes past the Chicago center fielder to maintain the clean slate. A groundout and two fly outs got Joss through the eighth, setting up the climactic final frame. Hanging on for a critical win in a spine-tingling pennant race was enough cause for excitement, but Joss was on the threshold of a much loftier accomplishment.

Doc White started the inning with a grounder to Lajoie at shortstop—the manager's tenth play in the field on the afternoon. Up next was Jiggs Donohue, and Joss recorded just his third strikeout of the game. With the crowd eerily silent, both appreciating and adding to the tension, White Sox pinch-hitter John Anderson stepped into the box, batting for Walsh. He ripped a line drive down the left-field line that landed inches foul, and the Naps and their fans let out a collective sigh of relief. With two strikes on him, Anderson then sent a sharp grounder to third, where Bill Bradley scooped up the first ball hit to him all day. He fired across to George Stovall at first, but the ball bounced before getting there. Stovall scooped it up and umpire Silk O'Loughlin called Anderson out. Despite wild protests by the White Sox, who claimed Anderson had not only beaten the throw, but that Stovall hadn't had control of the baseball, the call stood, securing the Naps' 1–0 victory. More importantly, it completed just the third perfect game in the three-decade history of organized baseball.

Fans rushed onto the field and pursued Joss, hoping to carry him to the clubhouse. The cautious Joss bolted away. "I am taking no chances," he said. "Suppose they had let me drop. The season is not over yet." Outside League Park, fans rejoiced with a pennant-clinching fervor and started their journeys home with a bounce in their step. "Three great sets of emotions filled the hearts of Cleveland people yesterday," the *PD* boldly declared. "Cleveland won the game. Joss pitched a no-hit game. Cleveland will win the pennant." The paper's excitement carried over to its front-page headline: "Cleveland Fans See Greatest Game in History of Big League Baseball."

"All the people who lived within a radius of ten blocks of East 66th Street and Lexington Avenue knew that Cleveland had won," the paper noted, "and ran out—nursemaids, janitors, grocers, housewives, saloon keepers, doctors, lawyers, ministers, children—all ran out to ask the score from the first man who passed with a smile."

One man who wasn't smiling was Walsh, who had put forth an incredible effort only to go down in history as a footnote. He'd allowed just one run on four hits and struck out a whopping fifteen, setting a new record. "Walsh was pitching the game of his life," Joss said afterward. "I never saw him have so much." Walsh was equally impressed with his counterpart. "Yes, I pitched a fairly good game myself," he said, "but Joss pitched better." The difference in the game was a wild pitch that "may have won a pennant for Cleveland," the *Plain Dealer* suggested. "There is no telling."

Yet the pennant was decided by an even wilder pitch.

With a chance to see their team leapfrog the Tigers, Cleveland fans were greeted with disappointing news that evening as Detroit had rallied for a ninth-inning victory over St. Louis that kept the Tigers a few meager percentage points up on the Naps. Chicago would bounce back the following afternoon for a 3–2 victory that, combined with another Tiger win, dropped Cleveland a game and a half out of first. A tie game called because of darkness in St. Louis on Sunday followed by a 3–1 loss to the Browns the following afternoon doomed the Naps, who finished a half game back of Detroit, which played one less game than the Naps.

Though the pennant drive would prove for naught, Joss's unforgettable performance would be remembered. He would go down in history as one of the great tragedies of baseball, dying of tubercular meningitis at the age of thirty-one after winning 160 games in nine seasons with a career 1.89 ERA. And he was never better than on a Friday afternoon at League Park, when he took part in the ultimate battle of aces.

White Sox	0	0	0	0	0	0	0	0	0	=0
Naps	0	0	0	1	0	0	0	0	x	=1

CHICAGO

	AB	R	H	RBI
Hahn rf	3	0	0	0
Jones cf	3	0	0	0
Isbell 1b	3	0	0	0
Dougherty lf	3	0	0	0
Davis 2b	3	0	0	0
Parent ss	3	0	0	0
Schreckengost c	2	0	0	0
Shaw c	0	0	0	0
White ph	1	0	0	0
Tannehill 3b	2	0	0	0
Donahue ph	1	0	0	0
Walsh p	2	0	0	0
Anderson ph	1	0	0	0
TOTAL	27	0	0	0

	IP	H	R	BB	SO
Walsh (L)	8	4	1	1	15

CLEVELAND

	AB	R	H	RBI
Good rf	4	0	0	0
Bradley 3b	4	0	0	0
Hinchman lf	3	0	0	0
Lajoie 2b	3	0	1	0
Stovall 1b	3	0	0	0
Clarke c	3	0	0	0
Birmingham rf	3	1	2	0
Perring ss	2	0	1	0
Joss p	3	0	0	0
TOTAL	28	1	4	0

	IP	H	R	BB	SO
Joss (W)	9	0	0	0	3

Attendance: 10,508

#14

INDIANS 1, BALTIMORE ORIOLES 0 (11 INNINGS)
OCTOBER 15, 1997

A Story That Wrote Itself

On a goodwill trip to Venezuela, President Bill Clinton couldn't get over the amount of interest he encountered surrounding the Major League Baseball playoffs. While much of Washington, D.C., was abuzz with the rise of the neighboring Baltimore Orioles, in Latin America the talk was all about the Cleveland Indians. With five key Latino players leading the way, the 1997 Indians had defied logic and shocked the baseball world by pulling to within a single victory of the World Series.

After a disheartening loss in Baltimore in Game One of the American League Championship Series, the Tribe sprang to life with three straight stunning, late-inning victories to put itself in the driver's seat. But when the Orioles rebounded with a clutch win at Jacobs Field in Game Five to stay alive, Cleveland's momentum was suddenly gone. The teams would now return to Camden Yards, where Baltimore would saddle up dominating pitcher Mike Mussina with the hopes of riding him into a deciding Game Seven. The Indians would counter with struggling Charles Nagy, who had compiled a 7.71 ERA in two playoff starts in 1997 and had been shelled by the Orioles in a Division Series encounter the previous year. As the teams took the field under a gunmetal Maryland sky on a warm October afternoon for Game Six, Baltimore seemed a lock for an easy victory.

True to form, Mussina cruised through four innings, retiring the first twelve Cleveland batters while Nagy continually skated on thin ice. Baltimore's leadoff hitter reached base in each of the first four frames, but the Orioles were unable to score. A double play ended the threat in the first, then a clutch groundout ended the third with Orioles on second and third. Another great chance came in the fourth when Cal Ripken Jr. led off with a double but stayed there as Nagy retired the next three batters. The scoreless game toiled on into the falling dusk.

Cleveland's David Justice ended Mussina's string with a double to start the fifth, but like Nagy, Mussina escaped. Nagy got his first 1-2-3 inning in the sixth, but then ran into big trouble in the seventh. Shortstop Mike Bordick started the inning with a single to center, then moved to second on a hit by center fielder Brady Anderson. The capacity crowd began to make noise, anticipating a big inning. But it was quickly silenced by the play of the day.

Baltimore manager Davey Johnson called for second baseman Roberto Alomar to move the runners with a sacrifice bunt. Alomar got the bunt down successfully, but the Indians countered it with perhaps the most beautiful play in baseball. As third baseman Matt Williams charged the ball and scooped it up along the third-base line, shortstop Omar Vizquel scampered over to third. Williams turned and fired the ball to Vizquel, "turning the wheel" for a force out and changing the complexion of the inning. The threat came to an end on the next pitch when Geronimo Berroa grounded into a double play and the Indians once again had wiggled off the hook. The Orioles threatened again in the eighth, putting runners on first and second with one out, but Cleveland relievers Paul Assenmacher and Mike Jackson enticed two consecutive groundouts—the second just barely forcing B. J. Surhoff at second—to keep the game scoreless.

Mussina was relieved after eight innings after surrendering just one hit for the game. The Indians quickly put two runners on in the ninth, but Baltimore's Randy Myers quelled the threat, and the teams continued to joust through the tenth as the contest neared the four-hour mark. "The game seemed to go on forever," Paul Hoynes would write. "A delicate strip of icy perfection that stretched to the horizon." The end would finally come in the eleventh.

Baltimore reliever Armando Benitez, who had already lost two games in the series, replaced Myers and retired the first two Cleveland batters. Up stepped second baseman Tony Fernandez, who wasn't even supposed to play that day. Bip Roberts had been scheduled to start at second, but during batting practice Fernandez hit a line drive that struck Roberts on the thumb. Roberts was scratched and Fernandez was penciled into the lineup. Now in his fifth at-bat of the game, Fernandez swung at the first pitch and drove it into the Baltimore night. The ball sailed over the tall scoreboard in right field and landed in the seats for the first run and just the Indians' third hit of the marathon contest. Even the most disbelieving disbeliever couldn't help but see meaning in Fernandez's homer—his first in thirty-eight career postseason games. "It was from the man above," Roberts said. "He wanted somebody in there who could win the game for us." But the game wasn't won yet.

As had been the case a year earlier, it would be up to Jose Mesa. In Game Four of the 1996 AL Division Series against Baltimore, Mesa first gave up a game-tying two-out RBI single to Roberto Alomar in the ninth, then surrendered a game-winning homer to Alomar in the twelfth. Now he was a mere three outs away from sending the Indians to the World Series. Mesa struck out Chris Hoiles swinging, then quickly got catcher Lenny Webster to ground back to him at the mound. Baltimore's hopes were down to Anderson, who was batting .333 for the series with a pair of home runs. He rifled Mesa's second pitch to right for a single, bringing the winning run to the plate in—appropriately—Roberto Alomar.

It was the chance at redemption for which Mesa had waited an entire year. Firing fastballs with every ounce of his strength, he fell behind Alomar 2-and-0; then the Orioles' second baseman swung and missed at another and fouled off two more. Mesa's next pitch, a sinking fastball, missed outside, and the count ran full. Anderson would be off with the next pitch. With thousands of fans' hearts pounding back in Cleveland, Mesa wound up and delivered the seventh pitch of the at-bat. It was a fastball that started inside, and Alomar gave up on it, even started to back out of the way. As he did, though, the fastball broke over the inside of the corner of the plate. Umpire Mike Reilly thrust his fist forward to signal strike three and at 8:08 P.M., the Indians had won the pennant.

Sandy Alomar, Roberto's older brother, sprinted to the mound and leaped on a jubilant Mesa. His teammates soon gathered around him, much as they'd done nine days before when Mesa had shut the door on the Yankees in the deciding game of the Division Series. Somehow, the 86–75 Indians had upset the mighty Yankees and Orioles and were headed back to the World Series after a spine-tingling ALCS that saw all four Cleveland victories decided by one run, three in the Tribe's final at-bat. "After a while, I just couldn't watch our games," Justice said. "They were so tense, so close. I had to get up and walk around. This series killed me. I feel like I'm forty-seven years old."

Which is about how old many of the Orioles felt after essentially giving away the game. Despite outhitting the Indians 10–3, Baltimore stranded a whopping fourteen runners as it went zero-for-twelve with runners in scoring position. Even more of a waste was Mussina's dominance. In two appearances in the ALCS, Mussina had pitched fifteen innings, struck out twenty-five batters, allowed just one run, and yet hadn't won a game. Meanwhile, the Indians struck out sixty-two times in six games and hit just .193 for the series—and won. Nagy, who'd carried a 7.17 career postseason ERA into the game, had pitched the game of his life to pave the way for one of the most memorable wins in Indians history.

It was a series—and an October—that defied logic. Each game had become a chapter in an increasingly unbelievable tale, capped by Nagy's gutsy showing, an unusual turning-of-the-wheel play, and Fernandez's surprise appearance and unlikely heroics. "I think it's a story," Mike Hargrove noted, "that's almost writing itself."

Indians	0 0 0	0 0 0	0 0 0	0 1	=1
Orioles	0 0 0	0 0 0	0 0 0	0 0	=0

CLEVELAND

	AB	R	H	RBI
Vizquel ss	5	0	0	0
Fernandez 2b	5	1	2	1
Ramirez rf	4	0	0	0
Justice dh	3	0	1	0
Williams 3b	4	0	0	0
Thome 1b	4	0	0	0
S. Alomar c	4	0	0	0
Giles lf	3	0	0	0
Grissom cf	4	0	0	0
TOTAL	36	1	3	1

	IP	H	R	ER	BB	SO
Nagy	7⅓	9	0	0	3	4
Assenmacher	⅓	0	0	0	0	0
Jackson	1⅓	0	0	0	1	3
Anderson (W)	1	0	0	0	1	2
Mesa (Sv)	1	1	0	0	0	2

BALTIMORE

	AB	R	H	RBI
Anderson cf	5	0	2	0
R. Alomar 2b	5	0	1	0
Berroa rf	5	0	2	0
Walton rf	0	0	0	0
Baines dh	3	0	1	0
Davis ph-dh	1	0	0	0
Palmeiro 1b	3	0	0	0
Hammonds pr-lf	1	0	0	0
Ripken 3b	3	0	2	0
Surhoff lf-1b	5	0	0	0
Hoiles c	5	0	0	0
Bordick ss	4	0	2	0
Webster ph	1	0	0	0
TOTAL	41	0	10	0

	IP	H	R	ER	BB	SO
Mussina	8	1	0	0	2	10
Myers	2	1	0	0	1	2
Benitez (L)	1	1	1	1	0	2

Attendance: 49,075

#13

INDIANS 3, TORONTO BLUE JAYS 0
OCTOBER 19, 2016

Shaking in His Boots

Throughout the 2016 season, there was a strangeness that kept inserting itself into games between the Indians and Toronto Blue Jays.

A casual Canada Day matinee in Toronto turned into an epic six-hour, nineteen-inning saga, won by the Indians when Carlos Santana finally broke a 1–1 tie with a game-winning home run. Six weeks later in Cleveland, they won another dazzler when Tyler Naquin came all the way around the bases on an inside-the-park walk-off home run—the first time the Indians had won a game in this fashion in a hundred years.

So when the teams met again in October in the American League Championship Series, it was little surprise that the bizarre encounters continued. The Indians cruised to victories in the first two games in Cleveland despite collecting only ten total hits and four total runs. Game Three in Toronto proved even odder. Indians starting pitcher Trevor Bauer took the mound in his first appearance since badly cutting the pinkie finger on his throwing hand on an off day while fixing the propellers on one of his robotic drones. Four batters into the game, the wound began seeping blood and Bauer was forced to leave the game after just twenty-one pitches. The Cleveland bullpen rode to the rescue, recording the remaining twenty-five outs as the Indians somehow pulled out a 4–2 victory to take a three-games-to-none lead in the best-of-seven series.

After the Blue Jays staved off elimination in the fourth game, there was an air of desperation surrounding the Indians going into Game Five. With Bauer sidelined and two other pitchers in their starting rotation out of action following injuries in the final month of the season, the Indians were literally out of options. Needing one more win to reach the World Series, they would hand the ball to twenty-four-year-old Ryan Merritt, who had made just one career

Cleveland first baseman Carlos Santana drops to his knees in celebration after catching the final out of Game Five of the 2016 American League Championship Series, a 3–0 victory over the Toronto Blue Jays that sent the Indians to the World Series. © Nick Turchiaro/USA TODAY NETWORK via Imagn Images.

start at the major-league level. As the ALCS had begun, Merritt was essentially playing pickup games at the team's spring training facility in Arizona to stay sharp just in case of an emergency. And now the emergency was at hand.

"We tell everybody that you're a hamstring, an elbow or something away from being on Field 4 in Goodyear to being on TV," manager Terry Francona said. In this case, not just TV—on the national stage trying to get your team to the World Series.

As word spread of the Indians' finger-in-the-dike solution, the Blue Jays began licking their chops. "With our experience in our lineup," Toronto slugger José Bautista said, "I'm pretty sure he's going to be shaking in his boots more than we are."

If not actually quivering, Merritt certainly had cause for anxiety. In addition to facing a powerful lineup with the baseball world watching and expecting a batting-practice exhibition, the seating capacity of the raucous Rogers Centre where the Blue Jays played was eight times the size of Merritt's hometown of Celina, Texas.

While he would be the center of attention, Merritt's teammates made it clear he wouldn't be alone.

"Before the game, they came and told me they had my back, everybody had my back, good or bad," he said. "So that takes some pressure off."

A little more pressure was alleviated when the Indians plated a run in their first at-bat. Cleanup hitter Mike Napoli pounded a two-out double off the wall in left, and, aided by Toronto outfielder Ezequiel Carrera bobbling the ball as he fielded it, Cleveland shortstop Francisco Lindor came around to score from first. As nice as the start was, one run wasn't going to make much of a difference if Merritt melted under the pressure.

But stunningly, from the outset, he looked like a seasoned veteran. He retired the Blue Jays in order on just thirteen pitches in each of the first two innings. It took him a mere five pitches to get three outs in the third, and after he enticed a fly ball from Bautista to open the bottom of the fourth, Merritt had retired ten straight batters to start the game. After he finally surrendered a single, he promptly enticed a ground-ball double play to end the inning.

In the meantime, Cleveland extended its lead. In the third, just as he had to end the marathon back in July, first baseman Santana smashed a homer to make it 2–0, then an inning later, outfielder Coco Crisp—a fifteen-year veteran acquired from Oakland at the trading deadline two months earlier—hit his second homer of the postseason to make it 3–0. Somehow, the desperate Indians were controlling a game the sports world expected them to lose heartily. And the shaking boots Bautista had predicted were suddenly on the other feet.

After Merritt allowed a one-out bloop single in the fifth, Francona decided not to push his luck any further. Merritt had delivered more than anyone could have expected, lasting 4⅓ scoreless innings, allowing just two hits, walking none, and striking out three while silencing the Toronto bats with a variety of slow but well-placed pitches that rarely topped 85 miles per hour.

As he'd done throughout the postseason, the Cleveland manager turned to his triple-threat bullpen. Bryan Shaw took the baton from Merritt and delivered a scoreless inning. He was replaced by dominant left-hander Andrew Miller, who'd been virtually unhittable in October. And he remained hot, permitting just one baserunner over 2⅔ shutout innings.

Finally, in the ninth, Cody Allen took the mound to try to close out the triumph. Bautista raked a double to start the inning, but Allen then struck out power hitters Josh Donaldson and Edwin Encarnación. One out away, Allen enticed a soft pop up into foul territory from Troy Tulowitzki. Santana drifted over from first base and settled under the baseball. He caught it, then dropped to his knees and spread out his arms in triumph. For the sixth time in their 116-year history, the Indians were going to the World Series.

While Merritt didn't get the victory in the box score—statistically speaking, it went to Shaw—he was both the primary reason for the win and a reflection of the philosophy of the entire franchise. "It just demonstrates this was an organizational win," owner Paul Dolan said. "We've built a system, so when we needed somebody to step up in a crucial moment, we have people behind them." Still, reflecting the out-of-nowhere heroics Merritt had provided, Dolan roamed through the champagne-soaked clubhouse afterward to find the rookie and introduce himself.

Even as fans back in Cleveland began their own celebration, there was a grass-roots effort to show their appreciation for Merritt's clutch performance. Word spread on social media that the young pitcher was engaged to be married in the offseason. A handful of industrious fans were able to determine where the couple was registered for gifts and proceeded to purchase items off the list and send them to Merritt.

The bridegroom and his bullpen had combined to shut out the Blue Jays for the second time in the series, combining to allow only six hits and not allowing a single runner to get past second base. Incredible as the performance was, it was nothing new. In Cleveland's four victories in the series, Toronto had scored a grand total of two runs. At the vanguard was Miller, who was named ALCS MVP, tossing 7⅔ shutout innings with fourteen strikeouts.

For his mastery, even Miller struggled to explain how the Indians had pulled this off. "I think 'it' is the right word," he said. "We just have 'it.'"

And in this case, "it" had delivered a trip to the World Series.

Indians	1	0	1	1	0	0	0	0	0	=3
Blue Jays	0	0	0	0	0	0	0	0	0	=0

CLEVELAND

	AB	R	H	RBI
Santana 1b	4	1	1	1
Kipnis 2b	4	0	0	0
Lindor ss	4	1	3	0
Napoli dh	4	0	1	0
Ramírez 3b	4	0	0	0
Chisenhall rf	4	0	0	0
Crisp lf	2	1	1	1
Davis ph-lf	1	0	0	0
Naquin cf	3	0	0	0
Pérez c	3	0	0	0
TOTAL	33	3	6	2

	IP	H	R	ER	BB	SO
Merritt	4⅓	2	0	0	0	3
Shaw (W)	1	2	0	0	0	2
Miller	2⅔	1	0	0	0	1
Allen (Sv)	1	1	0	0	0	2

TORONTO

	AB	R	H	RBI
Bautista rf	4	0	2	0
Donaldson 3b	4	0	1	0
Encarnación 1b	4	0	0	0
Tulowitzki ss	4	0	0	0
Martin c	3	0	1	0
Upton dh	1	0	0	0
Saunders ph-dh	1	0	1	0
Navarro ph-dh	1	0	1	0
Carrera lf	3	0	0	0
Pillar cf	3	0	0	0
Barney 2b	3	0	0	0
TOTAL	31	0	6	0

	IP	H	R	ER	BB	SO
Estrada (L)	6	5	3	2	0	7
Cecil	1	0	0	0	0	1
Biagini	1	0	0	0	0	1
Osuna	1	1	0	0	0	1

Attendance: 48,800

#12

INDIANS 4, BOSTON BRAVES 3
OCTOBER 11, 1948

Just Wonderful

The long, black locomotive sat silent on the tracks like a giant black snake waiting to creep out of its hole. Down through the steamy corridors of the station came word of what was happening up at Cleveland Stadium, and railroad employees reluctantly began to scramble into action.

The workers, like most Clevelanders that Sunday, were hoping the afternoon would end in a massive civic celebration instead of a rapid preparation for an unwanted road trip. After surging to a three-games-to-one lead in the 1948 World Series, the Indians needed just one more triumph to end the baseball season and capture their first world title in twenty-eight years. With Bob Feller on the mound for his second World Series start in a career at its pinnacle and the Boston Braves countering with unknown journeyman pitcher Ned Potter, the table was set for a celebratory feast for Cleveland. Though Feller struggled early, the Indians roared to life with a four-run fourth inning and took a 5–4 lead into the sixth.

Eleven outs away from the title, Feller gave up a game-tying homer to Boston catcher Bill Salkeld then allowed the Braves to take the lead with a pair of hits in the seventh. When the frame was complete, Boston led 11–5, and the orders were sent to get the train ready. Barring a miraculous Tribe comeback, the Indians and Braves would travel back to Boston that night for Game Six the following afternoon. When Boston wrapped up the victory, disappointing the largest crowd ever to witness a baseball game, the Indians players and coaches rapidly showered and changed clothes, then hustled to Union Terminal. Some phoned their wives and instructed them to meet them at the station with their luggage, others made the trip with nothing more than their wallets—all had agreed it would have been bad luck to pack for a trip they hoped wouldn't be necessary. "We had better finish it tomorrow and come back home," one Indian whispered to a reporter as they boarded the train. He pulled a comb from his pocket and added, "This is all I've got with me."

Though better than 10,000 fans followed the team to the station and sent them off with cheers of encouragement, dark clouds of doubt began to form over Cleveland's plans for a victory parade. The Braves had battered Cleveland's best pitcher, halted the Tribe's momentum with a blowout victory, and now would return to their own park for the sixth and possibly seventh game. The Indians' storybook season suddenly appeared headed for an unwelcome surprise ending.

But they still had one potent bullet left in the chamber. Rather than playing the odds, Lou Boudreau would pull out all the stops for the sixth game and decided to start pitcher Bob Lemon on three days' rest. Already nursing a sore arm, Lemon used heat pads throughout Sunday night, hoping to loosen up his aching muscles. If Lemon faltered and the Indians were to lose, Boudreau would admit later, he had no plan for Game Seven. The entire Cleveland season rested on the left arm of Lemon, who'd played a monumental role in the team's 1948 success, winning twenty games with a 2.82 ERA. Having used the dynamic pitching duo of Warren Spahn and Johnny Sain in the previous two games, Boston would counter with seasoned-but-not-spectacular veteran Bill Voiselle, who'd pitched 3⅔ innings of one-hit relief in Game Three. It seemed an appropriate end for a series dominated by pitching.

Yet in the early going, both pitchers looked shaky. Voiselle allowed a single by Larry Doby and then hit Boudreau in the first before retiring Joe Gordon and Ken Keltner. Lemon used a double play to end a potential rally in his half of the inning, then gave up a leadoff single to third baseman Bob Elliott in the second and was called for a balk that sent Elliott to second. After advancing to third on a long fly, Elliott could only watch as Lemon got Salkeld to pop out to first and then Mike McCormick to ground out to Keltner at third. The Braves had squandered the game's first golden scoring opportunity.

Moments later, the Indians made them pay. Left fielder Dale Mitchell led off the third with a double to left, then scored on Boudreau's double to right. The Braves threatened again in the bottom of the third, putting runners on the corners with one out. But again, Lemon came up big when he had to, getting shortstop Alvin Dark to ground into a double play to end the inning and preserve the lead. Cleveland wasn't so fortunate in the fourth. With runners at first and second with two out, McCormick delivered a single to center to bring home the tying run. The crowd at Braves Field roared to life, especially when Lemon walked second baseman Eddie Stanky to load the bases. With another base hit, Boston could take control of the game. But Lemon rebounded and got Voiselle to ground out to second to end the fourth.

Both pitchers settled in the fifth, then the Indians delivered another knockout punch in the sixth when Gordon blasted a fastball over the left-field wall—the first home run of the series at Braves Field. After Keltner popped out, center fielder Thurman Tucker walked and moved to third on first baseman Eddie Robinson's single. Catcher Jim Hegan then sent a grounder to third which Elliott threw to Stanky for the force at second, but Robinson's slide nudged Stanky enough to ensure the relay throw was unable to get Hegan at first. Tucker scored to make it 3–1, but the Indians weren't out of the woods yet.

With the New England sky becoming darker and more ominous, both teams had potential rallies snuffed out by double plays in their next at-bats, but Cleveland scratched together another run in the eighth on three consecutive singles by Keltner, Tucker, and Robinson. The Indians blew a chance to add to the lead when the Braves thwarted a double steal and Tucker was tagged out at the plate. The miscue appeared particularly costly when Boston plated two runs in the bottom of the eighth, chasing a tiring Lemon. Clinging to a 4–3 advantage with Braves on second and third with two out, the Indians' hopes now rested on rookie knuckleballer Gene Bearden, who'd come on in relief. With the dangerous McCormick at the plate, Bearden snared a sharply hit grounder right back up the middle and threw to first for the third out. Had Bearden not made the play, the Braves would have taken the lead and been three outs away from Game Seven. Instead, Bearden returned to the mound for the bottom of the ninth up by one.

It started badly when Stanky walked, but then Hegan made the play of the day. Attempting to lay down a bunt, pinch-hitter Sibby Sisti—one of the best bunters in baseball—popped the ball up. Hegan pounced out from behind the plate and lunged forward to catch the ball, then instantly fired it down to first to double up Stanky, who'd already bolted for second. Silence flooded through Braves Field as the tide of momentum had once again turned. Bearden and the Tribe were now just one out away. And at 3:17 P.M., when Tommy Holmes lofted a lazy fly to left, where it was caught by Bob Kennedy, the Indians were the champions of the world.

Boudreau and Gordon hugged at second base, while Cleveland players swarmed to Bearden and carried him off the field. "Everything is wonderful," an overwhelmed Bearden would say, "just wonderful." Kennedy returned the historic baseball to Bearden, who promised to give it to his young sons. In eight days, Bearden had suddenly become a legend. He'd won the one-game playoff for the pennant, then won one World Series game and saved another.

"It was Bearden's series all the way, all his," a humble Boudreau proclaimed. "Gene was the key to our success." In the locker room, coach Bill McKechnie kissed Boudreau on the cheek with tears streaming down his cheeks, yelling, "It's the best yet, Louie!" Both contemporary scribes and Tribe historians would agree with that assessment. A *Plain Dealer* editorial announced, "Cleveland fans will not be content with poor baseball teams after this glorious season."

Back home, the celebration was even more voracious, where cheers echoed through the steel canyons of downtown Cleveland. "Windows along Public Square and Euclid Avenue fairly trembled with the vibration of automobile horns, boat whistles, cannon firecrackers, shouts, cheers," Roelif Loveland wrote. Many fans got in their cars and simply drove around town to soak in the occasion. A victory parade was hastily scheduled for the following morning when the team would return from Boston. Parochial schools announced they would be closed on Tuesday in honor of the celebration. While Cleveland's public schools would stay open, children would be excused from class with a note from their parents.

It would be the last such day Cleveland would experience for the remainder of the century, but the memories would endure. "Our hats are off today to worthy champions of the world," Gordon Cobbledick wrote that day, "the Cleveland Indians. Our Cleveland Indians."

Indians	0 0 1	0 0 2	0 1 0	=4
Braves	0 0 0	1 0 0	0 2 0	=3

CLEVELAND

	AB	R	H	RBI
Mitchell lf	4	1	1	0
Kennedy lf	1	0	0	0
Doby rf	4	0	2	0
Boudreau ss	3	0	1	1
Gordon 2b	4	1	1	1
Keltner 3b	4	1	1	0
Tucker cf	3	1	1	0
Robinson 1b	4	0	2	1
Hegan c	4	0	1	1
Lemon p	3	0	0	0
Bearden p	1	0	0	0
TOTAL	35	4	10	4

	IP	H	R	ER	BB	SO
Lemon (W)	7⅓	8	3	3	4	1
Bearden (Sv)	1⅔	1	0	0	1	0

BOSTON

	AB	R	H	RBI
Holmes rf	5	1	2	0
Dark ss	4	0	1	0
Torgeson 1b	4	1	1	0
Elliott 3b	3	1	3	0
Rickert lf	3	0	0	0
Conaster ph-cf	1	0	0	1
Salkeld c	2	0	0	0
Masi ph-c	1	0	1	1
M. McCormick cf-lf	4	0	1	1
Stanky 2b	1	0	0	0
Ryan pr	0	0	0	0
Voiselle p	1	0	0	0
F. McCormick ph	1	0	0	0
Spahn p	0	0	0	0
Sisti ph	1	0	0	0
TOTAL	31	3	9	3

	IP	H	R	ER	BB	SO
Voiselle (L)	7	7	3	3	2	2
Spahn	2	3	1	1	0	4

Attendance: 40,103

#11

INDIANS 7, ATLANTA BRAVES 6 (11 INNINGS)
OCTOBER 24, 1995

The Forty-Seven-Year Itch

It had become like Bigfoot or a four-leaf clover, something people had heard of but really didn't believe in because they hadn't seen it for themselves: a World Series game in Cleveland.

Fathers had told sons of it, of the mania that had gripped Northeast Ohio three different times as the Indians won memorable pennant races and then participated in the Fall Classic. But after four decades of utter ineptitude, the concept of the Tribe reaching the World Series seemed more like science fiction than a genuine possibility. The Series—and postseason in general—was intended for other teams and other cities, not for the long-suffering denizens of Cleveland. Yet after a forty-one-year sabbatical in misery, the World Series finally returned to Cleveland on a cold, crisp October night.

It mattered little that the juggernaut Indians, winners of 100 games in a shortened 144-game season, were down two-games-to-none to the Atlanta Braves after losing back-to-back contests at Fulton County Stadium over the weekend. That Tuesday in Cleveland became a civic holiday as citizens tried to contemplate the notion that a World Series game would be played in their town that night. More than 43,000 fans would pack into sparkling Jacobs Field—where the Tribe was 89–34 over the previous two seasons—to see if the Indians could win a World Series contest for the first time since Harry Truman was president. And, almost as a subplot, if the Tribe could claw back to life in the '95 Series.

The rambunctious energy of the crowd, feeding off the almost religious atmosphere of the evening, carried over to the field. After Cleveland's Charles Nagy, pitching for the first time in eleven days, retired the first two Atlanta batters, third baseman Chipper Jones laced a double to left center then scored on a single by cleanup hitter Fred McGriff. Before the Braves could build any momentum, the Tribe answered right back. Kenny Lofton, the only Indian who excelled in the first two games, led off the game with a single off John Smoltz, then soft-hitting shortstop Omar Vizquel laced a triple into the right-field corner to score Lofton and tie the game. The roar of the crowd grew even louder when Carlos Baerga brought Vizquel home on a grounder to first to give the Indians a 2–1 advantage. As the opening inning concluded, it felt as though the night belonged to Cleveland.

Nagy settled and shut the Braves out for the next four innings. Meanwhile, the potent Cleveland offense got cooking again in the third when catalyst Lofton led off with a double off the wall in right center, then advanced to third on Vizquel's perfect bunt single. Baerga followed with a soft liner that Braves shortstop Luis Polonia couldn't handle, and Lofton scored. Then Albert Belle ripped a single up the middle to bring home Vizquel to make it 4–1 and knock Smoltz from the game. The Tribe squandered a chance to add to the lead when Manny Ramirez grounded into a double play with the bases load, but with Nagy cruising, it appeared Cleveland already had all the offense it would need.

McGriff hit a solo homer in the sixth to cut the margin to 4–2, then designated hitter Ryan Klesko belted the first pitch of the seventh into the bleachers in left to pull the Braves within a run. With the capacity crowd beginning to titter with nervousness, the Indians added a crucial insurance run in the bottom of the inning when Lofton reached base for the fourth time on the night with a walk, moved to second on a hit-and-run, then stole third and scored on an infield single by Baerga. Six outs away from a critical victory, it appeared time to turn the contest over to Cleveland's spectacular bullpen.

Yet Mike Hargrove opted to stick with Nagy in the eighth, later citing Nagy's low pitch count as the rationale for his decision. When Atlanta center fielder Marquis Grissom blasted a double off the wall in right to start the inning, Hargrove visited the mound but left Nagy in the game. Polonia singled to score Grissom and, two batters too late, the Cleveland manager decided to lift Nagy. Things didn't get much better for reliever Paul Assenmacher as Polonia stole second, then Jones walked. After McGriff was retired on a long fly to center, an error by Baerga enabled David Justice to reach base and allowed Polonia to score to tie the game. A magical night had suddenly turned sour, and things got even worse when pinch-hitter Mike Devereaux hit a single to score Jones and give Atlanta a 6–5 lead.

An uneasy silence worked its way through Jacobs Field. The Indians were on the verge of giving away a game that was rightfully theirs. If they couldn't muster a comeback in the final two innings, they would fall down three-games-to-none and face the very real danger of being swept in stunning fashion—just as had happened to the last Indians team to reach the World Series in 1954. But trailing in the late innings was nothing new to the '95 Tribe, having collected thirty come-from-behind wins. Thus it came as no surprise when the Indians began to work their clutch magic in the bottom of the eighth. "We told each other, if we're going to lose, we're going to go down fighting," said catcher Sandy Alomar.

Ramirez reached on a one-out walk, then advanced to third on a single by first baseman Paul Sorrento. Atlanta manager Bobby Cox rolled the dice and brought in closer Mark Wohlers an inning early, hoping to douse the Cleveland rally. On Wohlers' first pitch, Alomar shot a line drive just over first base and into the right-field corner to score Ramirez and tie the game. The Indians and their fans were back in it. Wohlers came back to strike out Vizquel and then got Baerga to ground out, and Game Three of the 1995 World Series moved to the ninth inning, where it evolved into a chess match.

Like Cox moments before, Hargrove took his own gamble, calling for closer Jose Mesa in a nonsave situation. He immediately got into trouble by giving up a leadoff single to Mark Lemke, then faced the powerful Jones with two out and men on first and second. Jones pounded a hard grounder down the first-base line, apparently destined for right field to give Atlanta the lead. But new Cleveland first baseman Herbert Perry—a ninth-inning defensive replacement for Sorrento—made a remarkable one-handed grab of the baseball coming off a bad hop and outraced Jones to the bag to retire the side. After the Indians went down in order in the ninth, the game moved into extra innings and the tension level at Jacobs Field rose even higher. Mesa dodged another bullet in the tenth when, with a man on second and two down, Baerga made a terrific play behind second to throw out Javier Lopez. The Indians threatened in their half of the tenth when Ramirez walked and reached third with two out, but Vizquel grounded to second and the game shuffled into the eleventh, twisting and writhing "like the bodies of the fans in their torment," Bill Livingston wrote.

For the third straight inning, Atlanta's leadoff batter singled off Mesa, but again Mesa recovered by inducing a double play. Baerga led off the bottom of the inning with a double to left center and the Cleveland fans, worn down by nervous exhaustion, began to taste victory once again. Utility infielder Alvaro Espinoza replaced Baerga, and Belle was walked intentionally, bringing ageless veteran Eddie Murray to the plate. Murray, one of the key veteran acquisitions who played a critical role for the '95 Indians, had struggled in Game Three, going zero-for-five with three strikeouts. But with the game now on the line, he ripped the first pitch from Alejandro Peña to center field, bringing Espinoza around third. Grissom's throw from center was off-line and Espinoza arrived at the plate with a head-first slide, capping Cleveland's twenty-ninth victory of the season in its last at-bat. After four hours and nine minutes—the longest game in World Series history—and forty-seven years, the Indians had finally won a game in the World Series.

Now the Tribe could turn its focus to the task at hand. "It's nice to get this little World Series jinx over with and get on with the series," Murray said. In the glowing aftermath of a desperately satisfying victory, Murray was perhaps the only person in the world who could get away with referring to a five-decade drought as a "little jinx."

Braves	1 0 0	0 0 1	1 3 0	0 0	=6
Indians	2 0 2	0 0 0	1 1 0	0 1	=7

ATLANTA

	AB	R	H	RBI
Grissom cf	6	1	2	0
Polonia lf	4	1	1	1
Jones 3b	3	2	1	0
McGriff 1b	5	1	3	2
Justice rf	5	0	0	1
Klesko dh	3	1	2	1
Devereaux ph-dh	2	0	1	1
Lopez c	5	0	0	0
Lemke 2b	5	0	2	0
Belliard ss	2	0	0	0
Smith ph	1	0	0	0
Mordecai ss	1	0	0	0
TOTAL	42	6	12	6

	IP	H	R	ER	BB	SO
Smoltz	2⅓	6	4	4	2	4
Clontz	2⅓	1	0	0	0	1
Mercker	2	1	1	1	2	2
McMichael	⅔	1	1	1	1	1
Wohlers	2⅔	1	0	0	3	2
Peña (L)	0	2	1	1	1	0

CLEVELAND

	AB	R	H	RBI
Lofton cf	3	3	3	0
Vizquel ss	6	2	2	1
Baerga 2b	6	0	3	3
Espinoza pr	0	1	0	0
Belle lf	4	0	1	1
Murray dh	6	0	1	1
Thome 3b	4	0	0	0
Ramirez rf	2	1	0	0
Sorrento 1b	4	0	1	0
Kirby pr	0	0	0	0
Perry 1b	1	0	0	0
Alomar c	5	0	1	1
TOTAL	41	7	12	7

	IP	H	R	ER	BB	SO
Nagy	7	8	5	5	1	4
Assenmacher	⅓	0	1	1	1	0
Tavarez	⅔	1	0	0	0	0
Mesa (W)	3	3	0	0	1	3

Attendance: 43,584

#10

INDIANS 1, CHICAGO WHITE SOX 0
APRIL 16, 1940

"I Just Pitched"

More often than not in northern American cities, the first day of baseball season doesn't mark the arrival of spring. April generally still packs some of winter's icy punch, thus opening day often leans toward damp and cold rather than bright and balmy. Such was the case in 1940, when the Indians opened the season at Chicago's frosty Comiskey Park. Though it felt nothing like baseball season, one of the most significant achievements in the history of the game would take place on this gray afternoon in the Windy City.

Coming off a breakthrough twenty-four-win season, twenty-one-year-old Bob Feller was looking for even better things in 1940, and he could start things off with a strong performance in the opener. With a raw wind coming off Lake Michigan, both Feller and his counterpart, Chicago hurler Eddie Smith, struggled with their control early. Smith walked two batters in the top of the first, then Feller sandwiched a walk between two strikeouts in the bottom of the inning. The frigid conditions then affected the defenders in the second as each team committed an error—Chicago on a muffed grounder, Cleveland on a dropped fly ball to center. When Feller then followed with back-to-back walks, the White Sox had the bases loaded and were poised to break the game open early. Feller rebounded to strike out third baseman Bob Kennedy, then, after surrendering a leadoff walk in the third, Feller decided that he would only use his fastball for the remainder of the game, unable to trust his grip on a slick, moist ball. From that point on, Feller became dominant.

Feller would retire twenty straight Chicago batters, though the fireballer struck out only three. Though Smith was not quite as dominant, he was effective in keeping the Indians from stringing together a rally. Only once could Cleveland rattle Smith—in the fourth, left fielder Jeff Heath scored on a two-out triple by catcher Rollie Hemsley to give the Tribe a 1–0 advantage. The way Feller was pitching, the Indians knew one run might be enough. But by the time the game reached the late innings, winning became a secondary objective. Bob Feller now had a chance for baseball immortality.

He'd already thrown a trio of one-hitters in his young career, yet he'd never gone the distance without allowing a hit. As the game marched through the somber cold, his place in history became more and more clear. Only twice had Chicago batters made good contact—liners by Luke Appling and Taffy Wright to Cleveland right fielder Ben Chapman in the third and fourth. There was a scare in the eighth when pinch-hitter Larry Rosenthal ripped a grounder to second, and Ray Mack's off-balance throw to Hal Trosky at first was just barely in time. Feller then got Kennedy to fly out and struck out first baseman Joe Kuhel to end the inning. He was now three outs away from baseball's first-ever opening-day no-hitter, and the partisan Chicago crowd of nearly 14,000 gave him a standing ovation. But Feller was remarkably calm. "I knew I had a chance for a no-hitter in the ninth, but I tried to put the thought out of my mind by reminding myself you never have a no-hitter until the last man is out," Feller said. "I got to thinking I'd just pitch my own ball game. A pitcher can't be any better than he really is. So I just pitched."

Conversely, tension dripped off the walls of the Cleveland dugout. Manager Oscar Vitt's stomach began churning when Feller opened the ninth with two straight balls to center fielder Mike Kreevich. After a strike, Kreevich lifted a towering pop fly that was gathered in by Mack near second. Two more outs. Feller would now have to face an old nemesis. Former Indian Julius Solters had twice spoiled Feller no-hit bids and now was in a position to do it a third time. This time, however, he slapped the third pitch to Lou Boudreau at shortstop, who then threw on to Trosky. One more out.

Up stepped Appling, one of the craftiest hitters in the game. While Feller focused on the task at hand, Vitt was busy requesting divine intervention. "I sat there with [coach] Luke Sewell and just prayed," he said. "I remember once saying to Luke, 'Oh, God, just let him get by Appling.'" Appling wouldn't comply. When Feller got two strikes, Appling fouled off four pitches as the at-bat stretched on. Finally, on the tenth pitch, Feller decided he was in a battle he couldn't afford to lose. With a full count, he purposely misfired, allowing Appling to take first on a walk—the first Chicago base runner since the third inning. Feller had craftily kept the no-hitter alive and would take his chances with Taffy Wright—another specter from his past. Twice while with the Washington Senators, Wright had delivered a clutch hit to hand Feller a tough defeat. Now, Wright had the chance not only to keep Feller from winning but also to keep him out of the record books.

Feller missed the strike zone with his first pitch, but Wright cut at the next, sending a low line drive between first and second. It was Chicago's hardest hit ball of the day, and Mack made an athletic move just to knock the ball down at the edge of the outfield grass. With Wright sprinting down the line, Mack hurriedly scooped up the baseball and fired it to first, beating Wright by a half step.

Bob Feller had done it.

His teammates swarmed him near the mound and quickly ushered him back to the warmth of the clubhouse, where the significance of what had just happened began to sink in. "The thing that had to happen sometime happened here this chilly afternoon," Gordon Cobbledick wrote.

"Bob Feller, the Iowa hurricane, rapped at the door of baseball's mythical Hall of Fame yesterday for the fourth time during his brief but meteoric career with the Cleveland Indians," the *Plain Dealer* proclaimed, "and finally was admitted."

Two more no-hitters would follow in Feller's illustrious career, but none matched the magnitude of his first. And though several have flirted with the possibility, in the six-plus decades since that glacial afternoon in Chicago, no one has pitched a no-hitter on opening day.

Indians	0 0 0	1 0 0	0 0 0	=1
White Sox	0 0 0	0 0 0	0 0 0	=0

CLEVELAND

	AB	R	H	RBI
Boudreau ss	3	0	0	0
Weatherly cf	4	0	1	0
Chapman rf	3	0	0	0
Trosky 1b	4	0	0	0
Heath lf	4	1	1	0
Keltner 3b	4	0	1	0
Hemsley c	4	0	2	1
Mack 2b	4	0	1	0
Feller p	3	0	0	0
TOTAL	33	1	6	1

	IP	H	R	ER	BB	SO
Feller (W)	9	0	0	0	5	8

CHICAGO

	AB	R	H	RBI
Kennedy 3b	4	0	0	0
Kuhel 1b	3	0	0	0
Kreevich cf	3	0	0	0
Solters lf	4	0	0	0
Appling ss	3	0	0	0
Wright rf	4	0	0	0
McNair 2b	3	0	0	0
Tresch c	2	0	0	0
Smith p	1	0	0	0
Rosenthal ph	1	0	0	0
Brown p	0	0	0	0
TOTAL	28	0	0	0

	IP	H	R	ER	BB	SO
Smith (L)	8	6	1	1	2	5
Brown	1	0	0	0	0	0

Attendance: 14,000

#9

CHICAGO CUBS 8, INDIANS 7 (10 INNINGS)
NOVEMBER 2, 2016

Until There Was Nothing Left

Considering how long everyone involved had waited, it only seemed right that this World Series would last as long as it possibly could. And, as it turned out, then some.

Altogether, the two teams squaring off in the 2016 World Series had been waiting a combined 176 years for a championship. Sixty-eight for the scrappy, smoke-and-mirrors Cleveland Indians and a whopping 108 for the heavily favored Chicago Cubs. No other World Series had matched more long-suffering franchises—the previous record had been a combined ninety-two years when the Cincinnati Reds and Boston Red Sox played in the 1975 World Series. Appropriately, that one had gone down in history as one of the greatest Fall Classics ever played. And as it happened, so would this one.

Plagued by injuries that saw two of their starting pitchers lost for the season in September and another's effectiveness diminished when he cut his pitching hand fixing a drone during the playoffs, the Indians had somehow cruised to the American League pennant. They then stunned oddsmakers by taking three of the first four games of the World Series over the Cubs, who'd won 103 games during the regular season and were expected by most to overwhelm Cleveland and snap their long title drought.

With a chance to clinch in Wrigley Field, the Indians dropped a tight 3–2 decision in Game Five, then returned to Cleveland and dug a deep hole early in Game Six as the Cubs rolled to a 9–3 win to knot the series and set up a deciding—and considering the two team's histories, perhaps inevitable—Game Seven.

On a fittingly surreal warm November evening in downtown Cleveland that saw the gametime temperature hover around 70 degrees, the Indians would hand the ball to star pitcher Corey Kluber, who'd won eighteen games during

Rajai Davis rounds the bases after hitting the most memorable home run in Cleveland baseball history—a two-run, game-tying blast in the eighth inning of Game Seven of the 2016 World Series. © Michael Chritton/ USA TODAY NETWORK via Imagn Images.

the regular season and had been nearly unstoppable in the postseason. But this would mark the second time in the World Series Kluber would be starting on three days' rest, and from the outset, it was clear Kluber was running on fumes. On his fourth pitch, Chicago leadoff hitter Dexter Fowler blasted a home run to center, setting a clear tone. Still, the stalwart Kluber endured, muscling through the rest of the inning and then two more without allowing another run.

Meanwhile, the Indians' bats came alive in the bottom of the third. Coco Crisp led off the inning with a double, then scored on an RBI single by Carlos Santana a batter later. Yet the tie score didn't last long as the wheels finally started to come off the wagon for Kluber in the fourth. A leadoff single and a hit batter set up a sacrifice fly, followed by an RBI double by Cubs catcher Willson Contreras to make it 3–1. When Javier Baez led off the fifth with another homer, Kluber had finally run out of gas. Cleveland manager Terry Francona replaced him with reliever Andrew Miller, who had been equally dominant throughout the playoffs. But now even Miller's tank was running low as he surrendered two hits and a walk that enabled the Cubs to push their lead to 5–1. The game appeared to be heading toward a clear conclusion as the Indians' hopes for a title dimmed.

Yet as they had all season, the Indians didn't give up. After two quick outs in the bottom of the fifth, Santana turned an 0–2 count into a walk. Second baseman Jason Kipnis then nubbed an infield single and advanced to second on a throwing error by David Ross, who'd subbed in at catcher for the Cubs, that enabled Santana to take third. And a pitch later, things got wilder.

Pitcher Jon Lester threw a curveball in the dirt that bounced off Ross's catcher's mask and ricocheted sideways toward the Cubs dugout. Santana came home to score and Kipnis, seeing the jagged path of the ball as Ross sprinted to retrieve it, never slowed coming around third and sped toward the plate. As Ross retrieved the ball and fired it to Lester, Kipnis slid headfirst into home just below the tag as the Progressive Field crowd roared back to life. The Indians had cut the lead in half on one of the zaniest plays in postseason history—marking the first time two runners had scored on a wild pitch in a World Series game since 1911.

But just as had been the case after the Indians had tied the game in the third, the Cubs immediately halted Cleveland's momentum. Ross atoned for his error minutes earlier by cracking a one-out homer in the top of the sixth that stretched the Chicago lead to 6–3. It was the first homer Miller had allowed in the postseason and yet another indication that the Indians' magical flight to Neverland had run out of pixie dust.

The game marched into the bottom of the eighth, and the Cubs retired the first two Cleveland batters. With the Indians down to their final four outs, third baseman José Ramírez slapped an infield single, and, wanting to prevent any trouble, Chicago manager Joe Maddon called on super closer Aroldis Chapman. Arguably the hardest-throwing pitcher ever to play the game, Chapman had been acquired by the Cubs at the trading deadline for just this scenario. He'd racked up a total of thirty-six saves during the regular season with a minuscule 1.55 ERA, and had been equally dominant in the postseason, racking up nine strikeouts in just over six innings of work in the World Series and nineteen total through the playoffs.

Often-overlooked Cleveland right fielder Brandon Guyer, who was quietly having a sterling postseason, worked the count full against Chapman, then drove a double into the gap in right-center field that scored Ramírez and cut the lead to two. It brought to the plate Rajai Davis, a journeyman outfielder who'd signed with the Indians as a free agent the previous offseason and filled a key role in center, leading the team in stolen bases. But Davis wasn't necessarily known as a clutch hitter, certainly not as a power hitter. And now he'd be facing baseball's ultimate power pitcher as the Indians' last best chance to save their season.

As Guyer had done before him, Davis battled with Chapman, taking two fastballs for balls, then fouling off four straight—three over 97 miles per hour and the fourth clocking in at 100. Knowing he'd need every ounce of advantage he could get facing such high-octane pitches, Davis had slid his hands higher up the handle of the bat, choking up enough to give his swing that much extra speed to try to catch up with Chapman's fastballs. And on the next one, a 97 miles-per-hour beauty Chapman tried to sneak in low over the outside corner of the plate, Davis thrust the bat at it, connecting with the baseball just as he had on the previous four. But this time was different.

The ball arched high and deep to left field, as the buzz of the ballpark momentarily ebbed. Fans' eyes widened and their breathing stopped as they gradually realized the possibility of what appeared to be happening. In a moment that seemed to stretch out longer than it actually could have, the baseball carried through the November night and cleared the nineteen-foot wall in left field just inside the foul pole.

Rajai Davis had just tied the game, but it was much more than that. He'd just hit the most dramatic home run in the 116-year history of the Cleveland Indians and delivered one of the most incredible World Series moments ever—the first time a game-tying home run had been hit in the eighth inning or later of a Game Seven.

He floated around the bases as if in a dream, pounding his chest with his right fist and thrusting it into the air as he came around second base. "You could just feel the crowd, the volume, like it was just beating in your heart," Davis would say. "Except I felt like I was flying higher than that."

The Indians players exploded into a frantic celebration, leaping over the railing of the dugout like bursting popcorn kernels, reacting from utter disbelief as much as jubilation. Progressive Field—which just minutes before had largely only echoed the cheers of a solid contingent of Cubs fans who'd been counting down the outs toward their long-awaited title—now erupted in a manner never before seen. Even though the stadium had been the site of more than its fair share of dramatic moments in its two-decade history, in that moment, as MLB.com columnist Richard Justice described, Cleveland fans "rocked the ballpark to its bones."

The Cubs' countdown to a title had been halted. Game Seven, for all intents and purposes, would begin again.

Chapman recovered to get out of the inning, and as they'd done all night, the Cubs immediately responded to a big Cleveland inning. A walk and a stolen base compounded by a throwing error by Cleveland catcher Yan Gomes put a Chicago runner on third with one out. Trying to surprise the Indians with a safety squeeze, Maddon called for Javier Baez to bunt with two strikes, hoping to catch the Indians off-guard enough to enable Jason Heyward to come home from third. Instead, Baez's two-strike bunt attempt went foul, and by rule, resulted in an out. Cleveland relief pitcher Bryan Shaw then enticed a ground ball to end the inning. The Indians would have a chance for a walk-off championship in the bottom of the ninth. But Chapman, recovered from his shaky eighth, needed just fourteen pitches to retire Santana, Kipnis, and shortstop Francisco Lindor to send the game to extra innings.

But first, almost as if Mother Nature itself demanded a break from the tension, the heavens opened. From a sky that had been littered with threatening clouds all night, a downpour fell upon Progressive Field. The umpires ruled a rain delay, and the tarp was rolled out onto the infield. In what had already been a suspenseful and unusual night, this was perhaps the most surreal development. With a world championship hanging in the balance, the teams returned to their respective clubhouses, trying to stay loose and focused amidst the crescendo of drama swelling around them. There, players found sheets of plastic covering the lockers in both clubhouses, placed there in preparation for the impending celebration that one of these teams would soon partake in.

After seventeen minutes that felt as long as the 176 years the teams had been waiting, the field was cleared and the game resumed. And as they had for the previous three games, the Cubs went on the attack. A leadoff single in the tenth sparked a rally capped by RBI hits from Ben Zobrist and Miguel Montero that pushed Chicago back ahead, 8–6.

The Indians, running on fumes both physically and emotionally, made one final push. After the first two batters in the tenth were retired, Guyer walked, bringing Davis back to the plate for the first time since his heroics in the eighth. And while maybe not as dramatic, he came through again, lacing a single to center that scored Guyer after he'd advanced to second base on defensive indifference. It cut the margin to 8–7 and brought the potential winning run to the plate.

Cleveland's last gasp was little-known Michael Martinez, a utility player who'd entered the game as a defensive replacement in the ninth inning and had only made three plate appearances during the playoffs, striking out each time. With the Indians and their fans imploring the baseball gods for just one more miracle, Martinez tapped a slow grounder to Bryant at third. He snagged it, threw across the infield to Anthony Rizzo at first, and the Cubs' 108-year title drought was over. The Indians' wait for a championship, meanwhile, would continue.

It was little solace at the time, but Cleveland fans would eventually recognize and appreciate that their team had just participated in one of the most memorable baseball games ever played.

"Game Seven was a murder mystery wrapped inside a Western inside a sci-fi thriller," Michael Rosenberg wrote in *Sports Illustrated*, "one what-just-happened moment on top of another." Rosenberg's SI colleague Stephanie Apstein described it as "exhilarating, crushing, dreamlike, stunning," and noted that the game had taken "at least a year off the life of everyone who participated."

Few World Series games approached the inherent drama and represented the emotional battlefield of this contest. The result was an electricity that was potent throughout each second of the game's four hours and twenty-eight minutes. "Even when things looked so against us it felt like there was magic in the air," Andrew Miller said afterward. "Unfortunately there wasn't quite enough."

"That was an incredible game to be a part of," Francona added, while acknowledging the pain his players were feeling. "It's going to hurt. It hurts because we care, but they need to walk with their heads held high.

"They tried until there was nothing left."

Cubs	1	0	0	2	2	1	0	0	0	2	=8
Guardians	0	0	1	0	2	0	0	3	0	1	=7

CHICAGO

	AB	R	H	RBI
Fowler cf	5	1	3	1
Schwarber dh	5	0	3	0
Almora pr-dh	0	1	0	0
Bryant 3b	4	2	1	0
Rizzo 1b	3	1	1	1
Zobrist lf	5	1	1	1
Russell ss	3	0	0	1
Contreras c	2	0	1	1
Ross c	1	1	1	1
Coghlan pr	0	0	0	0
Montero c	1	0	1	1
Heyward rf	5	0	0	0
Báez 2b	5	1	1	1
TOTAL	39	8	13	8

	IP	H	R	ER	BB	SO
Hendricks	4⅔	4	2	1	1	2
Lester	3	3	2	1	1	4
Chapman (W)	1⅓	3	2	2	0	2
Edwards	⅔	1	1	1	1	1
Montgomery (Sv)	⅓	0	0	0	0	0

CLEVELAND

	AB	R	H	RBI
Santana dh	4	1	1	1
Kipnis 2b	5	1	1	0
Lindor ss	5	0	0	0
Napoli 1b	5	0	0	0
Ramírez 3b	5	1	2	0
Chisenhall rf	2	0	1	0
Guyer ph-rf-lf	2	2	2	1
Davis cf	5	1	2	3
Crisp lf	4	1	2	0
Martínez rf	1	0	0	0
Pérez c	1	0	0	0
Naquin pr	0	0	0	0
Gomes c	1	0	0	0
TOTAL	40	7	11	5

	IP	H	R	ER	BB	SO
Kluber	4	6	4	4	0	0
Miller	2⅓	4	2	2	1	1
Allen	2	0	0	0	1	2
Shaw (L)	1	3	2	2	2	1
Bauer	⅔	0	0	0	0	1

Attendance: 38,104

#8

INDIANS 3, NEW YORK YANKEES 2
SEPTEMBER 12, 1954

A Yankee Funeral

At the dawn of autumn 1954, the city of Cleveland did not take on a hard-luck, woe-is-us mentality. As it had throughout the first half of the century, it was thriving. It was the seventh-largest city in the nation, reflected by booming industry, a thriving downtown, and the best baseball team on the planet.

With just twelve games remaining, the '54 Indians were on the brink of clinching the pennant. Despite the bitter second-place finishes of the previous three seasons, there was no sense of impending doom surrounding the team as it prepared for the biggest day of the year. The here-we-go-again defeatist mentality that would soak into the soul of Cleveland was still decades away. On a sunshiny September afternoon, Cleveland felt like the glimmering capital of the world, anticipating a dramatic knockout punch that would deliver the Indians' third American League pennant. And on the first Sunday of fall, six days after Labor Day, the Tribe would have a perfect chance to deliver.

Riding a four-game winning streak and now holding an astonishing 102–40 record, the Indians would host the second-place Yankees for a dramatic double-header at Cleveland Stadium—the twenty-first and twenty-second times the teams would meet in 1954. Holding a 6½-game lead over New York, its largest lead of the season, Cleveland was in control of the pennant race. A split would knock the Tribe's magic number down to six with ten games left, but a Yankee sweep would pull the AL's five-time reigning champion to within four games in the loss column and perhaps set the wheels in motion for one final New York push toward a sixth consecutive pennant. Though future generations of Clevelanders would sit back and wait for the worst to occur, after the most amazing regular season in franchise history, the citizens of 1954 only expected the golden summer to continue.

Bob Lemon and Early Wynn would face New York's Whitey Ford and Tommy Byrne. When thousands of fans poured to the Stadium ticket office that morning to snatch up the few tickets that remained, team officials anticipated a big crowd, maybe even better than 75,000. The Cleveland Transit System organized "Baseball Specials," running added trains between the suburbs and downtown. True enough, many fans with tickets came from the outer burgs and arrived early that afternoon, "giving the city the air of a midwest college town on a Saturday afternoon," the *Plain Dealer*'s Murray A. Seeger noted, "as they milled around the streets, restaurants, and hotels waiting for game time." And when game time arrived, even before the first pitch was thrown, history was made. When the turnstile tally was completed, it stood at 86,563—breaking the attendance record set at the Stadium in the 1948 World Series and standing as the largest crowd to ever attend a baseball game. And these fans would not be disappointed.

Ford and Lemon faced off in a pitchers' duel in the first game. The Indians broke a scoreless tie with a run in the fifth, then the Yankees tied it in the sixth with a run of their own. When Ford was lifted after six innings, the Indians plated three runs off replacement Allie Reynolds to secure a 4–1 win. The Tribe's magic number was now down to six, and as the teams prepared for the second game, Cleveland fans at the ballpark and those tuned in on the radio glowed with satisfaction. There would be no disaster, no last-minute collapse. The Indians' primary objective of the afternoon had been accomplished. "But what if," a playful *PD* editorial wondered, "they should win the second game, too? That's almost too much to expect."

So it seemed when New York catcher Yogi Berra blasted a two-run homer off Wynn in the first inning and Byrne held the Indians scoreless through four. Cleveland scratched out a run in the fifth on an RBI single by red-hot second baseman Bobby Avila, but the rally appeared quelled with little-used Wally Westlake stepping up. Westlake, a journeyman outfielder purchased from Cincinnati two years previous, had been substituted for injured Larry Doby. The magic of the entire campaign was reflected in the next few moments as Westlake pounded a double to left center to score Avila and Al Smith and give the Indians the lead. The roar of the historic crowd sounded like water running into a bathtub. Like in the standings, the Indians were now in charge.

As the game wore on, Wynn became dominant. Following Berra's homer, Wynn caught fire, allowing just one hit for the remainder of the game while collecting twelve strikeouts. He mowed down Yankee batters through the sixth, seventh, and eighth but would have to face the heart of the New York lineup in the ninth. Wynn opened by fooling veteran Enos Slaughter and getting a called third strike but now would face the Yankees' two primary power hitters: Berra and twenty-two-year-old Mickey Mantle. Wynn faced down the blonde-haired youngster and struck him out swinging. Now one out away from a crowning victory, he would face Berra, the only man to inflict any damage in the game. And, again following the magical script that kept unfolding, Berra also struck out swinging to end the game.

The Cleveland players swarmed onto the field, drowned in a raucous ovation from their adoring fans. There were still ten games to play, but it didn't matter. "They knew they had done it," Dan Cordtz wrote in the *Plain Dealer*, "battered the cocky Yankees hopelessly out of the pennant race." The Indians swaggered into their clubhouse shouting, singing, clapping, and banging bats. Their great nemesis had been vanquished on the largest stage baseball had ever seen. "No gambler, actor, or politician ever had a funeral like the one that 86,563 persons saw in the Stadium yesterday," Seeger wrote.

As had been the story all season, Cleveland's pitching was utterly fantastic. Both Lemon and Wynn pitched complete games, surrendering just nine New York hits in eighteen innings. Mantle, who would hit .300 on the year with twenty-seven homers and 102 RBI, struck out in six of his seven at-bats. Conversely, Avila collected five hits on his own, raising his season average to a league-best .340. "What a day, what a day," Avila cooed afterward. "Maybe I've had better hitting days, but never one that meant as much as this."

The sentiment carried over to the team itself. There had been—and would be—better days statistically and symbolically, but no day ever held as much promise as the one of that emphatic Sunday sweep that capped the greatest summer in Cleveland history.

Yankees	2	0	0	0	0	0	0	0	0	=2
Indians	0	0	0	0	3	0	0	0	x	=3

NEW YORK

	AB	R	H	RBI
Bauer rf	4	0	1	0
Carey 3b	2	1	1	0
Slaughter ph	1	0	0	0
Mantle cf	3	0	0	0
Berra c	4	1	1	2
Robinson 1b	3	0	0	0
Noren lf	2	0	0	0
McDougald 2b	3	0	0	0
Rizzuto ss	3	0	0	0
Byrne p	3	0	0	0
TOTAL	28	2	3	2

	IP	H	R	ER	BB	SO
Byrne (L)	8	7	3	3	3	5

CLEVELAND

	AB	R	H	RBI
Smith lf	2	1	2	0
Avila 2b	4	1	3	1
Doby cf	1	0	0	0
Westlake cf	3	0	1	2
Majeski 3b	4	0	0	0
Wertz 1b	3	0	0	0
Rosen ph	0	0	0	0
Glynn pr-1b	0	0	0	0
Philley rf	4	0	0	0
Strickland ss	4	0	0	0
Hegan c	3	0	0	0
Wynn p	3	1	1	0
TOTAL	31	3	7	3

	IP	H	R	ER	BB	SO
Wynn (W)	9	3	2	2	2	12

Attendance: 84,587

#7

INDIANS 15, SEATTLE MARINERS 14 (11 INNINGS)
AUGUST 5, 2001

The Sunday-Night Miracle

"Cover up those eyes. Head for shelter. Here come the Seattle Mariners, and this could be big-time ugly."

Burt Graeff's words in Friday's *Plain Dealer*—while true—hit a sore spot. A promising 2001 season for the Indians had soured as July turned to August. After rallying from a five-game deficit to the Minnesota Twins two weeks before to take over first place in the American League Central Division, the Tribe began to fall apart, losing six of seven games. In those six defeats, Cleveland's offense was invisible, only managing to score seventeen runs. "The firepower to mace their way to victory simply isn't there anymore," Bill Livingston noted. Luckily, the Twins also floundered and Cleveland clung to a half-game lead going into the first weekend of August. But coming into town that weekend for a four-game set was the best team in baseball—a squad looking to distinguish itself as perhaps the finest ever to play the game.

The Seattle Mariners had been competitive throughout the late 1990s, but in 2001, everything fell into place. They roared to a 20–4 start and never slowed, capturing their seventy-fifth win at the end of July. Gunning for the all-time single-season victory record set by the Yankees three years before, the Mariners arrived in Cleveland having won six of their last seven and holding a 78–30 record and a twenty-game lead in the AL West. They were two teams headed in opposite directions, so it came as no surprise when Seattle had its way with Cleveland in the first two games, improving its winning percentage to an astonishing .727. Consequently, the Indians now dropped out of first and fell a game and a half behind Minnesota. Though the third game of the series would be televised nationally by ESPN on a Sunday night, neither the

Indians nor their fans could generate much excitement. Primarily, they seemed to wince and prepare to absorb Seattle's next blow. And it was a doozy.

The Mariners rocked Cleveland starting pitcher Dave Burba for four runs in the second inning, then chased him from the game in an eight-run, thirteen-batter third that made it 12–0. Unfortunately for the Indians, this type of meltdown was nothing new. In the previous week they'd lost games 11–2 and 17–4, so this Sunday-night massacre simply was the continuation of a disturbing trend. Burba was removed in the third, and Cleveland manager Charlie Manuel sent forth a sacrificial lamb—rookie Mike Bacsik, making his major-league debut. Not surprisingly, he was battered as well to the tune of seven runs and nine hits in six innings of relief, though he accomplished his primary mission: eat up some innings, save the bullpen for another day, and try not to let things get too ridiculous.

The Indians prevented the shutout when Jim Thome hit a two-run homer in the fourth, but the businesslike Mariners came right back with another pair in the fifth to make it 14–2. Seattle starting pitcher Aaron Sele then cruised through the next two innings, retiring the Indians in order in the fifth and the sixth, by which time Manuel had removed a handful of starters to get some playing time for guys on the bench. Still up by twelve in the bottom of the seventh, it seemed inconsequential when Sele hit some turbulence, surrendering a leadoff homer to Russell Branyan, then loading the bases with two out. Indians replacement second baseman Jolbert Cabrera then delivered a two-run single, but when the dust settled, Seattle got out of the inning still leading by nine.

Bacsik did his part, hurling his third consecutive scoreless frame, then things started to get interesting in the bottom of the eighth. Thome led off with his second homer of the night, and after Branyan was hit by a pitch, right fielder Marty Cordova blasted a home run to left. In just a few minutes, a twelve-run lead had been cut to six, and what remained of the sellout crowd began to stir. At the very least, the lethargic Indians were showing signs of life. And the hits just kept on coming.

Catcher Einar Diaz and Kenny Lofton hit back-to-back one-out singles, then Omar Vizquel brought home Diaz with a double to make it 14–9. Cleveland's sudden momentum appeared quelled when Lofton was thrown out at the plate trying to score on a wild pitch and Cabrera struck out, stranding Vizquel in scoring position. The Mariners took a very comfortable five-run lead into the bottom of the ninth, when reality began to melt away into fantasy.

Pinch-hitter Eddie Taubensee led off with a single to center, but then Thome lifted a fly to right and Branyan struck out, and the Mariners were one out away from yet another victory. Cordova then seemed to simply delay the inevitable with a double to left to send Taubensee to third. Still, Seattle manager Lou Piniella was concerned enough to lift veteran reliever Norm Charlton for Jeff Nelson, who'd anchored the Yankee bullpen for the previous five seasons and had played a huge role in delivering four championships. Nelson worked the next batter, Wil Cordero, to a full count, but then walked him, loading the bases for Einar Diaz, who followed with a two-strike line drive to left to score Taubensee and Cordova and make it 14–11. The tying run would come to the plate in Lofton, and Piniella made a move that an hour before would have seemed ludicrous: he called for his closer, Kazuhiro Sasaki.

Lofton grounded Sasaki's second pitch into left for the fourth hit of the inning, loading the bases again. The crowd, by now a skeleton crew, had whipped itself into a frenzy. A twelve-run lead had been chipped to three, and the go-ahead run stood at the plate in Omar Vizquel, one of the best clutch hitters ever to don a Cleveland uniform. The former Mariner battled Sasaki, and again the Indians were one strike away from defeat. But once more, they endured. Vizquel ripped a line drive down the first-base line and the ball rolled into the right-field corner. Cordero scored. Diaz scored. And Lofton scored all the way from first as Vizquel motored into third with perhaps the biggest triple in team history. The Indians, down by twelve runs just two innings before, had come back to tie the game. The roar of the fans was deafening. "It was as loud as '95," Manuel would say later, recalling a spectacular Indians summer that by 2001 seemed decades past. Cabrera's groundout to end the inning did little to quell the enthusiasm.

Now with new life, the Cleveland bullpen was reenergized. Bob Wickman cruised through the tenth, and the resurgent Indians offense had a chance to end the game in the bottom of the inning with runners on first and second with two out. But Cordero struck out to extend this surreal game into the eleventh. Recently acquired reliever John Rocker struck out the Seattle side in the top of the frame, and the Indians got cooking again in the bottom when Lofton and Vizquel hit back-to-back singles. It brought up Cabrera, who swung at the first pitch from Jose Paniagua. The contact shattered his bat, sending splinters spiraling into the infield, but the ball lofted into left field and fell for Cleveland's twenty-third hit of the night. Lofton, still possessing his legendary speed, tore around third and sailed headfirst into home ahead of the throw from left fielder Mark McLemore. At 12:19 A.M. Monday, after four hours and eleven minutes of zaniness, a game for the ages was finally over. Technically, it was nothing more than an August regular-season game. But to the Indians and their fans, it seemed like so much more. "It felt like winning the seventh game of the World Series," Wickman would say later.

Reflecting that emotion, Taubensee, the on-deck hitter, met Lofton at the plate and jubilantly lifted him upside down onto his shoulders like a sack of potatoes and carried him off the field as their teammates smothered them in celebration. "I caught him and I wasn't going to let him go," Taubensee said. "He was the king of the night and I was going to let him get all the credit he deserved." The team as a whole deserved to share the credit. There were too many heroes to single out just one: Lofton, Vizquel, and Cordova each had four hits, while Vizquel knocked in four runs and Cabrera and Thome drove in three. Cleveland's last three pitchers—Rich Rodriguez, Wickman, and Rocker—only permitted one base runner in the final three innings of the game, giving the offense time to put together the historic rally. And what a rally it was.

They'd matched the greatest comeback in baseball history. The only other times a team had rallied from a twelve-run deficit were in 1925 and 1911, but in both cases the comeback began before the seventh inning. No team had ever come from so far back with so little time to do so. "A game unlike any other came droning along last night," Livingston wrote, "starting as just another blowout by Seattle against an Indians team whose season was going down the tubes."

The Sunday-night miracle reenergized the Tribe for the stretch drive, as it pulled away to win the Central Division by six games. But even without the reward of a playoff berth, what happened that August night was so incredibly unlikely as to be considered impossible—maybe never to be seen again. "The biggest lesson this game teaches you," Manuel said, "is to never give up and to keep on swinging."

Mariners	0	4	8	0	2	0	0	0	0	0	0	=14
Indians	0	0	0	2	0	0	3	4	5	0	1	=15

SEATTLE

	AB	R	H	RBI
Suzuki rf	3	0	1	3
Gipson rf-lf-rf	2	0	0	0
McLemore 2b-lf	5	2	2	0
Martinez dh	4	2	2	1
Javier ph-dh	2	0	0	0
Olerud 1b	3	1	2	1
Sprague 1b	3	0	1	1
Martin lf-rf	6	2	3	1
Wilson c	0	0	0	0
Cameron cf	6	2	3	3
Guillen ss	6	1	1	2
Bell 3b	5	2	1	0
Lampkin c	4	2	1	1
Boone ph-2b	1	0	0	0
TOTAL	50	14	17	13

	IP	H	R	ER	BB	SO
Sele	6⅔	8	5	5	3	3
Halama	⅔	5	4	4	0	0
Charlton	1⅓	3	2	2	0	2
Nelson	0	1	2	2	1	0
Sasaki	⅓	2	1	1	0	0
Rhodes	1	1	0	0	1	2
Paniagua (L)	⅓	3	1	1	0	0

CLEVELAND

	AB	R	H	RBI
Lofton cf	6	3	4	0
Vizquel ss	6	0	4	4
Alomar 2b	2	0	0	0
Cabrera 2b	5	0	2	3
Gonzalez dh	2	1	1	0
Taubensee dh	4	1	1	0
Thome 1b	5	2	2	3
Burks lf	2	0	0	0
Branyan lf-3b	3	2	2	1
Cordova rf	5	2	4	2
Fryman 3b	2	0	0	0
Cordero lf	3	1	0	0
Diaz c	6	3	3	2
TOTAL	51	15	23	15

	IP	H	R	ER	BB	SO
Burba	2	7	7	7	1	2
Bacsik	6	9	7	6	1	2
Rodriguez	1	0	0	0	0	0
Wickman	1	1	0	0	0	0
Rocker (W)	1	0	0	0	0	3

Attendance: 42,494

#6

INDIANS 5, BOSTON RED SOX 4 (13 INNINGS)
OCTOBER 3, 1995

2 A.M. Lightning

For better or worse, a magnificent, majestic summer was now officially over and it was time for the Indians and their long-suffering fans to discover what the 1995 edition was truly made of. On a dreary, drizzly Tuesday evening in downtown Cleveland, the Indians would play a postseason game—a mere 14,965 days since their last one.

To say the city was ready would have been the understatement of the century. More than 20,000 fans piled into Jacobs Field at 10:30 Monday morning to watch the Indians go through the motions in an informal practice. The typical cynical Cleveland skepticism had largely been replaced by unbridled optimism. "People aren't even entertaining the thought that we could lose," Cleveland coach Dave Nelson said. Even those who did weren't prepared for what the Indians had in store for them in their long-awaited playoff opener.

The Tribe would face another tough-luck franchise in the Boston Red Sox in a best-of-five Division Series. Though a regular playoff contender, the Red Sox hadn't won a world title in nearly eighty years. Clearly, with two powerful hexes colliding, something had to give. The Indians, some fourteen games better than Boston during the regular season, were clear favorites going into the series but would have to face a longtime nemesis in the opening game: Boston starting pitcher Roger Clemens, who had utterly dominated Cleveland in his ten-year career.

After the start of the game was postponed nearly forty minutes by rain (two more delays would follow in the coming hours), both Clemens and his counterpart, Cleveland starter Dennis Martinez, cruised through the first two innings. Boston surged ahead in the third when shortstop John Valentin blasted a two-run home run to right, and Clemens continued to shut down the Indians' heralded offense. After he retired the first two Cleveland batters in the bottom of the sixth, an uneasy silence settled over Jacobs Field. To win 100 of 144 games in the regular season and then get handled at home in the first game of a short playoff series had all the earmarks of yet another Cleveland postseason collapse.

Things changed in a hurry when Omar Vizquel walked and moved to third on a Carlos Baerga single. It brought up Albert Belle, the hottest and most feared hitter in baseball in 1995, and he blasted Clemens's second pitch off the wall in left center to score both Vizquel and Baerga to tie the game. The crowd was back to life, reminded that these Indians had come from behind countless times already in 1995, winning twenty-seven games in their last at-bat. The collective worry faded into the damp October night, apparently for good when Eddie Murray followed with a single to score Belle and give the Indians a 3–2 lead. With baseball's best bullpen now primed for action, the game was the Indians' for the taking.

Reliever Julian Tavarez set down Boston in order in the seventh, and the Tribe crept closer to victory. Leading off the eighth, light-hitting Boston second baseman Luis Alecea launched a homer just over the right-field wall to tie the game again. Paul Assenmacher and Eric Plunk combined forces to thwart another Boston threat in the inning, and then Plunk pitched his way out of a two-on, one-out jam in the ninth. With the crowd buzzing, anticipating yet another dramatic finish, three of the Indians' power threats—Jim Thome, Manny Ramirez, and Paul Sorrento—each went down meekly in the ninth, and the game was extended into extra innings. Little did anyone know the drama was just beginning.

Jose Mesa, fresh off an amazing season as Cleveland's closer in which he racked up forty-six saves, instantly got into trouble in the tenth when he walked the first two Boston batters. After Red Sox cleanup hitter Mo Vaughn flew out to center, Thome snared a Jose Canseco liner to third for the second out, then fired to second to double up Dwayne Hosey and end the inning. With clocks passing midnight, the Indians squandered a scoring chance in the bottom of the tenth, then appeared to once again be snake-bitten in the eleventh.

Boston third baseman Tim Naehring, who'd hit just twenty-three home runs in his six-year major-league career, hit a one-out homer to left off Jim Poole to give the Red Sox a 4–3 lead. The Jacobs Field fans, now nearly exhausted and running solely on nervous energy, again hoped against hope for another comeback. Leading off the inning against Rick Aguilera, one of the game's finest closers, Belle rocketed a line drive into the darkness that sailed over the nineteen-foot wall in left field for a dramatic game-tying home run.

After crossing home plate to a rousing ovation, Belle was informed that Boston manager Kevin Kennedy had requested Belle's bat be confiscated and checked for cork—an infraction for which Belle had been suspended the previous season. Later that night, AL Commissioner Bobby Brown had the bat sawed in half. It came out clean and Belle was vindicated. Kennedy tried to shrug off the move, claiming the Boston front office had instructed him to have the bat checked. "It's just a desperate effort to throw a monkey wrench in our season," Belle would say. More memorable was his reaction. Belle glared into the Boston dugout, flexed his right arm, and pointed to his bulging biceps with his left hand. "Right there!" he screamed. "Right fucking there!"

For all the theatrics, the game was far from over.

Aguilera gave up two more hits but Boston got through the eleventh, then threatened again in the twelfth when Alicea led off with a double. Poole struck out Hosey, then, after an intentional walk to Valentin, whiffed Vaughn on three pitches. With two down, Ken Hill was called on to face the dangerous Canseco, and Hill responded with a four-pitch strikeout to end the threat. The Tribe then clawed to the cusp of victory in the bottom of the inning when Lofton was hit by a pitch and moved to third on a Boston error. But Baerga popped out. Then after Belle was intentionally walked, Lofton was forced out at the plate on a Murray grounder and Thome grounded to first. Now it was the Red Sox who had new life. And once again, they threatened in the thirteenth with a leadoff single by Mike Greenwell, who then moved to second with two down. Hill got backup catcher Bill Haselman to ground back to the mound to end the frame.

It was 2 A.M. when the Indians came to bat in the bottom of the thirteenth. Much of the capacity crowd—which had been electric at the game's outset six hours before—had departed, and both teams were running on fumes. Each pitching staff had endured the lethal portion of the opposition's batting order, and it seemed as though the game might spiral toward dawn, especially when Red Sox pitcher Zane Smith retired the first two Cleveland batters in the thirteenth. It brought up backup catcher Tony Peña, an eleventh-inning replacement for Sandy Alomar. Released by Boston in 1993 after four seasons with the Red Sox, Peña worked a 3-and-0 count on Smith and waited for the signal from Mike Hargrove as to whether he was to swing away or take the fourth pitch. Either torn by indecision or fatigued by the epic marathon the game had become, Hargrove hesitated. "I gave him the take sign," he would say later, "but I gave it real late."

Late enough that Peña never saw it. Instead, he cut at the pitch, a waist-high fastball, and sent it floating toward left center. It drifted in the cool autumn morning and, at 2:08 A.M., just cleared the left-field wall for possibly the most dramatic home run in Indians history. The remaining fans—exhausted and nearing delirium—roared with celebration and relief. Peña threw his arms into the air as he circled the bases, appearing as surprised as anyone. The least likely hero on the roster—with just five home runs and twenty-eight RBI on the season—had just delivered not only the Indians' twelfth game-winning homer of 1995 but also the team's first postseason victory in two generations in one of the most remarkable playoff games ever. It was a bizarre contest that had a little bit of everything and was perhaps the only kind of game that could have lived up to four decades of expectation.

"Forty-one years without playoffs," Michael K. McIntyre wrote in the *Plain Dealer*, "then a playoff game that felt like forty-one years."

Red Sox	0 0 2	0 0 0	0 1 0	0 1 0	0	=4
Indians	0 0 0	0 0 3	0 0 0	0 1 0	1	=5

BOSTON

	AB	R	H	RBI
Hosey rf	5	1	0	0
Valentin ss	4	1	2	2
Vaughn 1b	6	0	0	0
Canseco dh	6	0	0	0
Greenwell lf	6	0	3	0
Naehring 3b	5	1	2	1
Tinsley cf	5	0	0	0
Macfarlane c	3	0	0	0
Stairs ph	1	0	0	0
Haselman c	2	0	0	0
Alicea 2b	5	1	4	1
TOTAL	48	4	11	4

	IP	H	R	ER	BB	SO
Clemens	7	5	3	3	1	5
Cormier	⅓	0	0	0	1	1
Belinda	⅓	0	0	0	0	0
Stanton	2⅓	1	0	0	0	0
Aguilera	⅔	3	1	1	0	1
Maddux	⅔	0	0	0	1	0
Smith (L)	1⅓	1	1	1	0	0

CLEVELAND

	AB	R	H	RBI
Lofton cf	5	0	1	0
Vizquel ss	3	1	0	0
Baerga 2b	5	1	2	0
Belle lf	5	2	2	3
Murray dh	6	0	1	1
Thome 3b	6	0	1	0
Ramirez rf	6	0	0	0
Sorrento 1b	5	0	1	0
Perry ph	1	0	0	0
Alomar c	4	0	1	0
Kirby pr	0	0	0	0
Peña c	2	1	1	1
TOTAL	48	5	10	5

	IP	H	R	ER	BB	SO
Martinez	6	5	2	2	0	2
Tavarez	1⅓	2	1	1	0	2
Assenmacher	⅓	0	0	0	0	1
Plunk	1⅓	1	0	0	1	1
Mesa	1	0	0	0	2	0
Poole	1⅔	2	1	1	1	2
Hill (W)	1⅓	1	0	0	0	0

Attendance: 44,218

#5

INDIANS 3, TORONTO BLUE JAYS 0
MAY 15, 1981

A Great Story to Tell

In many ways it was a typical early season Indians contest: the crowd was small, the weather was cold and drizzly, and most baseball fans weren't really paying attention. By the time the night was over, however, fans across the country would be focused on Cleveland Stadium—specifically, on one man's quest for baseball immortality.

Big Lenny Barker was off to a good start in 1981. Picking up where he left off in 1980, the six-foot-five pitcher had posted a 1.67 ERA in the first month of the season, winning a pair of games. He'd won nineteen the year before in a breakthrough season after coming to Cleveland from Texas in a ho-hum 1978 trade for mediocre pitcher Jim Kern and slap-hitter Larvell Banks. With Barker leading the way, the Tribe was off to a quick start in '81, winning fifteen of their first twenty-three games and surging into first place in the American League East on the first of May. They'd remain there for the next seventeen days, raising hopes that this might be the Indians team that finally turned a corner. Though the two-month players' strike in midsummer imploded the season and the Tribe never put together enough momentum to get much over the .500 mark, on a damp Friday night Barker would ensure that the 1981 season would be remembered in Cleveland.

It started in the bullpen as Barker warmed up. Pitching coach Dave Duncan was amazed at how beautifully Barker's curve ball was breaking and told manager Mike Garcia he'd never seen it better. It was impossible for hitters to tell from the rotation of the ball whether the pitch was a fastball or a curveball. Duncan casually predicted Barker would turn in another good game. "I know that I had good stuff," Barker would say later, "maybe awesome stuff. I had total command. I could throw anything anywhere I wanted."

The Cleveland ace got rolling early, getting the first three Toronto hitters to ground out, then his offense vaulted out of the starting blocks. Center fielder Rick Manning led off the game with a single and scored on a sacrifice fly by Andre Thornton. First baseman Mike Hargrove then reached on an error and came home on a Ron Hassey single to right. The Indians were quickly up 2–0, and Barker had all the support he would need.

He mowed down the Blue Jays in order the first time through the lineup, then in the fourth inning started to overpower them. Effectively using his devastating breaking ball, Barker struck out two straight to end the fourth, then picked up two more strikeouts in the fifth and another pair in the sixth—by which time everyone in the ballpark knew what was taking place. After Barker collected his sixth strikeout, moments after Cleveland second baseman Duane Kuiper made a nifty play on a well-hit ball to retire Rick Bosetti, the realization began to spread through the stadium—Barker was pitching a perfect game. Eighteen batters had come to the plate and eighteen had been retired. Now the tension began to build. "In the dugout between innings we just tried to go about our business and not put any pressure on Lenny," Toby Harrah said, "but it was awfully tough. It's like having a great story to tell, but not being able to tell it."

Kuiper made another impressive play to open the seventh, but from then on, the Jays batters never came close to reaching base. As had become his custom, Barker whiffed the next two batters in the seventh, then two more in the eighth to bring his total to ten. Cleveland right fielder Jorge Orta added insurance with a solo homer in the bottom of the eighth but also postponed the climax that 7,290 were dying to witness.

Bosetti started the ninth with a foul pop to third, caught by Harrah. Barker then took matters into his own hands, collecting his eleventh strikeout against Al Woods, pinch-hitting for young Toronto third baseman Danny Ainge—who would go on to notoriety with the NBA's Boston Celtics in the coming years. With the fans on their feet and mesmerized, Barker faced another pinch-hitter, Ernie Whitt. Whitt swung at a fastball and lifted a lazy fly to center. "I didn't even look up when Whitt hit the last ball," Barker would say. He didn't need to. Manning casually jogged over and caught it, then leaped into the air and sprinted back to the infield to join the mauling his teammates were laying on the man who had pitched just the eleventh perfect game in baseball history.

It had been thirteen years since anyone had done it, seventy-three since Addie Joss had become the only other Cleveland pitcher to mark the achievement. Barker's teammates laid out a trail of towels leading across the floor to his locker and arranged a collection of beer cans into a large zero. Beside them was a bottle of champagne. As Lenny Barker gulped down the bubbly, longtime sportswriters could only shake their heads in amazement. This was the same man who had started his career with miserable control problems. "He used to throw one out of every five pitches back to the screen," Garcia said. "Now he is a complete pitcher who knows what he's doing." On this perfect night, Barker's control was immaculate. Not once did he reach three balls on any batter, and he never even fired five balls in an inning. Of his economic 103 pitches, a whopping eighty-four were for strikes. "I have never seen a better pitched game," Garcia admitted.

Barker's clean slate wound up providing the highlight of not only the season but of the entire decade—the one glimmering majestic moment in a dark forest of mediocrity. There wasn't much that Indians players or fans wanted to remember from the 1980s, but this May night would never be forgotten. "It was a tremendous thing—the only thing that would be more tremendous would be for us to play in a World Series," Hargrove said, "and that might happen."

It would, ironically, with Hargrove as manager, but it still couldn't completely overshadow Lenny Barker's perfect night. As Toby Harrah said, it was indeed a great story to tell—and once the final out was recorded, it could finally be shared with the world.

Blue Jays	0	0	0	0	0	0	0	0	0	=0
Indians	2	0	0	0	0	0	0	1	x	=3

TORONTO

	AB	R	H	RBI
Griffin ss	3	0	0	0
Moseby rf	3	0	0	0
Bell lf	3	0	0	0
Mayberry 1b	3	0	0	0
Upshaw dh	3	0	0	0
Garcia 2b	3	0	0	0
Bosetti cf	3	0	0	0
Ainge 3b	2	0	0	0
Woods ph	1	0	0	0
Martinez c	2	0	0	0
Whitt ph	1	0	0	0
TOTAL	27	0	0	0

	IP	H	R	ER	BB	SO
Leal (L)	8	7	3	1	0	5

CLEVELAND

	AB	R	H	RBI
Manning cf	4	1	1	0
Orta rf	4	1	3	1
Hargrove 1b	4	1	1	0
Thornton dh	3	0	0	1
Hassey c	4	0	1	1
Harrah 3b	4	0	1	0
Charboneau lf	3	0	0	0
Kuiper 2b	3	0	0	0
Veryzer ss	3	0	0	0
TOTAL	32	3	7	3

	IP	H	R	ER	BB	SO
Barker (W)	9	0	0	0	0	11

Attendance: 7,290

#4

INDIANS 4, SEATTLE MARINERS 0
OCTOBER 17, 1995

Silence in Seattle

For the majority of Clevelanders, this was the closest they had ever been to a World Series. With back-to-back clutch victories at Jacobs Field over the weekend, the Indians had surged to a three-games-to-two lead over the Seattle Mariners in the 1995 American League Championship Series and needed just one more win to secure their first World Series appearance in more than four decades.

Yet the excitement and anticipation surrounding the historic potential of Game Six was notably subdued around Cleveland, since the Indians would have to face baseball's most imposing pitcher in perhaps the worst venue in the league. The Mariners had enjoyed a Cinderella ride to the ALCS, rallying from a 12½-game deficit in late August to force a one-game playoff with the California Angels for the West Division title. On the mound in that critical contest was six-foot-ten-inch Randy Johnson, who held the Angels to one run over nine innings in a 9–1 stomping that gave Johnson his eighteenth victory of an abbreviated season and the Mariners their first-ever playoff berth. The excitement continued in the Division Series as Seattle rallied from a two-game deficit to defeat the Yankees in five thrilling games, two of which were won by Johnson.

Now Seattle would turn to its ace and request one more masterpiece performance against the Indians to force Game Seven which, like Game Six, would be played in the concrete bunker known as the Seattle Kingdome, where raucous sellout crowds had rocked and rattled opponents for the past six weeks. Neither the Indians nor their fans wanted anything to do with a deciding Game Seven 2,300 miles from home in which their starting pitcher would be Charles Nagy, who held a career 0–5 record in the Kingdome with a 6.82 ERA. But neither did they like the prospect of facing Johnson with the season on the line. Seattle was 30–3 in games Johnson pitched in 1995 and had won three contests he'd pitched in the previous fifteen days in which a loss would have concluded the Mariners' season.

"Enough already," Joe Dirck wrote in the *Plain Dealer*. "These games with Seattle have been anxiety-ridden, agonizing, tension-wracked torture sessions that leave me drained and exhausted no matter who wins." But, Dirck continued, he was loving every minute of it. "One game. The World Series is that close. This is what Cleveland fans have been dreaming about for forty-one years. We should be savoring every moment, reveling in the fun this unfamiliar experience offers."

Thrown out to counter Johnson like a sacrificial lamb was forty-year-old Cleveland pitcher Dennis Martinez, who, despite putting together a marvelous career, had never won a postseason game. "That would be the best gift that baseball has ever given me," Martinez said the day before.

Not surprisingly, with the home crowd snarling and rattling the foundation of the Kingdome behind him, Johnson began rolling early. He struck out the Cleveland side in the second and came up big in the first and fourth with three key outs with runners in scoring position. Much more quietly, Martinez was matching Johnson scoreless frame for scoreless frame, wiggling away from a leadoff double in the third by enticing three straight groundouts. "I was telling the guys on the bench, 'All we need is one run, that's all we need tonight,'" Cleveland catcher Tony Peña said later. "The way Dennis was throwing, that's all we needed."

The Indians caught a break in the fifth when third baseman Alvaro Espinoza reached base and advanced to second on a one-out throwing error. After Johnson retired Peña, Kenny Lofton ripped a single into left field to score Espinoza and temporarily subdue the Kingdome crowd. A double play got Martinez out of trouble in the bottom of the inning, and then he came up with the pitch of the night by striking out dangerous designated hitter Edgar Martinez with runners on second and third to end the sixth. "I threw a pitch I don't even know what it was," Dennis Martinez said. "A lucky pitch." He then cruised through the seventh and fans began to wonder if one unearned run might actually be enough. In the eighth, the suspense ended in dramatic fashion.

With Johnson finally beginning to show signs of fatigue, Peña led off with a double to right center and was replaced by pinch-runner Ruben Amaro. Lofton, who would bat a record .458 for the ALCS, was up next and laid down a perfect bunt along the third-base line that allowed Amaro to advance to third as he reached first. Lofton, energized by the realization that the Indians were now wearing on the mighty Johnson, promptly stole second—his fifth stolen base of the series. And his excitement would manifest itself a moment later in one of the greatest plays in Indians history.

Johnson's next pitch sailed past catcher Dan Wilson and rolled to the backstop. As Amaro sprinted home, a downtrodden Wilson casually jogged back to retrieve the ball, conceding Amaro's run. However, Wilson had forgotten who was on second base. Lofton motored into third and rolled around the bag still sailing at full speed. "I wasn't going to try and score at first," Lofton said. "I was just bluffing. But Wilson kind of took his time getting to the ball, so I just came home." Never slowing, Lofton flew down the third-base line just as Johnson lagged to cover the plate. Amidst the constant noise echoing through the Kingdome, Johnson couldn't hear the shouts of his teammates alerting him to Lofton's approach. Wilson realized what was happening as he scooped up the ball and quickly fired to Johnson. Just as the ball hit Johnson's glove, Lofton slid beneath Seattle's giant to score the third run. "Lofton turned Johnson into Wile E. Coyote," Bud Shaw wrote, "the keg of TNT exploding in the arm-weary Seattle pitcher's face."

In that instant, the roar that had sustained the Kingdome over the previous month was silenced once and for all. A jubilant Lofton returned to the Cleveland dugout and was embraced by his teammates, the pennant now firmly in their grasp. Carlos Baerga followed with a home run off Johnson, who was then taken out of the game to a standing ovation. The Seattle faithful knew the ride was over. Julian Tavarez and Jose Mesa cruised through the eighth and ninth, and when Espinoza fielded a Jay Buhner grounder and threw on to Herbert Perry at first for the final out, the Cleveland Indians were American League champions.

"The Indians not only exorcised the demons of their own four decades of futility," Dirck would write, "they energized a community that had grown sadly accustomed over the years to cruelly dashed hopes. . . . The Indians shooed away the jinx that has bedeviled Cleveland sports teams for as long as many fans can remember."

Back in Cleveland, the party began, with fans spilling into the Flats and downtown streets. Just past 11 P.M., church bells rang all over Northeast Ohio—symbolizing the almost religious significance of what had just occurred. "Disbelief," Mike Hargrove said afterward when asked to describe his emotions, "that this was the Cleveland Indians."

But it was, thanks to a gutsy performance by an aging veteran pitching the last great game of his career—seven innings, four hits, no runs. "After all I've been through in my career, this was the game I was looking for," Martinez said. "Finally, I did something we can all remember."

Indians	0	0	0	0	1	0	0	3	0	=4
Mariners	0	0	0	0	0	0	0	0	0	=0

CLEVELAND

	AB	R	H	RBI
Lofton cf	4	1	2	1
Vizquel ss	4	0	0	0
Baerga 2b	4	1	3	1
Belle lf	4	0	2	0
Murray dh	4	0	0	0
Ramirez rf	3	0	0	0
Kirby rf	1	0	0	0
Perry 1b	4	0	0	0
Espinoza 3b	4	1	0	0
Peña c	3	0	1	0
Amaro pr	0	1	0	0
Alomar c	0	0	0	0
TOTAL	35	4	8	2

	IP	H	R	ER	BB	SO
Martinez (W)	7	4	0	0	1	3
Tavarez	1	0	0	0	0	1
Mesa	1	0	0	0	1	1

SEATTLE

	AB	R	H	RBI
Coleman lf	4	0	1	0
Widger c	0	0	0	0
Cora 2b	4	0	0	0
Griffey cf	3	0	0	0
E. Martinez dh	3	0	1	0
T. Martinez 1b	3	0	0	0
Buhner rf	4	0	0	0
Blowers 3b	3	0	1	0
Sojo ss	3	0	1	0
Fermin ss	0	0	0	0
Wilson c	2	0	0	0
Diaz ph-lf	1	0	0	0
TOTAL	30	0	4	0

	IP	H	R	ER	BB	SO
Johnson (L)	7⅓	8	4	3	0	7
Charlton	1⅔	0	0	0	0	1

Attendance: 58,489

#3

INDIANS 8, BROOKLYN DODGERS 1
OCTOBER 10, 1920

A Day When Heroes Were Made

On a bright Sunday morning across downtown Cleveland, well-dressed families sat in hushed sanctuaries listening to peaceful sermons and homilies. But many of these religious soliloquies were suddenly interrupted by a commotion outside as packs of rabid baseball fans made their way through downtown toward League Park cheering and yelling enthusiastically for their Indians, set to play the fifth game of the World Series that afternoon.

In fact, many fans had saved themselves the round trip. After Cleveland's Game Four victory on Saturday, hundreds got right back in line at the League Park ticket office and spent the night to ensure they'd have seats for Sunday's matinee. Those who were among the 26,884 in attendance that Sunday would witness one of the most remarkable contests in World Series history, highlighted by a trio of historic plays.

On the mound for Cleveland was Jim Bagby, who'd exploded out of relative anonymity to win thirty-one games in 1920. After giving up a leadoff single to Brooklyn's Ivy Olson and a sacrifice bunt, Bagby retired Tommy Griffith and Zack Wheat to keep the Dodgers off the board. In the next few minutes, Bagby would get all the support he would need.

Facing Dodger star hurler Burleigh Grimes, who had silenced the Cleveland bats in a Game Two Brooklyn win, the Indians came out hot. Left fielder Charlie Jamieson led off with a single to left, followed by a hit to center by second baseman Bill Wambsganss. Player/manager Tris Speaker then laid down a perfect bunt to advance the runners and wound up on first base. With the bases loaded, up stepped right fielder Elmer Smith, who had hit twelve of Cleveland's thirty-five homers during the season. With the count 1-and-2, Grimes tried to sneak a splitter past Smith, and Smith smashed it toward right. It sailed over the wall, across Lexington Avenue, and into baseball lore as the first-ever grand slam in World Series history. The sellout crowd exploded into ovation, carrying over to the fans watching from atop buildings across the street from the ballpark who began hugging and dancing. The Indians led 4–0 and were already coasting to victory—but there were plenty of fireworks yet to come. "He was the first to be a hero on a day when heroes were made," the *Plain Dealer* would report.

Propelled by double plays in the second and third, Bagby kept the Dodgers at bay through the fourth, when the Indians' history-making machine warmed up once again, this time with Bagby at the controls. After first baseman Doc Johnston led off the bottom of the fourth with a single, Grimes intentionally walked catcher Steve O'Neill to face Bagby and try to quell the impending rally with one out. It was a major miscalculation. Bagby, a solid .252 hitter during the season, belted a majestic three-run homer to center—the first round-tripper by a pitcher in the seventeen-year history of the Fall Classic. The capacity crowd was now giddy with excitement. Not only was the home team ahead 7–0 but it had done so on a pair of plays no one would forget. But the best was yet to come.

The Dodgers threatened to make things interesting in their next at-bat as second baseman Pete Kilduff and catcher Otto Miller led off the fifth with singles. Both runners took off on the next pitch as replacement pitcher Clarence Mitchell then ripped a line drive up the middle, apparently destined for center field and an RBI hit. But Wambsganss took three quick steps onto the outfield grass and leaped into the air to make a remarkable catch to retire Mitchell. When he returned to earth, his baseball instincts informed him he still had work to do. He trotted to second and kicked it to retire Kilduff, who'd already reached third, then reached over and gently touched Miller, arriving at second, with his glove for the third out. The fans cheered wildly, knowing something good had happened, but it took a few moments to calculate precisely what. As the Indians came trotting off the field, an even louder roar began as realization dawned. Wambsganss had pulled off the rarest one-play feat in baseball—an unassisted triple play, just the third ever recorded. It was the first in major-league baseball in eleven years and would be Cleveland's last for eighty-eight more. And naturally, it was the first—and still only—unassisted triple play in the World Series.

With the afternoon now electric with excitement, the Indians added another run in the fifth on a Larry Gardner RBI single, and Bagby sailed through the late innings. The Dodgers tacked on a meaningless run in the ninth, but when Wambsganss gathered in a pop fly for the final out, the Indians put the finishing touch on a masterpiece. "Every thrill in baseball was crowded into the fifth game of the Series," Billy Evans wrote in the *PD*. "Figuratively, an entire season of baseball was crowded into eight and one-half innings of play."

While the Indians had surged to a three-games-to-two lead with a critical win, the trio of historic plays glistened from the series itself like jewels in a dark cave. “Had but one of those three events taken place yesterday, it would have been considered most notable,” wrote *PD* sports editor Henry P. Edwards, “but when three high spots in the chronicles of the national pastime come in such rapid succession, the historian runs out of adjectives.” Not that the scribes of the day still didn’t try. One noted that the Dodgers had been “crumpled and broken and just naturally obliterated” in “a kind of slaughter that almost curdled the blood of the most bloodthirsty fan and made him feel that the Indians’ victory was almost too easily earned.”

Though still in the midst of a pressure-packed World Series, Tris Speaker and his Indians understood the potential longevity of their actions. “We gave future teams playing in the world’s series something to shoot at,” the manager said. “It was one of the most remarkable games I ever took part in, and must have been a great game to watch. It surely was one of which I could feel proud to have participated in.”

Dodgers	0 0 0	0 0 0	0 0 1	=1
Indians	4 0 0	3 1 0	0 0 x	=8

BROOKLYN

	AB	R	H	RBI
Olson ss	4	0	2	0
Sheehan 3b	3	0	1	0
Griffith rf	4	0	0	0
Wheat lf	4	1	2	0
Myers cf	4	0	2	0
Konetchy 1b	4	0	2	1
Kilduff 2b	4	0	1	0
Miller c	2	0	2	0
Krueger c	2	0	1	0
Grimes p	1	0	0	0
Mitchell p	2	0	0	0
TOTAL	34	1	13	1

	IP	H	R	ER	BB	SO
Grimes (L)	3⅓	9	7	7	1	0
Mitchell	4⅔	3	1	0	3	1

CLEVELAND

	AB	R	H	RBI
Jamieson lf	4	1	2	0
Graney ph-lf	1	0	0	0
Wambsganss 2b	5	1	1	0
Speaker cf	3	2	1	0
Smith rf	4	1	3	4
Gardner 3b	4	0	1	1
Johnston 1b	3	1	2	0
Sewell ss	3	0	0	0
O'Neill c	2	1	0	0
Thomas c	0	0	0	0
Bagby p	4	1	2	3
TOTAL	33	8	12	8

	IP	H	R	ER	BB	SO
Bagby (W)	9	13	1	1	0	3

Attendance: 26,884

#2

INDIANS 4, SEATTLE MARINERS 3 (11 INNINGS)
APRIL 4, 1994

Starting All Over Again

Opening day had always been a special occasion in Cleveland—the day when weary citizens could officially declare victory over another brutal winter. Even the players would find new life in the process. "It means you're starting all over again," veteran Cleveland catcher Tony Peña noted on the final day of the 1994 training camp. But as that spring beckoned, the anticipation for the Indians' ninety-fourth opening day was something else again.

After four decades of painful frustration and four years of breathless anticipation, Cleveland fans awoke on a cold April morning to what they desperately hoped would be a brand-new era of Indians baseball. Cleveland Stadium, the rickety albatross that had symbolized the franchise's futility, was now a part of the Indians' past, and players and fans alike were eager to christen their new home: a shining jewel constructed at the corner of Carnegie and Ontario avenues known as Jacobs Field.

If this shimmering new ballpark couldn't shake the Indians out of their nearly half-decade slumber, nothing could. "Finally, there is a nice symmetry in the relationship between this town and its baseball team," Bud Shaw wrote. While expectations were clearly atmospheric for these new Indians and the crystal palace they now called home, even the most dewy-eyed idealist tempered his hopes for the opener. To turn around the fortunes of a franchise as sorry as the Indians would take more than one afternoon. However, Clevelanders would soon discover how extending this pathetic saga could indeed occur within the framework of one contest.

The Tribe's opponent for the christening of the new park would be the milquetoast Seattle Mariners, who, aside from a handful of top-tier players, had garnered little attention in their seventeen-year history. One of those stars was one of baseball's finest pitchers: six-foot, ten-inch Randy Johnson, who had come of age the year before to win nineteen games and establish himself as the most intimidating mound visage in the game. Though the Indians had gradually assembled one of the better lineups in the American League over the previous three seasons, they would be no match for Johnson in the early going.

After President Bill Clinton threw out the ceremonial first pitch, Cleveland dug itself an early hole on a sunny but chilly afternoon when veteran pitcher Dennis Martinez couldn't find his control in the first inning, walking two and hitting a batter, permitting Seattle to take a 1–0 lead. While Johnson also struggled in the first, walking a pair, he recovered to retire the Indians' top two up-and-coming hitters, Carlos Baerga and Albert Belle. The Mariners added another run in the third on a solo homer by left fielder Eric Anthony, and with Johnson starting to roll, it appeared that's all the offense Seattle would need. The "Big Unit" retired ten in a row into the fourth, then enticed a pair of double plays to wipe out walks in the fifth and sixth. Though Martinez had also settled and matched Johnson, allowing only two hits through the next four innings after Anthony's homer, by the end of the seventh, a chilling hush had settled over Jacobs Field. After Johnson retired Cleveland's three best hitters—Baerga, Belle, and Eddie Murray—in order on a mere nine pitches, it appeared he'd faced his last true threat of the game. That the Indians would lose on such a promising day was one thing, to get shut out another. But through seven innings, the imposing Randy Johnson had not allowed a single hit.

All thoughts of longtime Cleveland fans turned to Bob Feller, who fifty-four years before had become the only man to pitch a no-hitter on opening day. Now, with Feller's star-crossed franchise on the cusp of ridding itself of its miserable past, Johnson was about to not only rob Feller of perhaps his greatest historical distinction but also to utterly cripple the Indians franchise once again.

Veteran Candy Maldonado opened the bottom of the eighth with a walk, bringing catcher Sandy Alomar to the plate. Alomar, who had long represented the team's lone source of hope, stepped to the plate and ripped a 1–2 fastball through the right side of the infield for Cleveland's first hit of the day, season, and ballpark. The capacity crowd roared more with relief than satisfaction but began to crackle with unexpected enthusiasm moments later when Johnson uncorked a wild pitch that allowed the runners to move to second and third. Johnson's next pitch, a fastball, was belted into left field by twenty-one-year-old rookie Manny Ramirez. The baseball pounded off the signature nineteen-foot left-field wall for a double, scoring both Maldonado and Alomar to tie the game. Much like the franchise itself, the Indians had dug themselves out of a hole and earned a chance for ultimate triumph.

Johnson rallied to keep the score knotted, then after both teams threatened but were unable to score in the ninth, the historic contest went to extra innings. A pinch-hit, two-out RBI single by Seattle's Kevin Mitchell gave the Mariners a 3–2 lead in the tenth, and it appeared the Tribe's late-inning heroics would be for naught. After Ramirez drew a walk, another promising Cleveland farm-system product came through. Third baseman Jim Thome ripped a double down the first-base line to send pinch-runner Wayne Kirby to third, then after Seattle intentionally walked Kenny Lofton came what would go down as the most meaningful play of a day filled with portents.

With the bases loaded and one out, new Cleveland shortstop Omar Vizquel stepped to the plate to face his former team. He ripped a hard grounder up the middle which appeared destined to win the game. But Seattle second baseman Rich Amaral made a fantastic diving stop and flipped the baseball to second base, and, in that instant, the potential of the play turned 180 degrees. Thanks to Amaral's incredible play, the Mariners now had a chance to turn a double play that would win the game. Amaral flipped the ball up to Felix Fermin—the shortstop whom Cleveland had shipped to Seattle for Vizquel—and he caught it to force Lofton at second but then bobbled it in his attempt to fire the relay to first. Vizquel was safe, Kirby scored, and the game was tied once again.

After pitcher Eric Plunk cruised through the top of the eleventh, the Indians struck again in the bottom of the inning. Murray blasted a one-out double off the wall in left center, then moved to third on a sacrifice fly by Paul Sorrento. The Mariners opted to intentionally pass Alomar to face Kirby, who had been replaced as the starter in right field by Ramirez in spring training, then, coincidentally, replaced Ramirez in the tenth. He worked the count to 3-and-1 on Seattle reliever Kevin King, then laced a curveball into the shadows engulfing the left-field line. Murray raised his arms triumphantly as the ball floated over his head and jogged home for the winning run. After nearly four hours of tension and worry, the Indians had finally won their first-ever game at Jacobs Field, forever leaving their spotted past behind them. "The Rip Van Winkle era in Indians baseball is officially pre-empted," Shaw wrote. "The alarm clock: Jacobs Field. . . . They put opening day on the mantel with a bookend finish to the perfect beginning."

Fueled by the drama of the opener, the Indians suddenly became a force to be reckoned with. Winning time and time again in the late innings, they turned Jacobs Field into their own amusement park, and the synergy between team and stadium would create one of the most thrilling periods in franchise history, resulting in six division titles and two pennants over the next seven seasons. "The park and the team are exciting," a *Plain Dealer* editorial forecasted the next day, “ahead are a summer full of breezy, blue afternoon skies, and of traditions that will bind Jacobs Field to yesterday’s ballparks and today’s fans.”

All of it began with an epic eleven-inning victory on an unforgettable opening day. “You can say so many things about this game,” Maldonado said afterward. “But finally, when it’s over, it was just a beautiful ballgame.”

Mariners	1 0 1	0 0 0	0 0 0	1 0	=3
Indians	0 0 0	0 0 0	0 2 0	1 1	=4

SEATTLE

	AB	R	H	RBI
Amaral 2b	5	0	1	0
E. Martinez 3b	0	1	0	0
Blowers 3b	5	0	1	0
Griffey cf	4	1	1	0
Buhner rf	3	0	0	0
Anthony lf	4	1	1	2
T. Martinez 1b	4	0	1	0
Jefferson dh	3	0	1	0
Mitchell ph-dh	1	0	1	1
Wilson c	4	0	0	0
Fermin ss	5	0	0	0
TOTAL	38	3	7	3

	IP	H	R	ER	BB	SO
Johnson	8	2	2	2	5	2
Davis	⅔	2	0	0	0	0
Ayala	⅔	0	1	1	1	2
King (L)	1⅓	3	1	1	2	0

CLEVELAND

	AB	R	H	RBI
Lofton cf	3	0	0	0
Vizquel ss	4	0	0	1
Baerga 2b	5	0	0	0
Belle lf	5	0	1	0
Murray 1b	5	1	2	0
Maldonado dh	2	1	0	0
Sorrento ph-dh	2	0	0	0
Alomar c	3	1	1	0
Ramirez rf	3	0	1	2
Kirby pr-rf	1	1	1	1
Lewis 3b	2	0	0	0
Thome ph-3b	1	0	1	0
TOTAL	36	4	7	4

	IP	H	R	ER	BB	SO
Martinez	7	3	2	2	4	4
Swan	1	1	0	0	0	1
Mesa	1⅓	2	1	1	0	1
Lilliquist	⅓	1	0	0	1	0
Plunk (W)	1⅓	0	0	0	0	1

Attendance: 41,459

#1

INDIANS 8, BOSTON RED SOX 3
OCTOBER 4, 1948

Showdown in Beantown

As a cool autumn dusk began to settle over the lake, a huge Sunday crowd sat silent in cavernous Cleveland Stadium, hushed by a colossal disappointment that these fans and their future descendants would soon come to know all too well.

Their beloved Indians, who had won five of six and twelve of fourteen down the stretch in arguably the greatest pennant race in American League history, came into this Sunday matinee needing just one more win over the mediocre Detroit Tigers to clinch their first World Series appearance in twenty-eight years. "If all the fingernails which have been bitten off in the course of the pennant race were placed end to end," the *Plain Dealer* surmised, "they would reach from Cleveland to San Francisco." A throng of 74,000-plus packed into the ballpark expecting to witness a satisfying and glorious conclusion to a magnificent season. Instead, on a raw, windy afternoon they saw their Indians completely handcuffed by future Hall-of-Fame pitcher Hal Newhouser, who wrapped up his final twenty-win season with a dominating five-hit, 7–1 victory over Cleveland's own star hurler, Bob Feller. Meanwhile, 640 miles away in Boston's Fenway Park, the Red Sox were pounding the rival Yankees to pull into a tie with the Tribe atop the American League with identical 96–58 records.

The downhearted crowd filed out of the Stadium, slowly processing the reality of this new situation. The beleaguered Indians would board a train that evening and race the moon to New England, where on Monday afternoon they would face the Red Sox in the first American League one-game playoff. It was the scenario no one in Cleveland wanted. A trip to Boston, yes—to face the National League's Braves in the World Series, not to have to toil with the dangerous Red Sox in their quirky house-of-horrors ballpark, where, the

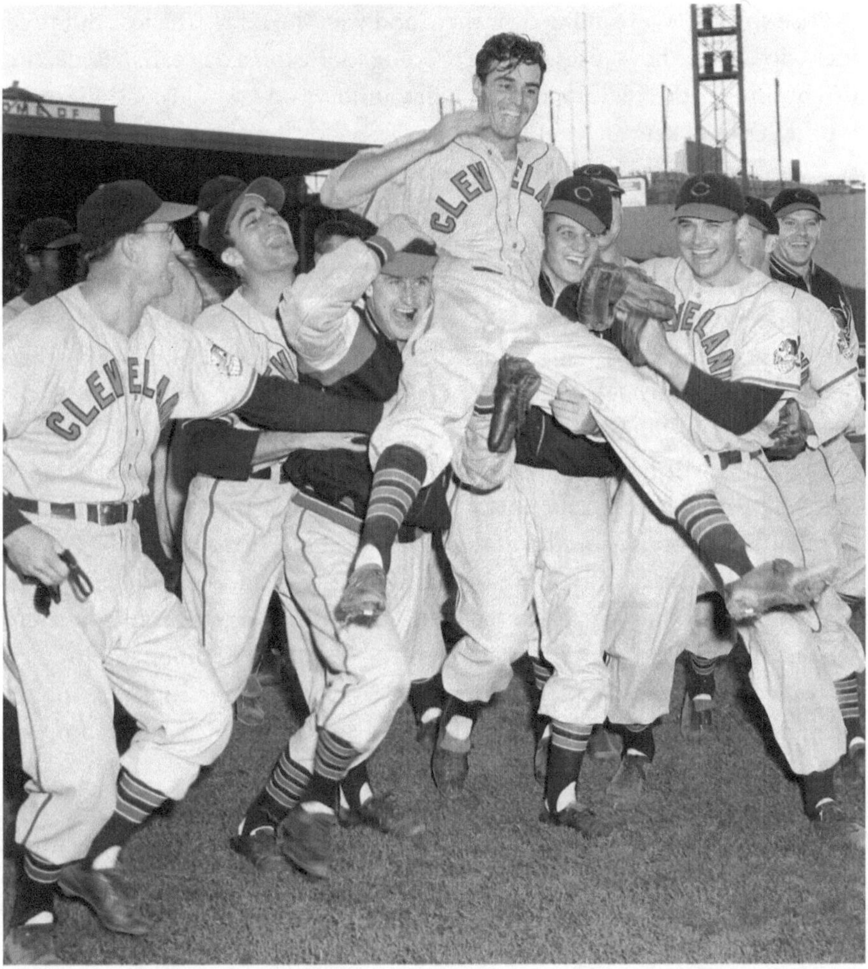

The greatest moment in Cleveland baseball history—pitcher Gene Bearden is carried off the field after the Indians defeated the Boston Red Sox at Fenway Park in a one-game playoff for the American League pennant on October 4, 1948. Cleveland State University Library's *Cleveland Press* Collection.

PD's Harry Jones suggested, "the Red Sox eat their young." Fenway Park, Jones went on, "is a structural monstrosity that through the years has proven to be a dreaded nightmare to its visiting baseball clubs."

Instead of a night of jubilation in Cleveland, it was a long, quiet Sunday evening. "The bride stranded at the altar, the boom that busted, Mudville when Casey struck out," Robert Drake wrote in the *Plain Dealer.* "All were one last night with the Indians and their rooters. . . . There never was a sport celebration like the one that did not happen here." Lou Boudreau did his best to raise spirits. "We're going over there and win," he said. "The loss didn't get them down. The boys just feel they're going to Boston a day early." Reflecting that optimism, the Cleveland ticket office announced it would continue to sell World Series tickets on Monday just as tickets for the playoff went on sale in Boston. The available 23,000 Fenway tickets sold out in just over two hours. Meanwhile, more than a thousand Cleveland fans met the team at Union Terminal as it boarded its 9 P.M. train, offering one final wave of support as the Tribe departed to play the biggest game in American League history.

While most Cleveland fans tried to put their best face on what was clearly a letdown, there was a sense of defeat, of a blown opportunity for greatness that permeated through the city. W. G. Thorpe, an editor at the *Plain Dealer*, was despondent Sunday night at the prospect of delivering the news of defeat to a baseball-mad city. But his wife, born with a caul over her face and prone to visions of the future, told him not to worry. The Indians would win Monday, she promised, and as if to prove her point, as the playoff began, she brought out the caul from a box in a dresser drawer and set it in front of the radio on which they'd listen to the game. And the Thorpes certainly weren't the only ones tuned in. Across Cleveland at 1:30 that afternoon, radios were turned on in homes, shops, restaurants, classrooms, and even prison blocks. Business slowed to a crawl on the Cleveland Stock Exchange, which dropped to its lowest level in six years.

Both teams shrouded their lineups in mystery, neither announcing its starting pitcher. Boudreau finally settled on rookie knuckleballer Gene Bearden, who had been magnificent in 1948, winning nineteen games. Though he would pitch on just one day's rest, Bearden had won ten straight games and would once again don the sweatshirt he'd worn beneath his jersey in all ten, now held together by nothing more than safety pins and the good luck he was sure it brought him. Mysteriously, Boston manager Joe McCarthy chose thirty-six-year-old journeyman Denny Galehouse, an Ohio native who had struggled as a member of the Indians through much of the 1930s, over apparently better candidates Mel Parnell and Ellis Kinder. With the thick tension of a marvelous pennant race now at its apex as the game began under sunny but cool skies at Fenway, Galehouse instilled some confidence by retiring the first two Cleveland batters. But after falling behind Boudreau 2-and-1, he served up a low curve that the Cleveland shortstop pounded over the Green Monster for a home run. In what would soon become the haunted cathedral of baseball, it was an ominous portent for the hometown nine. Bearden had his own struggles in the bottom of the first, giving up a one-out double to right center by third baseman Johnny Pesky, who then scored on a Vern Stephens single. A slugfest appeared eminent, particularly when third baseman Ken Keltner singled to lead off the Cleveland second. Galehouse worked out of it, then Bearden wobbled through the bottom half, giving up two walks and a single, but didn't allow a run. Both pitchers cruised through the third before the tension of a thrill-packed summer finally snapped.

Boudreau, the most valuable piston in the Tribe's pennant drive, led off the frame with a single to left, then advanced to second on a hit by Joe Gordon. With trouble brewing, Galehouse hunkered down to face Keltner, who'd enjoyed a fantastic season with thirty homers and 116 RBI. Galehouse worked a 2-and-2 count on Keltner and then made another critical mistake. Just as Boudreau had done three innings before, Keltner smashed the miscue into left field, where it settled into the screen netted above the iconic thirty-seven-foot wall. With one swing, a tie game turned into a three-run Cleveland lead. And the Indians weren't done.

Galehouse was yanked for Parnell, beginning a half century of Boston revisionist historical discussions. Larry Doby slapped a double off the wall in left center, moved to third on a Bob Kennedy sacrifice, then scored on a Jim Hegan ground out to make it 5–1. Bearden then quelled a Boston threat in the bottom of the fourth with a double play and spent the rest of the afternoon cruising. The Tribe added another run in the fifth on Boudreau's second homer of the game, but the Red Sox showed signs of life in the sixth when second baseman Bobby Doerr hit a two-run homer to cut the Cleveland lead to 6–3. Bearden enticed another key double play in the seventh, then the Indians added their seventh run on a Boston error in the eighth and their eighth when Eddie Robinson scored on a double play in the ninth.

Leading 8–3 and just three outs away from the pennant, Bearden efficiently extinguished the Red Sox in the ninth. He got Doerr to ground back to the mound, then after a walk, struck out Billy Goodman. Finally, at 3:54 P.M., Birdie Tebbetts hit a soft grounder to Keltner, who fired on to Robinson at first for the final out, and the Indians were headed to the World Series. "And if in answer," Roelif Loveland wrote in the *Plain Dealer,* "the city of Cleveland, which had waited long, went completely and noisily wacky."

In the Best Location in the Nation, the same fans who had all but accepted a season-ending defeat twenty-four hours before poured into the streets honking car horns, blowing whistles, and lighting firecrackers. "They had no place to go," the *Plain Dealer* reported, "but were basking in the reflected glory of the Tribe and making as much noise as possible." Paper and tickertape seesawed out of office windows, and young women were grabbed and kissed on the street by complete strangers. The Cleveland Board of Education allowed many employees go home an hour early. "What'd we do?" a young boy asked as he came upon an impromptu celebration. "Beat Russia?"

Back in Boston, the Indians were holding their own party. Bearden's teammates carried him off the field after a magnificent performance against the best offense in baseball, holding the Red Sox to just five hits and one earned run. Cleveland owner Bill Veeck limped across the Fenway infield on his one good leg and clutched Bearden's hand with tears spilling out of his eyes. "That Bearden! What a man!" Feller cried in the locker room. "He got me off the hook again, didn't he?" Ohio Governor Thomas J. Herbert, a lifelong Tribe fan who had been an usher at League Park during the 1920 World Series, wired a telegram of congratulations to Veeck. At bars all over Cleveland, patrons toasted boy manager Boudreau, who had gone four for four with the two huge homers and three runs scored.

It was a shining moment—one which would forever burn brightly in the annals of both the franchise and the city. Even that afternoon, long before Cleveland sports fans truly knew what suffering was, many were able to accurately forecast the magnitude of what had occurred—and how it would be remembered. "Shortly before four yesterday afternoon," Loveland wrote, "the sun trembled in his orbit and the stars shivered violently in the heavens. The earth gave itself a couple extra spins and a great voice cried: 'Behold the Cleveland Indians, winners of the 1948 American League pennant.'"

Indians	1 0 0	4 1 0	0 1 1 =8
Red Sox	1 0 0	0 0 2	0 0 0 =3

CLEVELAND

	AB	R	H	RBI
Mitchell lf	5	0	1	0
Clark 1b	2	0	0	0
Robinson 1b	2	1	1	0
Boudreau ss	4	3	4	2
Gordon 2b	4	1	1	0
Keltner 3b	5	1	3	3
Doby cf	5	1	2	0
Kennedy rf	2	0	0	0
Hegan c	3	1	0	1
Bearden p	3	0	1	0
TOTAL	35	8	13	6

	IP	H	R	ER	BB	SO
Bearden (W)	9	5	3	1	5	6

BOSTON

	AB	R	H	RBI
DiMaggio cf	4	0	0	0
Pesky 3b	4	1	1	0
Williams lf	4	1	1	0
Stephens ss	4	0	1	1
Doerr 2b	4	1	1	2
Spence rf	1	0	0	0
Hitchcock ph	0	0	0	0
Wright pr	0	0	0	0
Goodman 1b	3	0	0	0
Tebbetts c	4	0	1	0
Galehouse p	0	0	0	0
Kinder p	2	0	0	0
TOTAL	30	3	5	3

	IP	H	R	ER	BB	SO
Galehouse (L)	3	5	4	4	1	1
Kinder	6	8	4	3	3	2

Attendance: 33,957

www.ingramcontent.com/pod-product-compliance
Lightning Source LLC
LaVergne TN
LVHW090844190926
848329LV00024B/102
* 9 7 8 1 6 0 6 3 5 5 1 4 5 *